IN HONOR
OF JUSTICE DOUGLAS

WILLIAM O. DOUGLAS

THE HUMANIST AS LAWYER

· *a symposium* ·
*on individual freedom and the government
with papers, panel discussions, seminars
workshops & entertainments*

VINCE BLASI
university of michigan law school

CATHLEEN H. DOUGLAS
washington, d.c.

THOMAS EMERSON
yale law school

LINO GRAGLIA
university of texas

ANITA MILLER

ARVAL MORRIS
university of washington law school

ODETTA

HUMANISM IS THE WILL
TO SERVE OUR FELLOW
HUMAN BEINGS ·

APRIL 15 THRU 17 ·

FAIRHAVEN COLLEGE

*to register·contact
the douglas symposium
fairhaven college
bellingham, wa.
98225*

Poster for Douglas Symposium, Fairhaven College, 1977. Courtesy of the artist Tom Sherwood.

IN HONOR
OF JUSTICE DOUGLAS
A Symposium on
Individual Freedom
and the Government

————— Edited by ROBERT H. KELLER, Jr.

Contributions in Legal Studies, Number 12

GREENWOOD PRESS

WESTPORT, CONNECTICUT ● LONDON, ENGLAND

Library of Congress Cataloging in Publication Data

William O. Douglas Symposium, Fairhaven College, 1977.
    In honor of Justice Douglas.

    (Contributions in legal studies; no. 12 ISSN 0147–
1074)
    Includes index.
    CONTENTS: Murphy, J. W. Justice William O. Douglas'
humanism.—Emerson, T. I.   Government secrecy and the
citizen's right to know.—Blasi, V. A.   "Journalistic
autonomy" as a first amendment concept.   [Etc.]
    1. Civil rights—United States—Congresses.
2. United States—Constitutional law—Congresses.
3. Douglas, William Orville, 1898–   —Congresses.
I. Douglas, William Orville, 1898—   II. Keller,
Robert H. III. Title. IV. Series
KF4749.A2W55 1977   342'.73'085   78–22723
ISBN 0–313–20959–6

Library of Congress Catalog Card Number: 78-22723
ISBN: 0-313-20959-6
ISSN: 0147-1074

First published in 1979

Greenwood Press, Inc.
51 Riverside Avenue, Westport, Connecticut 06880

Printed in the United States of America

10   9   8   7   6   5   4   3   2   1

Copyright Acknowledgments

Dedication

This book is dedicated to Mr. Justice William O. Douglas of the United States Supreme Court. All royalties will go to Fairhaven College, Western Washington University, Bellingham, Washington, to support library acquisitions and a lecture series on Law and Society in memory of Scott Lane, 1954–77, a Fairhaven student of law, economics, and social values and an avid participant in the Douglas Symposium. Scott was killed in a hiking accident shortly after the Symposium.

Contents

Notes on the Contributors

Vincent A. Blasi studied law at the University of Chicago and now teaches at the University of Michigan. He has also taught at Stanford University, the University of Texas and the University of California. His principal interests are copyright law and the interpretation of the First Amendment; Blasi's publications include "Prior Restraints on Demonstrations," *Michigan Law Review* (1970), and "Requiem for the Warren Court," *Texas Law Review* (1970). He is the author of *Press Subpoenas: An Empirical and Legal Analysis* (1972).

Vine Deloria, Jr., is an attorney and a member of the Sioux Indian Tribe, Standing Rock Reservation. He holds a law degree from the University of Colorado and has taught at Western Washington University, UCLA, Colorado College, and the University of Arizona. Among his many publications on Indian affairs are *Custer Died for Your Sins* (1969), *God Is Red* (1973), *Behind the Trail of Broken Treaties* (1974), and *The Metaphysics of Modern Existence* (1979).

Thomas I. Emerson, Professor of Law at Yale University, is a member of the New York Bar, a past president of the National Lawyers Guild, and a Guggenheim Fellow (1953). He joined the Yale faculty in 1946 and subsequently taught as a visiting professor at the London School of Economics and the Brookings Institution. Widely published in legal periodicals, he is best known for his monumental works on civil liberties: *Political and Civil Rights in the United States* (3rd ed., 1967); *Toward a General Theory of the First Amendment* (1966); and *The System of Freedom of Expression* (1970).

Lino A. Graglia graduated from the City College of New York and Columbia University Law School, after which he practiced with the Justice Department and private firms for twelve years. He presently holds the Baker Professorship in Constitutional Law at the University of Texas, where he also specializes in antitrust law. His publications include "Antitrust and Small Business," *Texas Bar Journal* (1971); "Special Admission of the 'Culturally Deprived' to Law School," *Black Law Journal* (1974); and a book, *Disaster by Decree: The Supreme Court Decisions on Race and the Schools* (1976). He is a visiting professor at the University of Virginia School of Law, 1978–79.

Anita M. Miller is the executive director of the Institute for Studies in Equality, Sacramento, California. A graduate of Stanford University, she has served as an adviser to the United States Civil Rights Commission, as national vice-president of the American Association of University Women and, after July 1977, as president of the National Association of Commissioners for Women. She has been honored as California Woman of the Year and is the publisher of the *Equal Rights Monitor*.

Arval A. Morris is Professor of Constitutional Law and Jurisprudence at the University of Washington. He has been a Sterling Fellow at Yale University, a fellow at Oxford University, and a visiting professor at the University of Freiburg, West Germany. His specializations include criminal law, race relations, law and psychiatry, and local government. He has served on the board of directors of the American Civil Liberties Union of Washington. In addition to numerous publications in legal journals, Morris is the author of *The Constitution and American Education* (1974).

Jay W. Murphy, Professor of Law at the University of Alabama, has also taught at New York University and at Seoul National University, South Korea. He belongs to the Panel of Arbitrators, Federal Mediation and Conciliation Service, and since 1963 has served as a member of the Alabama Advisory Committee to the United States Civil Rights Commission. His special interests include collective bargaining, race relations, international law, and jurisprudence. Murphy has published *Labor Relations and the Law* (1960), *Legal Education in a Developing Nation* (1965), and *The Legal Profession in Korea* (1967).

Lloyd Meeds was the representative from the Second Congressional District in the state of Washington. **Marshall Forrest** is a Superior Court Judge, Whatcom County, Washington. **Donald J. Horowitz**, a former Superior

Court Judge, now practices law in Seattle. **Charles Bulger**, a native of St. Paul, Minnesota, is a senior completing an interdisciplinary concentration at Fairhaven College.

Preface

In our law school class on "Federal Courts" the final examination was the soul of simplicity. *Powell* v. *McCormick* was pending before the Supreme Court, and we were asked to write the majority opinion, a concurring opinion reasoned on different grounds, and two dissenting opinions. Depending on how closely we anticipated the final conclusion of the court, our legal careers and grades hung precariously between genius and mediocrity. One student wrote glowing majority and concurring reports sprinkled liberally with the boilerplate of gentlemanly rhetoric that so characterizes many Supreme Court opinions: "my esteemed brethren, learned in the law and paragons of civilized virtue" and so forth. His first dissenting opinion read: DOUGLAS, J. Dissenting: "Bullshit!"

William O. Douglas represents this stark no-nonsense, straight-from-the-guts analysis that distinguishes a person from the mysterious ethereal entities that inhabit the Supreme Court. He is not my thinker in judicial history, for I find in Cardozo a magnificently substantial mind and in Black a determined literalist driven to assert principles in defiance of legal fictions. Yet with Douglas one encounters the original role of the judicial mind, a function that has eroded with the centuries to the great detriment of civilization. Douglas presents the continual effort of the sensitive personality to strike beyond the confines of legal doctrine to grasp the world of organic existence and bring it gasping, struggling, and bleeding within the confines of polite institutions. This task is patently impossible in any generation and misunderstood more than it is appreciated. It is the arduous job of planting and seeding that the prophet Jeremiah found as the ultimate task of the prophetic personality.

Appendix B contains a bibliography that sketches in barest outline the life and thought of Douglas. Insofar as a person can leave a tangible memorial, this amazing list describes a life in touch with the diverse elements of human experience. Diversity alone is not represented here, but also the intuitive perception that the world of nature must somehow be reconciled with the universe of the mind. If the writings of William O. Douglas invoke visions of chaotic activity, and they certainly project that aspect if taken under close scrutiny, then the chaos is that of Creation Morning, when it was necessary to bring order and relationships to the plenitude of experience.

Douglas never reconciled his deepest intuitive thoughts about the world. Indians and conservation received unusual consideration in his intellectual horizon; yet, when the two clashed, invariably he would choose the conservation cause over the Indian pleas. The two, Indian law and environmental law, are not incompatible, but Douglas speaks of an even deeper wisdom: Our species is not separated from the rest of the organic world but simply a particular expression of its unity. Insofar as Douglas could not conceive of a manner of reconciling these two demanding aspects of law, he was a person of his time; to the degree that separately he gave them support and intellectual expression, his efforts remain a significant transformation of the reality of life into legal concepts and doctrines.

The Old Testament prophets correctly phrased their conceptions of divine law in poetic form, since only through this medium could the reality of emotional truth be adequately perceived. Legal minds in centuries following reduced this perception to a drabness of equality and similarity whereby human beings became interchangeable pieces of great institutions that dominated and defined all aspects of human experience. Insofar as Douglas stands within the intellectual heritage of great minds, he most certainly joins the prophetic tradition. His nonlegal writings cannot be divorced from the instances when he was called upon to articulate the doctrines, dogmas, and principles that order our public life. The combination of his writings, then, constitutes the Douglas understanding of the spirit of life and the heritage that he transmits to all succeeding generations.

This volume, therefore, must be experienced in the slightly disrespectful but substantial way that Douglas approached life and thought. All points must be considered as potential issues of rebellion, and a perpetual energy and first discovery of youth must accompany any reader's perusal of these pages. The human spirit must not be confined within these pages. Rather, the volume points ahead as did the old understanding of the law to new modes of experience and expression. American jurisprudence often suffers from the exaggerated dignity that we vest in personages of yesteryear in a frantic effort to escape the inevitable admission of our own mortality. If we can apply this technique of sanctification to other giants of the Supreme Court, we must quickly realize that William O. Douglas laughs at the suggestion. He cannot be contained within a well-ordered pantheon because even his most complete thoughts are not conclusions but beckonings to move forward into the unknown. A person cannot serve a greater function for either his community or human history, and in this sense we have only begun to experience and appreciate Douglas.

Vine Deloria, Jr.
Tucson, Arizona

Acknowledgments

In planning the William O. Douglas Symposium, we intentionally offered small honorariums to all participants. This means that contributors to the conference and to this volume have, in effect, volunteered their time and effort. We appreciate their interest in the Symposium, and we thank them for their contributions.

A number of persons not included here also volunteered papers, addresses, and commentary that enlivened the weekend of April 15–17, 1977. Among these are Cathleen Douglas, Superior Court Judge Norman Ackley, Professor Arthur Hicks, political writer Duff Wilson, and Seattle attorneys Donald Horowitz, Frederick Butterworth, and Alvin Ziontz. We had two active cosponsors in Janet Lutz of the Bellingham-Whatcom County League of Women Voters and Hubert Locke of the Institute for the Study of Contemporary Social Problems, Seattle. We are grateful to many other individuals in the local community who organized seminars and led discussions. William Pierron, Sr., of Bellingham assisted in countless ways from the first planning session to the final evaluation. Five artists—Tom Sherwood, Odetta, Earl Robinson, and Greg and Stephanie Ross—helped to decrease the distance between law and humanities, between lawyers and humanists.

Among the Fairhaven College students who watched over essential details were Jackie McClure, Simeon Dreyfus, Charlie Bulger, and

Scott Lane. Those of us associated with Scott Lane as a friend and co-worker since 1973 obtain special satisfaction in knowing that royalties from this book will honor his memory at Fairhaven College and will promote the discussion of those values to which he had dedicated his life.

The Douglas Symposium was made possible through a grant from the Washington Commission for the Humanities, an agency of the National Endowment for the Humanities. In addition to the commission's money, we received encouragement, enthusiastic support, and expert advice from Bill Oliver and Carola Norton of the staff in Olympia. Financial support was also provided by the International Longshoremen's and Warehousemen's Union, and by the Bridge Project of Fairhaven College.

Western Washington University offered the resources of the campus throughout the planning and the program. Staff members at the university and at Fairhaven College, as well as numerous members of the Bridge Project, donated hours of hard work. Our particular gratitude goes to Yvonne Calavan, Barney Goltz, Pat Karlberg, Kenneth Ott, Bessie and Wendell Robinson, Beth Powers, Jane Clark, and Florence Preder. The office staff in the Anthropology Department at the University of Arizona also generously assisted with final preparation of the manuscript.

Three months prior to the Symposium, James Sabin wrote to us that Greenwood Press would be interested in publishing the proceedings. His patient interest and encouragement have helped all of us in editing these papers. We thank him and Greenwood Press for joining in our tribute to the career of William O. Douglas.

Robert H. Keller, Jr.

Lynne Masland-Bettis

Larry Fehr

Rand F. Jack

Introduction

In 1977 at Fairhaven College, Bellingham, Washington, a symposium was held to honor Justice William O. Douglas after his retirement following thirty-six years on the Supreme Court. The program was in honor of Douglas but not about him, except in the sense that it was organized around ideas and conflicts central to the Justice during his tenure on the Court. The title of the symposium was "Individual Freedom and the Government," and the special theme was "William O. Douglas: The Humanist as Lawyer."

More than any other Justice within memory, Douglas' activism and convictions made him a controversial public figure. He wrote profusely, walked the earth as a world ambassador of democracy, preached a militant environmentalism, and relished his reputation as an absolute defender of the Bill of Rights. Douglas symbolizes the idea that a strenuous life and a devotion to principle yield social and personal reward. Raised in Yakima by a widowed mother, and crippled by polio, Douglas labored to support his family. He worked his way through Whitman College and Columbia Law School, and, as a professor of law at Yale, he attained distinction in the law of bankruptcy and corporate finance. It is a long, uncommon journey from the streets of sand-blown Yakima, 1915, to the chambers of the Supreme Court, Washington, D.C., 1939–75. In his sojourn, Douglas became an idol, a legend, a symbol—though exactly what he symbolizes cannot be agreed upon by his admirers or by his critics. What cannot be contested is that he made his imprint on the history of our time and he deserves our acknowledgment and attention.

As do all public heroes and symbolic figures, Douglas has his detractors. Even admirers, with casual inquiry, can see clay feet stumbling over the Japanese Relocation and treason cases during World War II, and over national security, war crimes, and polygamy after the war. Nor is his record uniform even in the areas of free speech, privacy, and freedom of association.[1] Scholars shudder at his simplistic reasoning to achieve desired ends, his pragmatism, and his subordination of procedure to substance. Even a friendly commentator had to concede that Douglas "was brilliant at raising issues . . . inept at solving them. . . . His willingnes to torture statutes, to disregard precedent, to bend logic, and to rewrite history so ignored the accepted canons of law as to be insulting."[2]

William O. Douglas had visited Fairhaven College in May 1969. Several courses subsequently covered his life and writings, his strengths and weaknesses, as a way of examining law and society. Many of us here felt a close identification between his spirit and that of the college; and we believed that a public symposium commemorating Douglas' retirement could reflect on the career of the Justice and the Supreme Court's role in our past, while seeking at the same time to understand the relationship among jurisprudence, the arts, literature, philosophy, and history. We attempted to bring together the legal profession and the public for an examination of how human values influence public policy and how these values determine our concepts of individual freedom.[3] Douglas believed, above all else, in the necessity of critical free expression. That virtue hardly produces social tranquility or peace of mind. The goal of the Douglas Symposium was to inquire into those intellectual issues that evoke conflict and inspire commitment. We aimed at controversy and criticism, not eulogy. For William O. Douglas, a gentle tribute would be inappropriate.

We sought to reflect Douglas' spirit in the structure and tone of the Symposium. No speaker received a large honorarium. Groups representing diverse persuasions, from the American Legion to the American Civil Liberties Union, were invited to lead workshops. Major speakers were expected to join seminars or workshops and attend coffee hours. For the three hundred persons who spent three days in

Bellingham, the Symposium provided a common format of panels, prepared papers, and a variety of small meetings. We desired both expert opinion and direct dialogue. A participant could choose from among a dozen formal addresses, six panel discussions, seven hours of film, more than thirty hours of workshops, and three different musical and theatrical performances. Through this book we try to capture a fraction of the Symposium's life.

It is difficult to express the varied and often spontaneous exchanges in workshops sponsored by groups such as the Republican and Democratic Parties, Evergreen Legal Services, an evangelical Christian organization, the Whatcom County Bar Association, Skagitonians Concerned About Nuclear Power, Bellingham Rape Relief, a runaway shelter, Planned Parenthood, and a local work-release program for felons. Among the issues debated in those workshops were: legal humanism, all-terrain vehicles and individual freedom, relegislating morality, civil rights, criminal procedure, prison reform and the American economic system, equal justice regardless of income, juvenile law, reverse discrimination, and Indian fishing and the federal courts. Although we have included a condensation of workshop dialogue as part of the conclusion to this book, the written word does not easily convey the emotion of involvement—the angry defense of Native American rights by a Lummi Indian woman, the relaxed conversation between Thomas Emerson and a high school junior from Sedro Woolley, Washington.

If the spirit of the Symposium remains elusive, the content of its major addresses does not. Jay Murphy takes Douglas as his subject for an approach to law that is humanistic and cosmic. In this bold undertaking, Murphy attempts to describe the principal elements of Douglas' humanism and to place these elements in a philosophical context. Drawing on Douglas' own writings, Murphy seeks to relocate the roots and implications of the values espoused by the Justice. In Chapter 2 the book turns from Douglas to a central topic in his judicial philosophy—limitation of the government's power to control the free flow of information. Through precise analysis and closely structured reasoning, Thomas Emerson develops a constitutional basis for curtailing the power of government to classify information as "secret." Critical of the Supreme Court, Emerson relies on Douglas' opinions to develop a citizen's-right-to-know doctrine in a brief the Justice would be quick to affirm. In another paper focusing on a critical First Amendment question, Vincent Blasi considers the regard the Supreme Court has had for the press's claim to special institutional protection. After rejecting traditional First Amendment values of diversity, individual freedom, and self-government as sufficient to justify "press autonomy," Blasi looks to the historical roots of the amendment for a rationale. He persuasively argues that checking government abuse of power is a constitutionally sound basis for affording the press enlarged protection in our society.

There is a peculiar affinity between Emerson and Blasi, on the one hand, and the address by Lino Graglia found in Chapter 4. Whereas Emerson and Blasi argued for First Amendment limitations on government power in a way Douglas would readily support, Graglia's position against another level of government intrusion stands in antithesis to Douglas' judicial career. Graglia speaks forcefully of a Supreme Court intruding into the lives of citizens, of the province of local governments, and of the constitutionally assigned role of Congress. Even where the result "sells," he is critical of judicial overreaching, including the greedy hands of Justice Douglas. Using school desegregation cases as his springboard, Graglia articulates a conservative judicial philosophy expressing a fear of government by the judiciary that matches Emerson's anxiety over government by secrecy. The restraint on judicial activism extolled by Graglia becomes, in a more restricted context, the concern of Arval Morris in his critique of recent decisions that narrow citizen access to the courts. With Douglas as his lance, Morris attacks the barricades that the Burger Court erects to confront citizens seeking entrance to the courthouse. For Morris, the point is that the powerless championed by Douglas, those most in need of judicial redress, are the most easily excluded. In the final Symposium paper included here, Anita Miller argues that women are just such victims of discrimination and that even when they gain access to the courts, judicial help has been at best only marginal. In a crisp attack, Miller finds sexism a recurring bias in Supreme Court decisions. She argues that this situation can only be remedied by women sharing the power of the judiciary. It would have certainly been a pleasing tribute to Douglas if he had been able to give up his seat to a woman.

The latter parts of Chapter 2 and Chapters 7 and 9 are edited transcripts of panel discussions—two of them planned and the third an outgrowth of a suppertime conversation between Emerson and Graglia on the Equal Rights Amendment. The panels shed light on important issues considered in other chapters, but most importantly they attest to the role of controversy and open debate for gaining understanding and firm convictions regarding difficult social questions.

In Chapter 10 Douglas speaks for himself through a television interview. Those of us who had used this interview in classes could think of no better way of letting the Justice have the last word. The scenic views of Goose Prairie, Washington, are missing in the transcript, but the rugged contours of Douglas' philosophy emerge undimmed.

The appendixes are given as a composite portrait of the man—without the sinews and muscles that make him real.

To the reader this is a book of ideas. It is for us also, but in addition it is our attempt to preserve the memory of an exciting event possible only when people cherish and join in the free exchange of ideas. President Gerald R. Ford, who had been invited to discuss the attempted impeachment of Douglas in 1970, expressed the intended spirit of the Symposium and this book in his letter to the conference:

I regret that I cannot be with you for this seminar focusing on the career of Mr. Justice Douglas.

Justice Douglas and I took decidedly different paths toward a goal I believe we hold in common: the protection of the rights, and the preservation of the worth, of the individual American citizen in an increasingly impersonal age.

In this spirit, and in recognition of his long years of devoted service to his country, I was proud to welcome Justice Douglas as a guest in the White House during my Presidency, and I am proud to join your tribute to him now.[4]

Notes

1. *Minersville School Dist.* v. *Gobitis*, 310 U.S. 586 (1940); *Viereck* v. *United States*, 318 U.S. 236 (1943); *Korematsu* v. *United States*, 323 U.S. 214 (1944); *Cramer* v. *United States*, 325 U.S. 1 (1945); *In re Yamashita*, 327 U.S. 1 (1946); *Cleveland* v. *United States*, 329 U.S. 14 (1946); *Columbia Broadcasting System* v. *Democratic National Committee*, 412 U.S. 94 (1973); *Village of Belle Terre* v. *Boraas*, 416 U.S. 1 (1974). For criticism of Douglas' motives, see Michael Parrish, "The Supreme Court and the Rosenbergs," *American Historical Review*, 82:4 (October 1977), pp. 805–42. Also

see Jospeh P. Lash, ed., *From the Diaries of Felix Frankfurter* (New York: Norton, 1975).

2. Robert J. Glennon, Jr., " 'Do Not Go Gentle': More Than an Epitaph," *Wayne Law Review*, 32:5 (September 1976), pp. 1304–34; quotations from pp. 1331–34.

3. These assumptions are not self-evident. Stephen Botein in analyzing the relationship between law and the humanities concludes that they have little to say to each other. "Reflections on the New Humanism in Law," *Wayne Law Review*, 32:5 (September 1976), pp. 1295–1303.

4. Gerald Ford to Lynne Masland, February 7, 1977.

Justice William O. Douglas' Humanism: A Copernican Revolution in Law

1

JAY W. MURPHY _____

Jay Murphy, whose classes at the University of Alabama School of Law include "Law and Extraterrestrial Intelligence," here portrays and praises "the humanist as lawyer." His rapid-fire delivery of a wide-ranging, imaginative, unorthodox address bewildered anyone not versed in the humanities, and it surprised those who believe that the legal profession should find its inspiration in casebooks, in the definition of terms such as "state action," and in the study of procedures. Just as the titles of Justice Douglas' books reveal the magnitude of his interests, Jay Murphy's scholarly résumé testifies to the eclecticism that the reader will discover in the following essay. In addition to his books about Korea, Murphy has written on "Free Speech and Atom Bombs," *Alabama Law Review* (1949); "Book Labeling—an Ominous Venture in Censorship," *Alabama Law Review* (1954); "John Dewey— a Philosophy of Law for Democracy," *Vanderbilt Law Review* (1960); "The Role of 'Non-practical' or 'Cultural' Courses," *Journal of Legal Education* (1962). Both Douglas and Murphy are unrestrained admirers of innovation and intuition; both consider world law the most critical task confronting humanity; and both would agree that lawyers, to be genuinely human, must have universal interests.

This address has been substantially shortened and rearranged from the form in which it was delivered.

> Knowledge is humanistic in quality not because it is *about* human products in the past, but because of what it *does* in liberating human intelligence and human sympathy. Any subject matter which accomplishes this result is humane and any subject matter which does not accomplish it is not even educational.[1]
>
> John Dewey

Overview

Each time I sat down to write these notes, I realized how limited I was and how vast the subject—requiring years of profound scholarship by many disciplines to reveal the limitless horizons of Justice Douglas' humanism. This is a great responsibility and I, of course, am not up to its fullest performance. Maybe I can point in a direction or two, and others, more qualified, can join to treat the subject with the true magnificence that it deserves.

As I concluded my brief study, I made a note to myself concerning my intuitive perception of Justice Douglas' motivating ideals and perspective. I put down: his massive optimism about the immense goals of which humans are capable; his recognition of powers and forces in society which interfere with the attainment of these goals; his keen perception of the historic struggle of mankind against great odds; his vast compassion for humankind and all living things; and his recognition of the judicial system as a powerful instrument for achieving his values through imaginative performance of its true function in a democratic society, while realizing that the judicial system alone cannot achieve an ideal rule of law without extensive aid from other persons, disciplines, and institutions in society. So Douglas alerts us to look beyond the judicial system and the legal profession to help human beings achieve their rightful potential. And, lastly, I noted, we are dealing with a superbly integrated personality.

The new humanism which springs forth in the last quarter of the twentieth-century world points to a unity of humanity through insights into the nature of people, life, environment, and being—from DNA to Black Holes; to the unity of art, music, and literature; to the unity of worldwide economic and political movements and systems. Actions taken at a corporate headquarters in New York affect what people think and eat; they affect the dimensions of their lives, their freedom of thought, of movement, of belief. This, too, reflects a new unity.

Correspondingly, there is a new need to expand our insights into the consequences of exercising power, the consequences of the protections afforded by the Bill of Rights in the United States Constitution upon the beliefs and actions of peoples within the United States and upon the world at large, including those vast areas not covered by a Bill of Rights but which are influenced by the existence of those freedoms and ideals in the United States.

I believe that Justice Douglas had this new vision of humanity, a vision of the unity of human beings: aesthetically, morally, physically, politically, socially, and economically. And, if we may call this vision macroscopic, he also had a microscopic lens in his perception, enabling him to see deeply within the United States to the local police station, the newspaper editor, the thousands of groups with diverse interests expressing their concerns in speech and action and belief; deeply within to the weak, the poor, the meek within the United States and also deeply within to the remote villages of mankind throughout the world.

He seemed to possess a social and individual microscope whereby he could feel and see the consequences of the application of laws and governmental action upon the individual human being, wherever humans exist—as those consequences related to his conception of the purpose of the constitutions, the law, the ideals of a national and a world society, and of the dignity of the individual human being.

Quotations of Justice Douglas on His Humanism

One can gain a much truer picture of Justice Douglas by letting him speak for himself through his many published lectures, books, and papers rather than attempting to summarize and substitute one's own words. In his book *Being an American*, published at the start of the cold war in 1948, one finds over and over expressions of ideals of American society and its role in the world and a faith in the democratic process. I have extracted passages from various chapters to capture and convey his humanism and the challenges which he persistently insists this country must face if it is to live up to its ideals.

We must reach behind the façade of ministers and cabinets and commissions and let the common people feel our warm handclasp. We must let them know that we understand their suffering. We must make sure they know that our desire is not to make them our satellites but to meet them as equals in a world where standards of decency and justice prevail.[2]

Yes, it takes courage to stand between an unpopular minority and the community, insisting that our Bill of Rights was designed for the protection of all people, whatever their race, creed, or political faith.[3]

For the goal of people of all races is toward a system that respects their dignity, frees their minds, and allows them to worship their God in their own way. None has yet designed an article of political faith more suited to those ends than our own Bill of Rights.[4]

The right of free choice on the part of all the people is the heart of our democratic philosophy.[5]

Government can have no nobler aim than securing justice for all people.[6]

Nothing could be more fallacious than the ancient theory that backward peoples can be exploited as outlets for industrially produced goods.[7]

We cheat ourselves, we rob ourselves of strength and vitality, when we deprive any segment of our people of opportunities, when we tolerate conditions that keep them in servitude.[8]

One of the most basic instincts in humanity is the desire for association with others in co-operative work.[9]

We have a place in the world. There is no choice about that. It is the position of moral leadership. Our only decision is whether we shall fill it well, or badly.[10]

Man's intelligence has unlocked the secrets of the universe. It has conquered vast domains of disease. It has harnessed the energies of nature and has made possible for a man a bountiful life. What the intelligence of man has made possible in the material and physical fields, it can likewise achieve in the field of government—that is, in human relations, and in law.[11]

. . . the legal system conceived for our people is designed to allow for full growth and development, not to protect a *status quo*.[12]

We are apt to think of peace as the absence of war. But peace is more than that: Peace is the presence of law, of justice, order, stability, and a method for orderly change. That is to say, peace is not merely the absence of war; it is the presence of government.[13]

World law is essential for world peace. The risks are far too great for us to entrust the cherished ideals of this great civilization to jungle techniques.[14]

For the common people of the world are on the move. And they are insisting that they come into their inheritance. If we do not do the job, others will. The job will, indeed, be done either on totalitarian terms or in the framework of democratic ideals.[15]

Let us identify ourselves with the common people of the world everywhere. Let us champion their causes. Let us show them how to be rid of the forces that have held them in slavery. . . . We can do so if we become practicing missionaries of the democratic faith. If that is our course, freedom and liberty, rather than regimentation, can become the dominant political pattern of the world.[16]

. . . the answer to the political program of the Communists is a dynamic and vital political program on the democratic front.[17]

America can continue to be the source of emotional and moral strength for the world on one condition. That condition is that this nation stays prosperous, progressive, civilized; that our program of justice moves progressively forward; that we continue to reduce the areas of injustice within our borders. The great challenge of the century is to find ways and means of extending a practical program of justice to the farthest regions of the world.[18]

Believe in your democratic faith, practice it, preach it and you can have a one world that is your kind of world.[19]

Some Sources of Justice Douglas' Humanism

What are the sources of Justice Douglas' humanism? How can we learn from his experiences and share his intense human insights? The question cannot be unerringly answered, although we may find hints spread throughout his autobiography, *Go East Young Man*. It would require a book-length study to comment upon the individual experiences which helped mold Douglas' warm feeling for humankind: an early intimate involvement with nature and mountains; early adversities; sharing the work and lives of the poor and the humble; overcoming polio; sharing his boyhood earnings with his family; humanistic teachers in high school and college for whom he felt profound gratitude; constant struggle during most of his early life; identification of himself with the great mass of strugglers in life.

The intensity of his contract with nature permeated his whole being. At an early age he seemingly became one with nature and could identify with flowers, rocks, winds, clouds, and stars. While reading his autobiography I felt the intimacy of nature. The Justice writes:

I took my early hikes into the hills to try to strengthen my legs, but they were to strengthen me in subtler ways. As I came to be on intimate terms with the hills, I learned something of their geology and botany. I heard the Indian legends associated with them. I discovered many of their secrets. I learned that they were always clothed in garments of delicate hues, though they seemed to be barren; though they looked dead and monotonous, they teemed with life and had many moods.[20]

And in speaking of an ideal Christmas gift he recalled a rare species of flower on the high ledges of Kloochman Rock near Yakima:

. . . One of these flowers—tenderly collected and carefully pressed—would make a Christmas gift unequalled.[21]

"Tenderly" collected and "carefully" pressed conveys a universe of meaning!

Justice Douglas' main criticism is that the "establishment" in the United States does to the common folk of America what George III and his friends did to the colonists:

George III was the symbol against which our Founders made a revolution now considered bright and glorious. George III had not crossed the seas to fasten a foreign yoke on us. George III and his dynasty had established and nurtured us and all that he did was by no means oppressive. But a vast restructuring of laws and institutions was necessary if the people were to be content. That restructuring was not forthcoming and there was revolution.[22]

Professor Page Smith reminds us:

It is thus of particular importance for all the nations of the modern world to understand our common revolutionary tradition and to recognize that the brute force of modern technology must be mastered and humanized, whether we call ourselves capitalists, socialists, communists, republicans, or democrats.[23]

Justice Douglas roars like a fighting scholar both within and without his ivory tower, as have his fellow humanistic colleagues through the centuries. And many have been admonished by their colleagues who were either unaware of the world outside or who were devoted to the comforts within.

As a law teacher dealing with the subjects of constitutional law, law in developing countries, international law, world peace and conflict resolution, labor law and philosophy of law, I concluded my study of Douglas with a feeling that he must, indeed, know deep remorse, despair, frustration, and sorrow over events in the world. But he has fought back to do something about that despair.

Perhaps it would be fitting to close this section of my exploration of the humanism displayed by Justice Douglas by quoting from the English historian Arnold Toynbee, who, when speaking to an American audience, remarked:

Your role in the coming chapter of the World's history is not yet irrevocably decided. It is still in your power to re-enter into your heritage. It is still within your power to recapture the lead in your own revolution. . . . The future is still open.[24]

When I encountered Douglas' discovery of a small violet, my mind leaped back to the wonderful seventeenth-century Japanese poet Bashō, and I at once realized that there was a unity here; Bashō's insights became transmuted into Justice Douglas', and with one leap the two vast threads of thought and feeling united. The spark that aroused my comparison came in his autobiography where the Justice says:

. . . Even a minute violet quickens the heart when one has walked far or climbed high to find it.[25]
And Bashō writes in his beautiful haiku poem:
Coming along the mountain path,
There is something touching
About these violets.[26]

I suspect that Justice Douglas and Bashō would find themselves to be great companions. Indeed, Blyth's words on Bashō help us see the kinship:

He has an all-around delicacy of sympathy which makes us near to him, and him to us . . . there is something in him beyond literature, above art, akin to what Thoreau calls homeliness. In itself, mere goodness is not very thrilling, but when it is added to sensitivity, a love of beauty and poetry, it is the irresistible force which can move immovable things.[27]

This "all-around delicacy of sympathy" has been the flame added to an immense catholicity of knowledge of the law, the world, and man.

These have made Justice Douglas our most humanistic Justice. In his autobiography, Douglas states, "That night I felt at peace. I felt that I was a part of the universe. . . ."[28]

About the Wobblies and other laborers he knew during his teenage years as a migrant worker, Douglas writes,

By the time my teenage years ended, I had met a different group of outcasts, who made a very deep impression on me. They were the Wobblies, or IWW's, of the Far West—the Industrial Workers of the World. Though Yakima denounced them as criminals, I came to know the Wobblies as people who deserved more than our society had meted out to them.[29]

And in writing of Blacky, a rather desperate member of the IWW who had earned a lifelong bond with the Justice through an act of friendship, Douglas continues:

There was no drive or ambition in Blacky. But there was a kindness, compassion, tenderness, and a desperate loneliness. I had seen that some loneliness under the railroad bridge over the Yakima River north of the city, where I used to sit with restless vagabonds, sharing coffee and stew, while the wrath of their discontents against society bubbled out. Their lives were mostly empty and filled with despair. I had been raised to believe in the Puritan ethic—that right was right and wrong was wrong, and that man, endowed with free will, could choose which he preferred. It was all a matter of good and bad, sin and righteousness, reward and punishment. Criminals were the product of the wrong moral choice. The poor were the product of lack of desire, energy, and will power. The rich were those who took advantage of their opportunities. Young as I was, I began to doubt the accuracy of this ethic. I sensed in this restless, lonely community, constantly pursued by the forces of law and order, personal tragedies that had somehow or other fragmented them.[30]

Some insight concerning the humanism of the Justice can be found in his descriptions of others whom he admired. He says of his father: "Father was one of the few truly good men I ever knew. Like St. Francis, he loved people and went humbly among them. Spiritual reward, not monetary gain, was his desire."[31] In speaking of Chicano migratory workers with whom he worked, he observed:

There were many Chicanos whom I came to love. . . . Having been one, I have an enduring love for migrant workers. They are still looked down upon as we were. Yet they are wonderful people who take care of their children and their wives and they are the direct descendants, spiritually, of our working people of the beginning of the century.[32]

He further suggests:

The American Indian . . . seems to have had an Oriental reverence for the land and its life, and when I was exposed to Hinduism and Buddhism in Asia, I realized that Eastern thought had somewhat more compassion for all living things.[33]

And thus, in describing others, the Justice describes his own profound humanism.

In speaking of Justice Brandeis, Justice Douglas likewise characterizes himself:

There is in Brandeis a universal note. We can reach the moon and top all secrets of the universe and yet not survive if we do not serve the soul of man. We serve the soul of man only when we honor individual achievements and respect individual idiosyncrasies. We serve the soul of man only when a man's worth—not his race, creed, or ideology—becomes our basic value.[34]

These quotations recalled to my attention a statement about culture made by John Dewey in his *Art as Experience*:

As the developing growth of an individual from embryo to maturity is the result of interaction of organism with surroundings, so culture is the product not of efforts of men put forth in a void or just upon themselves, but of prolonged and cumulative interaction with environment. . . .[35]

I mention this simply to show a glimpse of the aesthetic—the union with being which the Justice epitomizes, with culture, man, and nature. And, if indeed he should be required to stick to what he knows, as disgruntled critics and myopic politicians have asserted over the years, presumably he should have to eliminate the aesthetic from his responses to life and human beings. And, presumably, he would have to eliminate a concern for the vast interaction between law and culture. If judges are to stick to their jobs, then it is interesting to note that some other notable human beings strayed from theirs to the benefit of humankind: Copernicus and Mendel should have stuck to being priests; Gandhi to being a lawyer; Freud and Jung to medicine; Buddha to being a rich man's son; and Christ to carpentry. Professor Loren Eiseley should never have deviated from measuring human skulls to his concern with the plight of mankind, while the great astronomer Harlow Shapley should never have strayed from his observatory to write his book, *Beyond the Observatory*, and say:

To me it is a religious attitude to recognize the wonder of the whole natural world, not only of life. Is not the creed of Schweitzer too narrow, too selective? Why not revere also the amino acids and the simple proteins from which life emerged? Or why not go all the way and avow reverence for all things that exist, all that is touched by cosmic evolution, and reserve the greatest reverence of all for existence itself.[36]

Justice Douglas' Humanism and the American Revolution

Before beginning to study the Douglas materials for my comments here, I happened to read *A New Age Now Begins*, by Professor Page Smith, on the American Revolution. I eventually realized that no small part of Douglas' effort was to make the ideals of the American Revolution real to the modern reader. "We must realize that today's Establishment," Douglas has written, "is the new George III. Whether it will continue to adhere to his tactics, we do not know. If it does, the redress, honored in tradition, is also revolution."[37]

Professor Smith says of the Founding Fathers:

. . . I believe that they would have responded warmly to the notion of the "United States" . . . as a society that would be the vector of a new human order rather than simply a nation among other nations . . . I believe that the first American Revolution has an inexhaustible capacity to illuminate our own "soul" or "spirit" as well as the dilemmas of our times; and that America, forged once in the fires of adversity, may be forged once more and in that forging merge its great talents and energies, its gift for self-criticism and for visions of a better world, with the common metal of humanity.[38]

Justice Douglas was conscious of the relevancy of the American Revolution through his continuing study of what he called *An Almanac of Liberty*. He collected over 360 illustrations with commentary on significant laws, events, and situations in the achievement of and quest for liberty in the United States. He says: "I wrote for the common man, hoping I could help him see the main contours and, seeing them, better understand the high vantage point we have reached with our form of government."[39]

Here again, the Justice's efforts have been constructive efforts, efforts to help the nation and the world save and achieve their ideals, always with the offering of plans and alternatives where criticism is leveled. This is true on the world scene, as it is in the United States. I cannot find where he has made any criticism without an offer of solution or a hypothesis for alternative action.

Colleagues in Humanism from Other Disciplines

I see Justice Douglas united with the thesis of modern humanism expressed by John Dewey in his *Reconstruction in Philosophy:*

Government, business, art, religion, all social institutions have a meaning, a purpose. That purpose is to set free and to develop the capacities of human individuals without respect to race, sex, class or economic status. And this is all one with saying that the test of their value is the extent to which they educate every individual into the full stature of his possibility. Democracy has many meanings, but if it has a moral meaning, it is found in resolving that the supreme test of all political institutions and industrial arrangements shall be the contribution they make to the all-around growth of every member of society.[40]

It is a contribution of Justice Douglas that he refused to recognize anything immutable in the precepts of law and so entered the great stream of the scientific method applied to law. He has given the same challenge to law which Dewey gave to mankind. Dewey proclaimed:

When the liberation of capacity no longer seems a menace to organization and established institutions, something that cannot be avoided practically and yet something that is a threat to conservation of the most precious values of the past, when the liberating of human capacity operates as a socially creative force, art will not be a luxury, a stranger to the daily occupations of making a living. Making a living economically speaking, will be at one with making a life that is worth living.[41]

And in dealing with the same vast social crises which faced Douglas, Dewey asked himself:

... the experimental logic when carried into morals makes every quality that is judged to be good according as it contributes to amelioration of existing ills. And in so doing, it enforces the moral meaning of natural science. When all is said and done in criticism of present social deficiencies, one may well wonder whether the root difficulty does not lie in the separation of natural and moral science.[42]

And, as Justice Douglas sought growth in the national and world community, Dewey felt that a union of science` and its method with the humanities is indispensable to growth, not to fixed ends, but to an ever-flowering of ideals through intelligence. He says:

Not perfection as a final goal, but the ever-enduring process of perfecting, maturing, refining is the aim in living. Honesty, industry, temperance, justice, like health, wealth and learning, are not goods to be possessed as they would be if they expressed fixed ends to be attained. They are directions of change in the quality of experience. Growth itself is the only moral "end."[43]

This expresses the essence of Justice Douglas' philosophy of law, of the American experiment, and of the ideal world order.

A great Swiss psychoanalyst likewise agonized with these issues. Carl Jung, in *The Undiscovered Self*, described man's destructiveness and asked:

Considering that the evil of our day puts everything that has ever agonized mankind in the deepest shade, one must ask oneself how it is that, for all our progress in the administration of justice, in medicine and in technology, for all our concern for life and health, monstrous engines of destruction have been invented which could easily exterminate the human race.[44]

Jung's answer is that the modern person simply has not discovered his or her unconscious and refuses to acknowledge the evil within his capacity. This lack of recognition forces humans to project, or blame, others (nations and other human beings) for the evils which they refuse to see in themselves. Unless we learn to take conscious possession of such forces in our unconscious mind, we simply cannot control the catastrophes which might occur; by recognizing them, heaven knows the good and creativity which can follow. By explaining the unconscious, Jung helps us see the magnitude of the forces working for and against humanism.

In stating that "the task that faces our age is indeed almost insuperably difficult," Jung places great reliance on "those guiding and influential personalities in the world who have the necessary intelligence to understand the situation the world is in."[45] Justice Douglas is a leader in that category. The challenge to even such personalities, Jung says, is that:

Nature, as we know, is not so lavish with her boons that she joins to a high intelligence the gifts of the heart also. As a rule, where one is present the other is lacking, and where one capacity is present in perfection it is generally at the cost of all the others. The discrepancy between intellect and feeling, which get in each other's way at the best of times, is a particularly painful chapter in the history of the human psyche.[46]

Justice Douglas is a rare human being whose heart and intelligence have joined; he has utilized them both, as Jung has done, to attempt to alert mankind to evils and catastrophes.

This use of intelligence and heart, this dynamic urge to alert us to our evils, explains Justice Douglas' *Points of Rebellion*. What a wonderful event! A Supreme Court Justice writing about situations which can lead to rebellion! And available in paperback! What courage, joined with heart and intelligence, to write of the military industrial complex, the CIA involvement in universities, the forces encouraging conformity of ideas, the massive constraints imposed on government employees, the loyalty and security boards, the Vietnam crisis, the China Lobby, the ABM missile program with unending escalation, the plight of racial minorities, the bias against the poor, the destruction of the environment through strip mining, insecticides, wilderness exploitation, and coastal spoilage. Imagine a Supreme Court Justice not only with such detailed knowledge of the society, but writing about the evils which he sees! Indeed, why should he not be impeached? This is dangerous doctrine! Today, assuredly, he could not get a job with the FBI, or maybe not even have a rural mail route, let alone be appointed to the Supreme Court. As he states in *Points of Rebellion*: "There are only two choices: A police state in which all dissent is suppressed or rigidly controlled; or a society where law is responsive to human needs."[47]

This is the Copernican Revolution which Justice Douglas calls upon humanity to recognize. It is the same challenge Jung made in his *Undiscovered Self.* It is the same voice as John Dewey's urging mankind to test its precepts of the consequences which occur when they are acted upon. It is the same voice as that of psychotherapist Rollo May, who urges: "We now need to establish feeling as a legitimate aspect of our way of relating to reality. . . . For human beings, the more powerful need is for relationships, intimacy, acceptance and affirmation."[48]

It is the voice of anthropologist Loren Eiseley, who urges mankind to recognize that we are capable of love, when he writes:

Forty thousand years ago in the bleak uplands of southwestern Asia, a man, a Neanderthal man, once labeled by the Darwinian proponents of struggle as a ferocious ancestral beast—a man whose face might cause you some slight uneasiness if he sat beside you—a man of this sort existed with a fearful body handicap in that ice-age world. He had lost an arm. But still he lived and was cared for. Somebody, some group of human things, in a hard, violent and stony world, loved this maimed creature enough to cherish him.[49]

It is both our misfortune and our great challenge that things are now moving at a computer speed for us. We lack the leisure of adjustment which was given to humans following the year 1543 when Copernicus published his mathematical description of the heavens, *The Revolution of the Heavenly Orbs*, showing a single system moving around the sun. The adjustment, even so, was painful. The Inquisition excommunicated and burned Giordano Bruno at the stake in 1600. He had written an exposition of the Copernican theory and rejected, therefore, the Aristotelian astronomy, which did not allow for the possibility of innumerable worlds. Galileo's trial was in 1633. Bronowski records that: "Galileo thought that all he had to do was to show that Copernicus was right, and everybody would listen."[50] We all know that he was confined for the remainder of his life. Bronowski concludes: "The effect of the trial and of the imprisonment was to put a total stop to the scientific tradition in the Mediterranean. From now on the Scientific Revolution moved to Northern Europe."[51] And there are those in our society who would have silenced Justice Douglas. The silence heard among the bench and bar of the United States, with over 350,000 members in the legal profession, is a vast silent voice adding its weight to the prevention of the Copernican challenge which Justice Douglas sounded to the legal profession.

Unlike our friend Galileo, we know it takes more than just telling for everybody to "listen," and feel, and understand, and act.

Nobel Prize recipient, Professor Peter Medawar, and his wife, Jean Medawar, Trustee of the International Institute for Environment and Development, in their article, "Revising the Facts of Life—a Framework for Modern Biology," have not stuck to their discipline when they warn mankind that survival is conditioned on sensitivity to humankind and all living things. They say:

> Although it is widely regarded as frivolously superficial to suppose that the human predicament is remediable, nothing in reality could be more superficial than failure to realize that acquiescence in the notion of impending doom is a principal factor in helping it to come about. In spite of all its frightening groans and rattles, the great world machine can still be made to work, but not unless it comes to be accepted that the long-term welfare of human beings cannot be secured by policies that promote the interests of some people at the expense of others or even the interests of mankind at the expense of other living things. *The unity of nature* is not a slogan but a principle to the truth of which all natural processes bear witness. The lesson has been learned too late to save some living creatures, but there may just be time to save the rest of us.[52]

These "colleagues in humanism," as I have called them, all have a shared focal point of concern. Each in his or her respective way searches for a greater socialization, a greater community, and this, of course, demands enlightened concern by both leaders and the people, organization and dedication on many fronts. Humanism is not easy.

Legal Humanism

To speak of a judge as a "humanist" who writes of the love of humankind, the beauty of a mountain flower, and the evils of the military industrial complex, can receive a wide-eyed uncomprehending response among some of the legal profession and newspaper editors.

One may observe among many of one's acquaintances the same reaction to Harlow Shapley's remark that in his estimate there are at least "a hundred thousand million billion stars in the universe," and that

If only one star in a trillion has a planet that harbors life, there would be, nevertheless, a hundred million of them. Life is widespread. It evolves out of the lifeless as a natural product of cosmic evolution. Perhaps this natural evolution has produced elsewhere biological forms that excel in many respects anything that this planet can show.[53]

Most of us are caught in traps, immediate narrow confines of a quite limited existence, and therefore possess only very shallow perceptions of ourselves, of nature, and of the universe. Justice Douglas warned: "A man or woman who becomes a Justice should try to stay alive; a lifetime diet of the law turns most judges into dull, dry husks."[54]

If humanism is to come to law, it will not come from the legal profession as it presently exists, but from other forces: from disciplines that teach a sense of awe toward existence, love toward all beings; from enlightenment with a method of intelligence, an intelligence that sees social and moral issues by the consequences which flow from adopting a position, and which requires an openness of mind to view alternatives; from mental habits demanding to view the largest possible field of knowledge applicable to any given issue or problem; and from a habit of mind willing to abolish all final and absolute solutions, to be reconciled to the tentative until wiser solutions are discovered.

In speaking of his experiences with some judges when he served as chairman of the Securities and Exchange Commission, Justice Douglas stated:

I had had many experiences with judges prior to that time, but never before had I sat with them in conference. I realized then, and later on, that judges as a whole were the most reactionary group I had encountered, even more reactionary than investment bankers. The bankers were usually open to new ideas; the judges were anchored fast to the past. Precedents were their hallmark. What had once been done was hallowed; what had never been done was suspect.[55]

If this is what law can do to judges, one may ask, "Why is this so?" Is it because of the law school? Is it something deep in the system of litigation itself? In the litigiousness of society? In the worship of the rule of positive law? Now Justice Douglas was a superb craftsman in the law. There is nothing inconsistent with being a legal craftsman and at the same time seeing one's craft in the broadest possible dimensions. The simple answer to me is that judges are chosen not for their catholicity of knowledge about the world, nor for their humanism, but mostly because they have had a successful career in the law, or are favored by a political machine, and are not known to rock many boats by deviating from the customary norms of the community in action or in thought.

As a leader in the movement known as "Sociological Jurisprudence" and the "Realist"[56] movement at Columbia and Yale law schools, where he taught, Justice Douglas along with others sought to relate law to the larger society, to the diverse conflicting interests and demands of men and institutions, to bring into the study of law many other nonlegal disciplines which could add a richness of knowledge about forces which make and change law. He wanted to integrate social science and the humanities with the study and practice of law. He tried to study and perceive law beyond the rules and principles in the casebook on contracts, or labor law, or corporations, and to identify forces from which law emerges, the ends served by the law, to make law justify itself. Thus law was viewed not as immutable, but as a process.

As I view sociological jurisprudence, neither the law schools nor the legal profession has taken this view of the law to its logical consequences, namely, that a system of study be arranged to study systematically the needs of people in the local and world society and evaluate whether or not the legal code serves those needs. The study would begin with hypotheses concerning human needs, hypotheses concerning values and estimates of the resources available to a community, with the idea of human potential being uppermost in mind. Every discipline of knowledge capable of throwing light on the problem of law would be explored. A Copernican Revolution, indeed, in the study of law. And this is the challenge laid down to law, to the legal profession, to law schools, to colleges and universities, by Justice Douglas.

There is also a need for some means to capture, nurture, teach, and help mold a society which possesses a sense of humanism, a leavening, without which the end product continues to be lifeless. Humanity in general remains unaware of the vast implications of the earth floating in space around the sun, and of ten billion other galaxies in view of the Palomar telescope. With these physical facts widely unknown, and with the ethical implications far from explored, how can we deal with the vastly more complex issues of regard for human beings by human beings?

Given the present state of litigiousness in our society, students must be skilled to protect their client's interests and of course this requires knowledge of the rules, principles, and policies which courts follow in making decisions. But we are *not* free to meander along as before, as though the vast crises of our times do not exist. New dimensions have been added. All of us must in reality be reeducated to the crises, to determine the consequences if these crises are not solved. We must adapt our legal education and reform the legal profession so that new ways of teaching and practicing law will maximize the further creation and survival of the values of dignity and growth of the individual human.

The first step is to recognize that there *is* a problem. Justice Douglas joined with scholars of many disciplines to prove that there are problems for all to see. Unfortunately, many refuse to look through Galileo's telescope to see that Jupiter's moons do revolve around that planet; some see but do not believe because to believe is to upset accepted ways of doing things. If many of us sustain these illusions, the moons will continue to revolve around Jupiter but there will be no one to observe them.

Having taught international law for some years and feeling increasingly frustrated by my own and my students' lack of empathy with what happened at the human level, I began to emphasize the problem of world peace and how conflicts are resolved or not resolved. By so doing, we managed to catch a glimpse or two of some problems never disclosed by the traditional international law casebook. I conducted another experiment to shock myself and the students into an awareness of where and what we are in the universe. Our course is the philosophy of law is where Alabama students first deal with problems which Justice Douglas has raised about the endangered condition of the planet Earth. Then we study the major systems of legal philosophy to see what they can and cannot do about the situation, and we study methods of inquiry, applying intelligence to problem solving from Jung to Zen Buddhism. Students then write papers utilizing their undergraduate training and life's philosophies to develop philosophies of law equal to the problems we have encountered. They keep their philosophies of law to build on and reconstruct when the encounter other experiences, law, and society, knowing that the process will never end but conscious of that fact. The objective is simply that every student, every member of the legal profession, has "a philosophy of law" which is part of his or her own general philosophy of life and existence— hopefully as a growing humanist. These, of course, are minor palliatives, but they do make me feel good; they do open up a world of excitement; they challenge lawyers to participate in society's survival.

How to create legal humanists? Or humanists in the legal profession? In a course I teach called "World Peace and Conflict Resolution," after spending a month or so on problems and instruments of war, destruction of nature, pollution, population, famine, and then some time on hypothetical models for various types of world order, we then look at about twenty-five movies of villages in many areas of the world (produced by the American Universities Field Staff), making notes as we observe village life with all its vast poverty and despair; seeing children, with diseases which could be cured with ten cents worth of medicine, left uncured; barefoot potato planters watching their crops wither without fertilizer and water, and on and on. A hush comes over the class; we look at each other with different eyes. For an instant we have established contact with other human beings in need. The papers the students write show this. They show their feelings in words and expression. Then we spend a session or so on the evolution of life and see our various struggles from the osteolepis from which we grew, and on and on, and then marvel at the unique place *Homo sapiens* now occupies. And then we look at a beautiful book called *Behold* with some wonderful microscopic studies of the total body and see the vast spider webs and stream meandering and rope twistings of the human brain. Then we study something of the unconscious. And lastly we take some books, and sometimes my wonderful Questar telescope and look out beyond our galaxy to the nebula Andromeda. We watch it seemingly pulsate with life, a million light years away, with its 10 million suns and heaven knows how many planets. And then we have some beautiful photographs of the earth taken by the astronauts. The earth, blue and green, a beautiful sight which one would not think would contain so much human despair. And then we just sit and think. But, of course, this is just a two-hour course and Alabama students must study bankruptcy, torts, contracts, constitutional law to pass the bar examination—for there is no bar examination on law and humanism.

Will the knowledge that we are not alone make mankind more humanistic? My classes think so; although there are some bold spirits who say it will increase world militarization to fight off our extraterrestrial friends if they should decide to attack. One astronomer friend asked me if I was not "borrowing trouble" in speculating about this. I responded that this is what a lot of law should be about: borrowing trouble by thinking of possibilities. When I asked him whether he did not believe in other intelligent life in the universe, he responded, "Oh yes, but they are probably a hundred and fifty million years ahead of us, so why would they bother?" We laughed and parted. But my students and I have felt, if only for a moment, a greater kinship with all being, with astronomer Shapley's "Existence," with Tillich's "Ultimate Concern," and with Justice Douglas.

What if the American judiciary became involved in studying the present humans in the local, national, and world society and then spoke and wrote about their concerns? So far as I know, Justice Douglas is the only American judge who has written so widely and deeply about the conditions of modern man and the law. We have literate voices from ecologists, biologists, botanists, physicists, theologians, psychologists, psychiatrists, demographers, ethologists, and others who are concerned about the destruction of the environment, the pollution of the oceans, world illiteracy, the population explosion, famine facing the world, the destructiveness of atomic and biological warfare. Is it not strange that the literature is sparse from the legal community, from judges? It is as though the medical profession of the country, in the presence of a vast pestilence rising up throughout the world, would maintain an "objective" silence and go about their daily chores blandly practicing their profession in their offices. Judges and the legal profession in general are unaware of crisis literature, of what Professor Richard Falk writes about in his book, *This Endangered Planet*,[57] in which he assembles brilliantly a list of worldwide dangers threatening and offers hopeful suggestions in coping with them.[58]

A solitary Justice of one court in the United States has called out to the legal profession and to the law schools to listen. What is happening to mankind? He documented his examples with facts like a good trial lawyer. Then it is as though the Justice has given up on his colleagues and finds that he must appeal to the world community, over the heads of most of his associates, in order to alert the world to the dangers of lawlessness and the absence of reasonable rules of law. He advises alternatives to law in the form of conciliation and arbitration and mediation.

This is the present dilemma of President Carter with his task of alerting the American people to reaffirm their sensitiveness to humankind to provide him with a strong base from which to carry out his forcefully expressed beliefs in human rights throughout the world. A powerful base is indispensable to this task. And, indeed, the power base itself, the American people, must be made to see that their self-interest can be furthered only by a stable, humane world. As Professor Harold Lasswell has concluded in his essay, "Toward World Community Now," "it must be made apparent to leaders and potential leaders, old or young, socialist or liberal, that they have more to gain by intensifying the discovery of common interest than by playing a separated and parochial game in world affairs."[59]

It seems to me that Justice Douglas was well aware that in his duties as Justice of the Supreme Court his power did not extend to reshaping the massive ills of the world of which he was so conscious. So it is apparent that he utilized part of his time and the prestige of his high office to attempt in a herculean fashion to educate his contemporaries concerning the crises of the times, which, if unchecked, could lead humankind to self-destruction. Douglas saw the limitations of laws in statute books, of international law, of gaps in the Constitution. He carried his ideal and insights of humanism around the world and saw firsthand how human dignity suffered through the lack of laws respecting basic human needs. He saw multinational corporations operating without regard to the values of the foreign culture of which they played a large role in dominating. He explored alternatives to war and searched for a rule of law for humanity. He recognized that conflicts among nations were inevitable, and that "the atomic age has greatly limited man's ability to cope with them in the conventional way. That is why the search for the Rule of Law is the most pressing problem of this century."[60]

In 1971 Douglas wrote *International Dissent: Six Steps Toward*

World Peace, in which he stated: "This is a book about law, not law as it can be found in a library but law as it must be: and will be *if* we are to avoid the nuclear holocaust."[61] His six steps dealt with: an end to military alliances, the freeing of all colonies and the abolition of all protectorates, the recognition of China and its admission to the United Nations, the creation of an international regulatory body to govern the control and use of the ocean floor, the helping of developing nations to enter this technological age, and the agreement on the Rules of Law governing international relations. William O. Douglas concluded:

The area of international dissent covers emotional as well as economic, fiscal, population, nationalistic, and technological matters. The solution turns on the heart as well as the mind. If the search for international accord is to be successful, there must be a moral and ethical change; there must be a great sense of charity toward all people; there must be an increasing respect for the diversities and idiosyncrasies of the people; there must be a new respect for the earth itself.

Can we the people of Spaceship Earth, develop this new ethic and live by it? Are we, the people of the United States, dedicated enough to our Jeffersonian tradition that we can take the world leadership?[62]

The questions posed by the Justice may not be definitively answered by this generation, but we can ill afford not to grapple with them, following Douglas' splendid example, in our attempt to ferret out solutions to seemingly intractable issues.

Intractable? What, one may ask, is the alternative facing human beings if a firm basis is not immediately established for resolving the issues raised by William O. Douglas' questions?

Notes

1. John Dewey, *Democracy and Education* (New York: Macmillan & Co., 1926), p. 269.

2. William O. Douglas, *Being an American* (New York: The John Day Co., 1948), p. 12.

3. Ibid., p. 14.

4. Ibid., p. 15.

5. Ibid., p. 17.

6. Ibid., p. 113.

7. Ibid., p. 132.
8. Ibid., p. 140.
9. Ibid., p. 142.
10. Ibid., p. 167.
11. Ibid., pp. 169–70.
12. Ibid., p. 172.
13. Ibid., p. 176.
14. Ibid.
15. Ibid., p. 186.
16. Ibid., p. 187.
17. Ibid., p. 201.
18. Ibid., p. 208.
19. Ibid., p. 212.
20. William O. Douglas, *Go East Young Man* (New York: Random House, 1974), p. 34.
21. Ibid., p. 21.
22. William O. Douglas, *Points of Rebellion* (New York: Vintage Books, Random House, 1970), p. 95.
23. Page Smith, *A New Age Now Begins* (New York: McGraw-Hill, 1976), II, p. 1827.
24. Ibid., p. 1832, quoting Toynbee.
25. Douglas, *Go East Young Man*, p. 36.
26. R. H. Blyth, *Haiku* (Tokyo: Hokuseido Press, 1950), II, p. 379.
27. R. H. Blyth, *A History of Haiku* (Tokyo: Hokuseido Press, 1963), I, pp. 109–10.
28. Douglas, *Go East Young Man*, p. 37.
29. Ibid., p. 74.
30. Ibid., pp. 75–6.
31. Ibid., p. 12.
32. Ibid., pp. 82–4.
33. Ibid., p. 202–3.
34. Ibid., p. 447.
35. John Dewey, *Art as Experience* (New York: Minton, Balch & Co., 1932), p. 28.
36. Harlow Shapley, *Beyond the Observatory* (New York: Charles Scribner's Sons, 1967), p. 128.
37. Douglas, *Points of Rebellion*, p. 95.
38. Page Smith, *A New Age Now Begins*, p. 1821.
39. William O. Douglas, *An Almanac of Liberty* (Garden City, N.Y.: Doubleday & Co., 1954), p. vii.

40. John Dewey, *Reconstruction in Philosophy*, enlarged edition (Boston: Beacon Press, 1957), p. 186.

41. Ibid., p. 211.

42. Ibid., p. 172.

43. Ibid., p. 177.

44. C. G. Jung, *The Undiscovered Self* (New York: Mentor Books, The New American Library, 1959), p. 111.

45. Ibid., p. 106.

46. Ibid.

47. Douglas, *Points of Rebellion*, p. 92.

48. Rollo May, "Love And Will," *Psychology Today*, 3:3 (August 1969), p. 60.

49. Loren Eisley, *The Firmament of Time* (New York: Atheneum, 1960), pp. 144–5.

50. J. Bronowski, *The Ascent of Man* (Boston: Little, Brown & Co., 1973), p. 205.

51. Ibid., p. 218.

52. P. B. and J. S. Medawar, "Revising the Facts of Life," *Harper's*, 254:1521 (February 1977), p. 59.

53. Shapley, *Beyond the Observatory*, p. 123.

54. Douglas, *Go East Young Man*, p. 467.

55. Ibid., p. 410.

56. See generally Edgar Bodenheimer, *Jurisprudence*, revised edition (Cambridge, Mass.: Harvard University Press, 1974), pp. 111–33.

57. Richard Falk, *This Endangered Planet, Prospects and Proposals for Human Survival* (New York: Random House, 1971).

58. See also his study of plans for world order. Richard Falk, *A Study of Future Worlds, World Order Models Project* (New York: The Free Press, 1975).

59. Harold D. Lasswell, "Toward World Community Now," in Larry Ng, ed., *Alternatives to Violence* (New York: Time-Life Books, 1968), p. 121.

60. William O. Douglas, *Towards a Global Federalism* (New York: New York University Press, 1968), p. 2.

61. William O. Douglas, *International Dissent* (New York: Vintage Books, Random House, 1971), p. 8.

62. Ibid., p. 154.

Government Secrecy and the Citizen's Right to Know   2
THOMAS I. EMERSON_____

Thomas Emerson studied under William O. Douglas at Yale, 1928–31, and, like Douglas, he is no stranger to the inner workings of government bureaucracy. For fourteen years he was employed as counsel for various New Deal and wartime agencies in Washington, D.C. These included the National Recovery Administration, the Social Security Board, the Office of Price Administration, the Office of Economic Stabilization, the Office of War Mobilization, and the Department of Justice. After 1945, Emerson taught at Yale, where he earned the reputation of being an excellent teacher as well as a scholar involved in the era's most controversial social issues.

At the Douglas Symposium, Emerson participated in four panel discussions and delivered the conference's keynote address. In exploring the issue of government secrecy, his speech applies categories and assumptions that were earlier developed in his *System of Freedom of Expression* (1970). Emerson advocates an essentially conservative position, at least in the sense that Mill, Madison, Hamilton, Jefferson and Douglas are conservative: "It may be a reflection on human nature that such devices should be necessary to control the abuses of government. But what is government itself, but the greatest of all reflections on human nature? If men were angels, no government would be necessary. If angels were to govern men, neither external nor internal controls on government would be necessary. In framing a government which is to be administered by men over men, the great difficulty lies in this: you must first enable the government to control the governed; and in the next place oblige it to control itself" (*The Federalist*, No. 51).

For appreciative views of Emerson's contributions to American law, see L. H. Pollack, "Thomas I. Emerson, Lawyer and Scholar," *Yale Law Journal*, 85:463–9 (March 1976). For supplements to Emerson's remarks here, see Alan Reitman's "Freedom of Information and Privacy: The Civil Libertarian Dilemma," *American Archivist*, 38:501–8 (October 1975), and Sheldon Adler's "Toward a Constitutional Theory of Individuality: The Privacy Opinions of Justice Douglas," *Yale Law Journal*, 87:1579–1600 (July 1978).

There are few matters more urgently demanding our attention today than the problem of government secrecy and the citizen's right to know. In the past decade we have witnessed the military buildup in Vietnam, the bombing of Cambodia, the undermining of the legitimate government of Chile, the bribery of heads of government, and numerous other excursions into foreign affairs, all without the knowledge of the people of this country. On the domestic scene, the period has been marked by a vast increase in government surveillance over the political activities of the citizen, a disturbing amount of illegal conduct by the intelligence agencies, a massive effort by the Nixon administration to use the powers of government to suppress political opposition, again all buttressed by a policy of concealment and deception. Various proposals have been made, and are still being pressed, for more extensive controls over the dissemination of information which the government chooses to label as secret.

On the more positive side of the picture, we are today facing some very difficult decisions, which will call for a united effort on the part of the whole people. We must determine how to end unemployment and inflation, what energy policy to adopt, what to do about the decay of our urban centers, how to achieve disarmament, to name but a few. None of these tasks can be accomplished successfully without the understanding and participation of the ordinary citizen.

The question to which I address myself is what part the Constitution and the courts can play in solving these pressing issues of government secrecy and the citizen's right to know. An examination of the problem requires us to focus on most of the themes this conference was called to consider. It is necessary to explore the underlying values at stake and how far they should be translated into legal doctrine. Clashes between the rights of the individual and the rights of society are involved. Central to the issue is the question of how the Constitution is to be interpreted and what role, active or passive, the Supreme Court should play. We must also consider to what extent the courts ought to be bound by technical rules of law and to what extent humanistic values ought to be the guiding force.

We shall see that Justice Douglas, as usual, has been at the center of the action. Some of his ideas have prevailed; others have not. Those which have not been accepted, as in the case of all great dissenters, nevertheless lay the foundation for future progress.

The Value Structure

As Justice Douglas was fond of saying, "The starting point for decision pretty well marks the range within which the end result lies."[1] It is necessary, therefore, to be clear in our own minds as to the basic value structure from which we approach the constitutional decisions concerning government secrecy and the citizen's right to know.

There is one central point upon which all are agreed: Knowledge is power; and conversely ignorance is impotence. The words of James Madison, several times quoted by Justice Douglas, are still the best distillation of the point:

A popular Government, without popular information, or the means of acquiring it, is but a prologue to a Farce or a Tragedy; or perhaps both. Knowledge will forever govern ignorance: And a people who mean to be their own Governors, must arm themselves with the power which knowledge gives.[2]

Justice Douglas also quoted Patrick Henry to the same effect: "The liberties of a people never were, nor ever will be, secure, when the transactions of their rulers may be concealed from them."[3]

Something more, however, needs to be said. In a democratic state government secrecy is, as a general proposition, a form of *illegitimate* power. It is antithetical to all democratic values. This is true for a number of reasons.

In the first place, full information on public affairs is the right of the citizen, who is the ultimate source of political power. The Preamble to the Constitution explicitly states that it is "We the People of the United States" who "ordain and establish this Constitution." Dr. Alexander Meiklejohn has made clear to generations of readers the full implications of this elementary starting point, and Justice Douglas has consistently reiterated the same theme. The citizen is the master, and the government is the servant; and the servant has no political authority to withhold information from the master. On the contrary, the sovereign, the individual citizen, is entitled to all the facts available upon which to plan and direct the activities of his or her subordinates, the government servants.

Second, in public decision making the withholding of information from the persons directly affected is morally wrong, a denial of fair process. We have no doubt that in the case where the government institutes a proceeding against a single individual, that person should be entitled to a full and fair hearing before a decision is reached. Why should it be any different when the government decision concerns a large group of people, or perhaps the whole population? There, also, all those affected should have a right to full information before their lives and liberties are subject to government controls. This is only a just price asked by the individual for bowing to collective authority.

Third, government control through secrecy is a form of coercion, not persuasion. There is no opportunity for the persons involved to know the reasons for the government action. They must accept it as fiat, not by virtue of any rational process. This is authoritarianism, not democracy. Indeed, secrecy is the acknowledged hallmark of totalitarian government.

Fourth, secrecy is the frequently used instrument for hushing up bureaucratic errors. As Justice Douglas observed in the CIA budget case, "History shows that the curse of government is not always venality; secrecy is one of the most tempting coverups to save regimes from criticism."[4] Moreover, secrecy feeds the disposition of all bureaucracies to become impersonal and to lose the humanistic touch.

Fifth, secrecy is the source of much of the evil that governments engage in. The good things that governments do are usually done in the open. The bad things governments do are usually done in the shadow of secrecy. Witness Cambodia, Chile, Watergate. Government wrongs are kept secret because they are evil; and evil is done because it can be kept secret.

Finally, secrecy in government is politically destructive. It is responsible for the credibility gap and the consequent loss of faith in the government of the day and in the whole governmental process. Secrecy stirs fear, frustration, anger, and ultimately irrational response. Worst of all, secrecy is used to preserve an outworn status quo and to prevent necessary social change. In the end it leads to the resolution of social conflict by the resort to violence.

To sum up, in the words of Justice Douglas in the Pentagon Papers case, "Secrecy in government is fundamentally anti-democratic. . . . Open debate and discussion of public issues are vital to our national health."[5]

Also at stake, in addition to governmental withholding of information, is protection of the individual's right to acquire information from other sources, and the extent of government control over the dissemination by citizens of information which the government wishes to keep secret but which has escaped its grasp. Here, also, the fundamental values involved are the values of an open, democratic way of life.

On the opposite side of the equation, there are certain other values which must be considered. In some situations official secrecy may be justified and the public interest in knowing may be weak or nonexistent. The most important areas where such conflicts of value arise need to be mentioned briefly.

First, there are certain nondemocratic areas of national life where democratic values do not prevail, at least to the same extent as in the main sector. The most important of these is the military. Yet even here the parameters of any exception would be narrow. For the principle of civilian control over the military is a fundamental tenet of any democratic state. That principle would demand that secrecy in the military would not extend beyond the technical expertise of the military forces, the very narrow area in which the civilian state relinquishes its power to the compelling needs of military operations. This would limit military secrecy to the design of weapons, tactical operations of military units in the field, and the like. It would not include strategic or policy decisions, such as the decision to bomb Cambodia.

Second, our notions of the right to privacy are based upon a special set of values—the importance to the individual of maintaining a zone of privacy free from the intrusion of society and its rules. These values have to be protected. There will be some situations, for example, in which the government is entitled to obtain information about an individual, but privacy would be invaded if the information were released to the public. In most of these situations, the need of the public to know would be minimal.

Third, certain attributes of an economic system of free enterprise imply a degree of secrecy which does not apply to public enterprise. Thus information in the government's possession concerning the internal affairs of business corporations, which did not involve health, safety, fraud, or similar social concerns, would be entitled to some protection against public disclosure. Trade secrets, some aspects of financial institutions, and the like, would fall into this category.

Fourth, there are times when the government is in an adversary position with respect to some individual or group, and needs protection against premature disclosure of information in its possession. Such matters include law enforcement investigations, collective bargaining negotiations, and similar operations. Secrecy is necessary here, but for a limited time only.

Fifth, what has come to be known as the "advice privilege" is based upon values which run counter to the values of public disclosure. Officials in government are entitled to have full, frank, and freewheeling discussion from their subordinates in the decision-making process. It is a sad commentary on the bureaucratic personality, but unfortunately true, that such assistance is hampered if public disclosure is to be anticipated. This exception, which incidentally is the only justification for claims to "executive privilege," would be limited to matters of opinion and would not include factual information.

Finally, the area of diplomatic relations presents some problems. Here we are dealing with foreign nations which are outside our system and may be governed by a different value structure. Yet what happens in the field of foreign affairs is, of course, a matter of utmost importance for Americans. Valid reasons for concealing information would exist only in very limited circumstances, such as with respect to information obtained under a promise of confidentiality, matters relating to pending diplomatic negotiations, and perhaps some aspects of espionage operations.

Looking back over this survey of the value structure, it would appear that the basic concept of open government and full discussion of public issues remains paramount, and that competing values can best be reconciled by making a relatively few precise and narrow exceptions to that underlying principle. The next question is, to what extent does or should our Constitution, as interpreted by the Supreme Court, translate these values into governing rules of law.

The Original Constitution and the Current Reality

The original Constitution says very little about the subject of government secrecy and the citizen's right to know. It contains one provision mandating disclosure and one permitting secrecy. Article I, Section 9, Clause 7 states that "a regular Statement and Accounting of the Receipts and Expenditures of all public Money shall be published from time to time." On the other hand, Article I, Section 5, Clause 3 provides that "Each House shall keep a Journal of its Proceedings, and from time to time publish the same, excepting such Parts as may in their Judgment require Secrecy." That is about all that is said in express terms.

Nevertheless, the structure of the Constitution carries clear implications that open government is the norm, and secrecy the exception. As already noted, the Constitution was ordained and established by "We the People." It confers the franchise, limited though it originally was, upon citizens. Article IV, Section 4 guarantees a republican form of government to each state. More important, the First Amendment guarantees that "Congress shall make no law . . . abridging the Freedom of Speech, or of the Press; or the right of the People peaceably to Assemble, and to petition the Government for a redress of grievances." As Alexander Meiklejohn has pointed out, the First Amendment can be interpreted not only as a negative guarantee against government interference with freedom of expression, but as affirmative power reserved by the people in order to carry out their constitutional mandate as sovereign masters to control the activities of their servants, the government. Such an interpretation clearly implies the right of the citizen to have full access to government information.

Thus broad protection of the right to know is latent in the Constitution. Yet it must be acknowledged that for a century and three quarters no such constitutional right was formally recognized. The Constitutional Convention was itself held in secret. The Supreme Court remained silent. And the actual practice, from the time President Washington withheld information pertaining to the Jay Treaty from Congress, was to give the government full freedom to refuse disclosure of any matter it chose to withhold.

The onrushing times, however, have wrought important changes. The functions of government have greatly expanded. Hence government occupies a much more prominent place in our national life. This trend is likely to continue. Despite the demands of some groups to retreat to laissez faire, we are surely headed for some form of collectivism. The maintenance and development of individual freedom in a growing collective society is a central problem of our age. Success is possible only if full access to government information and open dissemination of facts and ideas are fully guaranteed and affirmatively promoted.

Other factors work in the same direction. Thus expansion of the government has brought expansion of the bureaucracy—and the problems of bureaucracy. These problems can be solved only through greater decentralization and, even more important, greater community control. This, too, is possible only with open government. Similarly, modern systems of communication, including the invention of Xerox machines, create many new opportunities for obtaining and disseminating information. These advances in communication make feasible a kind of participation in government decision making that has never been possible before. Finally, we can solve the manifold problems that confront us, without resort to force or violence, only if we remain united through open channels of information and discussion.

The need for open government in the modern world is reflected in the United Nations Declaration of Human Rights. Article IX of that document contains the provision:

Everyone has the right to freedom of opinion and expression; this right includes freedom to hold opinions without interference and to seek, receive and impart information and ideas through any media and regardless of frontiers.

In view of these considerations the question may be asked, "Should not the Constitution be interpreted as a living document and the concept of a constitutional right to know be brought to full fruition?" I believe the answer should be Yes.

Establishment of the Constitutional Threshold

The first steps toward creating an effective constitutional right to know have been taken. It was Justice Douglas who took the lead in bringing this about. This threshold position is the explicit recognition by the Supreme Court that the Constitution, more particularly the First Amendment, embodies not only a right to communicate, but also a right to receive communications—that is to say a right to listen, to observe, to read, and to obtain information.

As oftentimes happens, the first clear statement of the constitutional right to know came in a dissent. In *Zemel* v. *Rusk*, decided in 1965, the Supreme Court had before it a case involving the right of Louis Zemel, a citizen of Connecticut, to travel to Cuba in order to satisfy his curiosity and to educate himself on world affairs. The majority of the Court, in an opinion by Chief Justice Warren, upheld the authority of the State Department to refuse to issue a passport. Justice Douglas, dissenting, argued that the right to travel for purposes of informing oneself was one of the peripheral rights of a citizen under the First Amendment: "The right to know, to converse with others, to consult with them, to observe social, physical, political and other phenomena abroad as well as at home gives meaning and substance to freedom of expression and freedom of the press."[6] Characteristically, Justice Douglas made his point in global terms: "The ability to understand this pluralistic world, filled with clashing ideologies, is a prerequisite of citizenship if we and the other peoples of the world are to avoid the nuclear holocaust."[7] And he went on to quote Pope John XXIII's *Pacem in Terris*. Although there had been offhand references to the right to receive information in prior cases, this was the first real articulation by a Supreme Court Justice of the constitutional right to know.

Later during the same term, Justice Douglas, speaking for a unanimous Supreme Court, wrote the opinion which embodied the first actual holding that a constitutional right to know existed. In *Lamont* v. *Postmaster General*, Corliss Lamont challenged the validity of a federal statute which provided that, in order to receive materials from abroad which the government considered "communist propaganda," it was necessary to notify the post office that one actually wished to have such mail delivered. In this case, Lamont's copy of the *Peking Review* had been held up by the post office until he informed them in writing that he wished to receive it. The situation was one, of course, in which the persons seeking to communicate, the editors of the *Peking Review*, being in China, were in no position to complain. It was the recipient, the person wishing to be informed, who asserted his constitutional rights. The Supreme Court ruled that the statute, since it put a burden upon receiving communications, violated the First Amendment. Thus the constitutional right to know was born.[8]

Thereafter the right to know became accepted constitutional doctrine. Shortly after the *Lamont* case, Justice Douglas hammered home the principle in his opinion for the Supreme Court in *Griswold* v. *Connecticut*, the birth control case: "The right of freedom of speech and press includes not only the right to utter or to print, but the right to distribute, the right to receive, the right to read."[9] Later in *Stanley* v. *Georgia*, decided in 1969, the Court held that a state could not make it a criminal offense to look at obscene movies in the privacy of one's home.[10] In the *Red Lion Broadcasting* case, also decided in 1969, the Court ruled that the Federal Communications Commission's fairness doctrine was valid because radio and television viewers had a right to obtain a diversity of viewpoints in programs broadcast over the airways.[11] And very recently, in the *Virginia State Board of Pharmacy* case, the Supreme Court ruled invalid a Virginia statute which prohibited the advertising of prices of prescription drugs, on the ground that consumers were entitled to have access to the information.[12]

Thus the threshold has been crossed. The basic principle has been recognized and applied in a few elementary situations. Nevertheless, the Supreme Court, despite the urgings of Justice Douglas, has been unwilling to push the concept into frontier areas. The issues have arisen in three different contexts: where the government has refused to disclose information; where the government has imposed burdens on the efforts of the press or of ordinary citizens to obtain information; and where the government has attempted to control the dissemination of information it hoped to keep secret but which has escaped its grasp.

Forcing the Government to Disclose Information

Ever since the government started operations in 1789, it has been assumed that all branches of government could legally withhold whatever information they desired from the public. Why should this be? Why is not government business always, or virtually always, the public's business? On the basis of the analysis of democratic values, as sketched earlier, the citizen should have a right to know whatever his servants know.

The Supreme Court has never taken this position. There are not many cases in point, in fact only three of direct relevance. In those cases the Supreme Court has not advanced very far toward the position that the government has a constitutional obligation to conduct its activities in the open.

The issue was presented squarely in *United States* v. *Richardson*, decided in 1974. In fact, in that case the question arose under the only constitutional provision which expressly requires public disclosure. Richardson, a citizen of Pennsylvania and a taxpayer, brought suit against the United States to compel disclosure of the amount of the CIA budget, resting his claim upon the constitutional provision requiring a public accounting of the expenditures of all public money. The Supreme Court, in a 5–4 decision, dismissed the suit, upon the ground that Richardson had no standing to raise the issue.[13]

The result is hard to understand. Why should not a citizen and a taxpayer have the right to invoke a constitutional provision devised entirely for his enlightenment? And if not a taxpayer, who would have standing to enforce the constitutional guarantee? The decision represents a rather remarkable use of technical legal rules to reject an important substantive claim. Furthermore, beneath its employment of technical doctrine to avoid passing on the issue, the majority of the Supreme Court revealed that it was basically unsympathetic to the values of the right to know and oversympathetic to the values of national security. I do not believe the republic would fall if the CIA budget were revealed. The majority of the Supreme Court seems to think otherwise.

Justice Douglas' dissenting opinion brought the matter back to the basics: "The sovereign in this Nation are the people, not the bureaucracy."[14] But his views did not prevail.

In the second case the Supreme Court kept the door slightly ajar. The issue in *Pell* v. *Procunier*, decided the same term as *Richardson*, was whether the California prison system could forbid interviews by the press with specific inmates with whom the newspapers wanted to talk. A majority of the Supreme Court upheld the prison authorities. The major opinion, however, did indicate that the result would have been different if the prison officials had attempted to exclude all access by the general public. In other words, there was a strong implication in the Court's decision that the public does have a right to know what goes on inside the prison walls.[15]

Justice Douglas again dissented, along with Justices Brennan and Marshall. He asked a fundamental question: "Could the government deny the press access to all public institutions and prohibit interviews with all government employees?"[16] The majority did not answer directly. One would hope that the answer is No.

The third case bears on the issues less directly. *United States* v. *Nixon* involved a claim by former President Nixon that, under the doctrine of executive privilege, he could withhold the White House tapes from a grand jury investigating violations of criminal law by his associates. The Supreme Court unanimously rejected the Nixon claim, but held for the first time that an "executive privilege" did exist. The Court went on to say that the courts could review the executive's right to assert the privilege, and that the privilege could not prevail in this case against a grand jury investigation into crime.[17]

The issue in the *Nixon* case, of course, was not the right of the executive to withhold information from the public, but rather to withhold it from another branch of government, the judiciary. It would be expected, however, that a claim valid against the judiciary would also be valid against the public. The Court was thus, in effect, marking out one area of exception to the general right of the public to obtain government information, namely, the advice privilege. To this there would seem to be no objection. As already indicated, the advice privilege constitutes a legitimate exception to the citizen's right to know. The Supreme Court did not delineate the scope of the advice privilege, confining itself rather closely to the facts of the case before it. Again, the Court cannot be faulted for this. Its preference for proceeding slowly, on a case-by-case basis, has considerable merit.

This, then, is the record of the Supreme Court to date. In my judgment it is not satisfactory. I believe the Court should apply the right-to-know doctrine so as to impose on the government a constitutional duty to make government business the public's business. As the earlier analysis of value structure suggested, the starting point should be full disclosure. Thereafter narrow exceptions can be made. I believe that Justice Douglas would agree. Such an approach is clearly implicit in the Constitution. And it is demanded by the pressing needs of the day.

It should be noted, although it is beyond the scope of this writing, that much of this development is already being achieved through legislation, rather than constitutional interpretation. The Federal Freedom of Information Act and the recent federal sunshine law, along with similar state laws, have opened up many areas of government operations from which the public was formerly completely shut off. These laws show that open government is wholly workable. But statutes can be repealed or modified. They are not the equivalent of a constitutional mandate. The citizen's right to know is of such fundamental importance to a democratic society that it deserves constitutional protection.

The Right to Acquire Information

The constitutional right to know also plays an important role in cases concerned with the right to acquire information. One aspect of this involves situations in which the government attempts to prohibit or curtail the right to receive communications. Usually the Supreme Court has held such direct interference to be a violation of the First Amendment, as in the *Lamont, Stanley,* and *Virginia State Board of Pharmacy* cases already mentioned. Yet this is not always true. A right-to-know claim was rejected in the *Zemel* passport case, although the foreign affairs element in that situation injected some extraneous issues. *Kleindienst* v. *Mandel*, decided in 1972, is a clearer case where the Supreme Court refused to give weight to the constitutional right to know. That was a suit brought by various academicians and others to compel the attorney general to grant a visa to a Marxian economist, residing in Belgium, who had been invited to give a series of lectures in this country. A majority of the Court upheld the attorney general's ruling, virtually ignoring the argument that American citizens were being deprived of the right to hear a distinguished foreign scholar.[18]

Justice Douglas' approach is quite different. He considers such cases as vintage examples of improper government intrusion. The main purpose of the Bill of Rights, Justice Douglas says over and over, is to "take Government off the backs of people."[19] For him there is no more appropriate case for applying the Bill of Rights than when the government imposes a direct obstacle to the citizen's right to hear, read, or see. In fact Justice Douglas equates such government action with thought control. And thought control, Justice Douglas says in his dissent in *Kleindienst*, "is not within the competence of any branch of government."[20]

There is much to be said for the Douglas position that the right to know is entitled to full, or absolute, protection against direct government interference. The conduct of the citizen is far removed from any action with which the government can be legitimately concerned. Rather, the right to hear, read, or see, like the right to believe, is the source of all freedom. Control of those activities is a sure sign of a totalitarian society. Justice Douglas is correct, I believe, that interference with this function of the citizen is in essence thought control.

Another group of cases relates, not to government interference, but to the power or obligation of the government to promote affirmatively the acquisition of information. There are a number of aspects to this problem, but the most controversial, and the only one I shall discuss here, concerns the role of the government in creating greater diversity of opinion and information among the mass media.

The problem is obvious. The mass media in the United States, which are the most powerful instruments of communication in the country, tend to reflect a single political, economic, and social point of view. Ideally, a much greater diversity of ideas, opinions, and information, and a much wider access by individuals and groups not now represented, are necessary for a healthy system of free expression. Yet government-imposed diversity or access involves a paradox. Media subject to government control are no longer free. In attempting to improve the system, the system itself may be destroyed.

The Supreme Court has sought to solve this dilemma by distinguishing between the mass print media and the mass electronic media. As to the print media, the Court has excluded all forms of government control designed to achieve diversity or access, other than the antitrust laws. As to the electronic media the Court has allowed limited control. Thus, as mentioned earlier, the Court sustained the fairness doctrine in the *Red Lion* case. But not long afterward, in *Columbia Broadcasting System* v. *Democratic National Committee*, it rejected a claim that the First Amendment required broadcasting stations to accept paid political advertisements.[21]

Justice Douglas disagrees. He takes the same position as the majority of the Court on the print media. As to the electronic media, however, he will not permit any controls. In other words, he would treat both the same. Concurring in *Columbia Broadcasting System*, Justice Douglas observed that if the government owned radio and television, as it does the Corporation for Public Broadcasting, it would have to present all views. But the government has seen fit to license the stations to nongovernmental operators, and hence should keep its hands off:

. . . the fear that Madison and Jefferson had of government intrusion is perhaps more revelant to TV and radio than it is to newspapers and other like publications. That fear was founded not only on the spectre of a lawless government but of government under the control of a faction that desired to foist its views of the common good on the people.[22]

My own view diverges from that of Justice Douglas at this point. I share his position on print media and on government-owned radio and television. But I part company on *Red Lion* and *Columbia Broadcasting System*. In my view, the scarcity of wavelengths is the key factor. As long as there are not enough physical facilities for all to broadcast (and, while this is disputed, I think that scarcity does now exist), I believe the First Amendment should protect the rights of listeners to acquire a greater breadth of opinion and information. This would include acceptance of the fairness doctrine and a substantial degree of access. Were the scarcity to end, and cable television may bring that about, then I would revert to the Douglas hands-off doctrine.

A third issue concerned with a right to acquire information involves the matter of a reporter's privilege. The question is whether or not a news reporter who obtains information under a pledge of confidentiality can be forced by the government to reveal the information, or the source of the information, so acquired. Clearly a number of value conflicts may arise. On the one side is the interest of the reporter in protecting his sources and the interest of the public in having the reporter obtain inside information. On the other side there may be arrayed the interest of a legislative committee in acquiring the information; the interest of a grand jury or a prosecutor in investigating or prosecuting a crime; the interest of an accused in defending against a charge of crime; the interest of a party in civil litigation; and many other individual and social interests.

The Supreme Court dealt with the problem in *Branzburg* v. *Hayes*, decided in 1972. That decision involved three reporters; each had been subpoenaed by a grand jury to give testimony about material he had received in confidence, one with respect to the local drug scene and the other two with respect to the Black Panthers. Four justices of the Supreme Court resolved the conflict in favor of requiring disclosure of information to the grand jury, unless the reporter could show that the information was being sought not in good faith but for purposes of harassment. One justice voted to balance the conflicting interests involved on a case-by-case basis. Three justices, dissenting, thought that a balance should be struck in each case but that the balancing should be weighted on the side of the reporter. They would have required disclosure only when the government could show a compelling reason and could demonstrate that the information could not be obtained from any other source.[23]

Justice Douglas thought that the conflict should be resolved wholly in favor of First Amendment values. He held that the First Amendment barred any compulsory disclosure. The Douglas position, based upon a realistic assessment of the news-gathering operation and an unequivocal commitment to freedom of the press, rested upon three basic points: first, that the function of the press in a democratic society was not only to report the readily available news but to dig out and expose the less pleasant facts that lurked beneath the surface; second, that if a reporter was compelled to reveal confidential sources, this function could not be effectively performed; and third, that a process of balancing interests in each case would not protect the First Amendment interests at stake because sooner or later any test short of full protection got watered down to ineffectiveness, and also because the reporter would never know in advance when he could promise confidentiality.

Justice Douglas summed up his views as follows:

The function of the press is to explore and investigate events, inform the people what is going on, and to expose the harmful as well as the good influences at work. There is no higher function performed under our constitutional regime. Its performance means that the press is often engaged in projects that bring anxiety or even fear to bureaucracies, departments, or officials of government. . . .

Unless [a reporter] has a privilege to withhold the identity of his source, he will be the victim of governmental intrigue or aggression. If he can be summoned to testify in secret before a grand jury, his sources will dry up and the attempted exposure, the effort to enlighten the public, will be ended. If what the Court sanctions today becomes settled law, then the reporter's main function in American society will be to pass on to the public the press releases which the various departments of government issue.[24]

I think Justice Douglas makes the correct choice of values in this complex and difficult situation. The fate of investigative journalism is at stake. Although the results that Justice Douglas predicted have not yet come to pass on an extensive scale, the potential is there. A cloud hangs over the press which may someday develop into a destructive storm.

Government Controls over the Dissemination of Information That the Government Desires to Keep Secret

In an ideal democracy, for reasons already noted, there would be very little information which the government would be entitled to keep secret. Hence the problem of controlling the dissemination of such information would be a relatively minor one. But this is not now the case. As the government operates today vast amounts of information are classified, that is, kept secret and subject to strict security requirements. Most other information in the possession of the government is routinely withheld. At the same time large amounts of government information, classified and unclassified, are constantly being made public through leaks, investigative journalism, memoirs of former government officials, and in many other ways. Consequently, the question of what the government can or should do to control the dissemination of information it does not wish disclosed is a major problem for American democracy.

At the outset it should be made clear that there is no disagreement over the power of the government to punish traditional espionage, namely, the disclosure to a foreign government, with the intention to injure the United States, of information which would seriously jeopardize our national security. Nor is there any doubt that the government may impose sanctions upon those who obtain government information by burglary, the theft of documents, or similar criminal methods. Rather, we are concerned with what additional measures the government can take to prevent the circulation of information which it has the right to withhold and whose disclosure it believes may injure governmental or public interests, including the public interest in national security.

There are two main aspects to the problem. One concerns the internal controls which the government may exert over its own employees and former employees. The other relates to external controls which may be placed on persons outside the government, particularly the press.

As to the internal controls, here also there is a large area of agreement. No one disputes the power of the government to establish rules concerning the dissemination of information which it has authority to keep secret, or to set up a security system for safeguarding such information. Nor is it questioned that the government may impose administrative sanctions, ranging from mild discipline to dismissal, for violation of such regulations. The crucial question is whether it is constitutional or wise to impose *criminal* sanctions upon government employees or former employees for unauthorized disclosure of government information.

Present law on this subject, while not entirely clear, almost certainly does not provide now for any such criminal sanction, except in the case of traditional espionage. The government argued the contrary in the Ellsberg case, but the issue was never finally decided there. In any event, proposals have recently been advanced for the enactment of new legislation which would establish criminal sanctions, and the question is now before the American people for decision.

It seems to me highly doubtful whether criminal sanctions imposed upon government employees or former employees would be constitutional under the First Amendment. It is not necessary to pursue that issue at this time, however, because the enactment of such legislation seems to me clearly unjustified as a matter of policy under the value system that has been sketched previously. The reasons for this conclusion can only be briefly summarized here.

In the first place, it is clear that the imposition of criminal sanctions on government employees would result in a very close-mouthed, tight-lipped governmental structure. The possibility of criminal prosecution would frighten most government officials into deep silence. Indeed, the ordinary bureaucrat would tend to lean over backward out of an abundance of caution. If one adds to this the fact that, under the *Branzburg* decision, news reporters would be compelled to reveal their sources, and government employees who divulged information could thus be easily tracked down, it is clear that most government operations would be effectively sealed off from public scrutiny.

Second, in our system, control by the public of the government, or of factions in the government, depends to a major degree upon public access to information which the government wants to keep secret. A large percentage of news about the government is of this character. Without these sources of information the public would be, as Justice Douglas said in the *Branzburg* case, dependent on government handouts. This would be a mortal blow to the democratic process in America.

If one stops to consider what information, disclosed to the public over the past few years, would have remained suppressed if a rigid system of criminal penalties had been in force, it is possible to visualize the gravity of the proposed legislation. Much of the news about the Vietnam War, about the covert operations of the CIA, about the illegal activities of the FBI and other intelligence agencies, about cost overruns on military procurement, about our brush with the Russians over the *Glomar Explorer*, about the Watergate scandals, and a host of other matters might never have seen the light of day. The whole history of our country might have been quite different.

Third, criminal sanctions against government employees would never be administered fairly or evenhandedly. They would inevitably be used to punish or intimidate those within the bureaucracy who questioned or opposed the official policy of the moment or who blew the whistle on government corruption or incompetence.

Fourth, a system of criminal sanctions would mean that information coming from the government would be going all in one direction. Under such a system the government could declassify or leak information at will, in ways designed to manipulate public opinion. Anti-government leaks would be shut off.

Finally, the impact of the proposed legislation would be particularly severe as it was applied to former government employees. A healthy government structure should allow every government employee the option of resigning and telling all. Knowledge of this possibility has a salutary effect upon the government and the information disclosed can be of crucial importance to public understanding.

In sum, enactment of a system of criminal penalties for government employees who disclose government information, apart from the espionage laws, would cast a pall over the democratic process in this country. What the nation needs is not a closed structure in which the government can operate free from public watchfulness, but more looseness, more openness, and more opportunity for the people to control their government.

External controls over the dissemination of public information take two forms. One is through enjoining or otherwise preventing publication in advance, which raises the question of prior restraint; the other is making publication a criminal offense.

The question of prior restraint upon publication arose in the Pentagon Papers case. There the government sought an injunction against the *New York Times*, the *Washington Post*, and other newspapers to prevent them from publishing a Defense Department history of the Vietnam War. Three justices—Justices Black, Douglas, and Brennan—thought that prior restraint of the press was never permitted, or permitted only in the narrowest of circumstances where an ongoing military operation was involved. Two justices took the position that prior restraint would be constitutional where the publication would result in grave and imminent danger to national security, but that the government had not made a showing of such danger in the case then before the Court. Three justices would have adopted even less stringent rules. And one justice held against the government on other grounds.[25]

Thus no clear doctrine on prior restraint has been enunciated by the Supreme Court. In my judgment the only principle that satisfies the demands of our value structure is the one adopted by Justices Black, Douglas, and Brennan. Prior restraint is a draconian method of suppression. It is the way of the censor, the accepted method of the totalitarian regime. It should never be utilized in a democratic nation.

Criminal sanctions against the publication of material that has escaped the grasp of the government raise very much the same issues as have already been discussed in connection with proposed criminal sanctions against government employees. In the case of persons outside the government, however, the arguments against criminal penalties are even stronger. Such a system of attempted control would amount to an official secrets act; circulation of certain information would be made illegal. There is no better way to destroy the whole system of freedom of expression in America. The only safe rule is that information which the government has been unable to keep secret becomes information in the public domain and subject to no form of governmental restraint.

Conclusion

In the end one's approach to the problems of government secrecy and the citizen's right to know is determined by one's faith in the democratic process. Those who have confidence in the capacity of the American people to govern themselves will see little need for the government apparatus to conduct its affairs in secret. On these issues Justice Douglas has never wavered. In one of his last opinions, unfortunately again in dissent, he once again expressed his ultimate belief:

Secrecy and suppression of views which the Court today sanctions increases rather than repels the dangers of the world in which we live. I think full dedication to the spirit of the First Amendment is the real solvent of the dangers and tensions of the day.[26]

* * *

A panel responded to Professor Emerson's address. The following segments of that discussion include Vince Blasi's consideration of the First Amendment's historical basis, Lino Graglia's attack on Emerson's method of constitutional interpretation, and Congressman Lloyd Meeds' practical critique from a legislator's point of view. The conversation has been considerably edited and abbreviated.

MODERATOR: Let's begin with Mr. Blasi.

BLASI: I find myself in general agreement with most of what Mr. Emerson has said. . . . but I'd like to say it in my own way to cast a slightly different light on the subject. I think one can begin by asking why the right to know, and specifically the right to acquire information about the government, has not been treated as a core First Amendment right? Most of us, and most members of the judiciary, believe that the right to express oneself is at the heart of the First Amendment; that the speaker getting up on the soapbox, finding a forum and expressing himself or herself, is a core-protected First Amendment right. The competing interest must be very, very compelling for the government to regulate such speech.

In contrast, when we have a claim to acquire information, and particularly to acquire information about what the government is doing, the courts begin to get troubled [even though] the acquisition of information is very much what the First Amendment is about. The result is a pattern of decisions difficult to rationalize or justify. Professor Emerson did a good job of explaining some of those decisions, and showing how the Court seems to breathe hot and cold when dealing with the acquisition of information as opposed to self-expression.

Well, why is that? One might ask that question in light of the eighteenth-century history surrounding the passage of the First Amendment and the political tradition of the century before 1790. People in the eighteenth century thought about freedom of the press and freedom of speech primarily in terms of a need to check misbehavior by government, in terms of a limited government philosophy. The Framers were particularly impressed with how government power could be abused, and they thought of free speech as an antidote to that. Yet when these problems are presented to us today, we draw on a tradition that has a different emphasis which alters the way some judges and some people think about these questions.

Our more recent traditions stress individual self-fulfillment, it seems to me, more than the need to check dangerous government. Over the last fifty or seventy-five years we have rationalized our commitment to free speech primarily in terms of self-expression. Our models of free speech stress essentially humble, powerless, people expressing themselves, getting it off their chests, and individually participating in a decision-making process.

Also, we have stressed the idea that speech is harmless. Much of our marketplace-of-free-ideas metaphor, I think, is based on the premise that sticks and stones may break my bones but words will never hurt me. If everyone has his say, what emerges out of that marketplace supposedly will resound to the ultimate good of the society. Much discussion of landmark free-speech cases during the last fifty years has stressed the point that the regulatory interests present were not substantial.

But many recent First Amendment cases have dealt not with self-expression by individuals, but with the acquisition of information about the government by powerful forces in the society, the mass media or representatives of powerful reform movements. Then it's not so easy to say there are no substantial regulatory interests on the government's side. Professor Emerson has been perceptive in outlining for us some of the regulatory interests that are present in these disputes over information and in proposing ways of accommodating these regulatory needs with traditional First Amendment values. But I do not think we should start with the premise that the primary purpose of the First Amendment is to allow individuals to express themselves to find individual fulfillment, or even to nurture a system of direct democracy of the sort that Alexander Meiklejohn proposed.

Instead, *we should start with the premise that one of the major purposes of the First Amendment is to check the inherent tendency of government to do wrong*, to harm people in material ways—not just to deviate from an ideal of democracy, but to do concrete damage of the sort that was done by much of the secret government decision making about Vietnam. That is the different emphasis that I would place on this subject, although in terms of the basic conclusion Professor Emerson draws, namely, that the claim to acquire information deserves strong constitutional protection under the First Amendment, I find myself in full agreement. I would probably disagree with some of the line-drawing suggestions he makes, but they are not the essence of his paper.

MODERATOR: Thank you, Mr. Blasi. We'll move to Mr. Graglia.

GRAGLIA: I also am in a very large measure of agreement with Professor Emerson on the values of open government and the need to keep government secrecy to a minimum and as narrow as possible. He has identified very well the interests of such a policy. He has also in his typically accurate and thorough way identified some reasons why such a policy cannot be absolute—the reasons for having less than total full disclosure in many situations.

Like Mr. Blasi, my disagreements with Mr. Emerson on any particular problem would not be very wide or very great. For example, Mr. Emerson believes it is proper for government to control the content of the electronic media because of the alleged scarcity of the channels. Justice Douglas considers it improper because government should not control the content of the electronic media any more than it controls the content of newspapers. On that issue I agree with Justice Douglas, one of the few areas where Mr. Emerson disagrees with the Justice.

What I would like to emphasize and call to your attention, what is really involved here, and what is so difficult to keep in mind, is that we are discussing constitutional law. Mr. Emerson has not come before us and said, "I've thought about these problems." He indeed has studied and thought about them a long time and his recommendations are entitled to very great weight and are very valuable. He did not say, "I'd like to persuade you that the social policy we should urge our legislators to adopt is this rather than that." That's not what's being done here. What *is* involved here is a proposal that Mr. Emerson's preferred solutions and recommendations be imposed upon the country by the Court in the name of constitutional law.

Now that, I want to suggest to you (and it is the most important thing there is to understand about constitutional law), is a very different position than recommending a solution on the basis of its merit. It is one thing to think that a problem should be decided in a certain way. It is quite another thing to think that *courts* should decide how it should be settled and that what they decide should be required. Two very separate questions! It's like the minister who discovers the happy coincidence that God agrees with everything he wants, and finds that the Bible supports exactly his views. Well, that is Mr. Emerson and the Constitution. It so happens that for him, luckily enough, the Constitution requires all his solutions. This is our basic source of difference. That is also my chief difficulty with the work of Justice Douglas. Justice Douglas more than any other justice in our history was willing to remove decision making from the political process. Bear in mind that to say that a question should be decided as a matter of constitutional law is to say that it should be decided by judges—unelected, unremovable judges, who sit apart from the ordinary processes of representative democracy.

Justice Douglas was more willing to do that than any Justice who ever sat on the Supreme Court. It may be fair to say that Professor Emerson is more willing to do that than any eminent constitutional scholar in the country. That, I suggest to you, is the primary issue involved here. The ironic thing is that it's put forward in the name of democracy. "Get the government off the backs of the people," Justice Douglas tells us. But recall for a moment that the Supreme Court *is* government. It sits in Washington. It's federal government. It's not a moral or an educational institution. Its decrees are enforced. It is potentially on the backs of the people, and it is the most dangerous and the most irresponsible form of government, government by unelected and unremovable officials. Indeed, I would say that the most serious imposition on individual rights that takes place in this country today is imposed by the courts. I don't know of any more serious violation of individual rights than the busing requirement, the taking of children from the neighborhood of their homes and busing them to create racially balanced schools. This offends more rights than I could list. This is court-created and court-imposed. . . . Mr. Emerson concludes that one's feeling about this matter depends upon how strongly one has faith in democracy. That's ironic! I think faith in democracy would indicate, it indicates to me, that these problems should be left to the political processes—not taken from the public by the Court. . . .

There are two issues. The issue is not only, "What does the Court think, or is the Court's decision a good one?" but is the Court the *proper* institution to make the decision? Why is it? Because it's not government? That's not so. Why is it? Because the First Amendment answers these problems? That's silly! Only lawyers say such silly things as that; indeed, one could describe the process of learning law and practicing law as being a process of becoming inured to the ridiculous. The First Amendment says Congress shall make no abridgment of the freedom of speech. Mr. Emerson tells us, interestingly enough, that this means Congress cannot regulate the content of newspapers, but *can* regulate the content of TV. It means that a government agency can fire an employee who improperly discloses documents but it cannot punish him criminally. Now all those recommendations may be excellent, but to suggest that they are in the First Amendment is just silly! It is only an attempt to find higher authority for one's personal views, to relieve oneself of the obligation of having to persuade, a thumping on the Bible or the constitution.

MODERATOR: Thank you, Mr. Graglia. Congressman Lloyd Meeds. . . .

MEEDS: Thank you very much, I think.

I'm delighted to follow your bland and noncontroversial presentation. Maybe I could begin by first indicating to you, Professor Emerson, a very high degree of agreement with your paper, and while I am the recipient of some of this legislative power, I think on balance that the Supreme Court does a fairly good job of staying out of our business, though not always. My disagreements are slight, and I would just indicate some particulars.

First of all, I appreciated your statement about secrecy being politically destructive, responsible for the credibility gap and loss of faith. . . .but I'd like to point out that there are perhaps more problems than you indicate with the Freedom of Information Act. You mentioned problems with the free-enterprise system and trade secrets, plus some aspects of financial institutions. There are more problems than are readily apparent here, and we must continue to fine-tune the Freedom of Information Act so businesses do not have a ready resource for learning all the trade secrets of their competition. Let me give one illustration of where it has hurt.

The federal government is the trustee of the land and resources of the American Indians, and as trustee conducts research with regard to their property. Not long ago we found that coal companies and others used the Information Act to obtain records from the Interior Department and Bureau of Reclamation files. The firms used the information in negotiating with Indian tribes. It was like having total access to your competition's records. We plugged the loopholes. . . .

I totally agree with you on *Branzburg* v. *Hayes*. It shocked me when the Supreme Court failed to hold on the First Amendment, so I would go further than you do in that respect. . . .

MODERATOR: Thank you, Congressman Meeds. Mr. Emerson will have a short time to respond.

EMERSON: I agree with Mr. Blasi that the right to know has a somewhat different emphasis and approach than the traditional aspects of the First Amendment which prohibit interference with communication. Along with Justice Douglas I would say that communication is protected absolutely. Yet when we come to the right to know, we have to make exceptions, and therefore the legal rules are somewhat more difficult.

With respect to Mr. Graglia, I'm afraid that he's succumbed to the ridiculous in his own right. When he says that the most serious violations of individual rights today have been imposed by the courts, that statement really fails to stand up even if one takes his point of view on everything. The question he raises is, of course, a basic one in our constitutional structure, namely, "What is the role of the Supreme Court and of the courts?" To my mind, the way this structure has developed in our society is not antidemocratic. The Bill of Rights can be and has been enforced through an independent judiciary. And to say that the courts are on the other side of that issue does not make sense. It ignores the history of the Supreme Court, the Bill of Rights, and the approach which Justice Douglas has made.

With respect to Congressman Meeds, I agree that there are problems in the Freedom of Information Act. It should be called to our attention that we have made substantial progress in the right direction through legislation rather than through constitutional interpretation. . . . The Freedom of Information Act correctly starts with the position that every record should be available, and then we make some exceptions. . . . Also, the right of privacy does come quite clearly into conflict with the need to know. That's a whole area of law in itself which needs to be worked out very carefully, and of course we cannot do that now.

Notes

1. *Branzburg* v. *Hayes*, 408 U.S. 665, 713 (1972).
2. Letter from James Madison to W. T. Barry, August 4, 1822, in 9 *Writings of James Madison* 103 (G. Hurst ed. 1910); quoted in W. O. Douglas, *The Right of the People* (Garden City, N.Y.: Doubleday, 1958), pp. 19–20; *Branzburg* v. *Hayes, supra* note 1 at 723.
3. Quoted in Douglas, *The Right of the People*, p. 80.
4. *United States* v. *Richardson*, 418 U.S. 166, 198 (1974).

5. *New York Times Co.* v. *United States*, 403 U.S. 713, 724 (1971).

6. *Zemel* v. *Rusk*, 381 U.S. 1, 24 (1965).

7. *Id.* at 24.

8. *Lamont* v. *Postmaster General*, 381 U.S. 301 (1965).

9. *Griswold* v. *Connecticut*, 381 U.S. 479, 482 (1965).

10. *Stanley* v. *Georgia*, 394 U.S. 557 (1969).

11. *Red Lion Broadcasting* v. *F.C.C.*, 395 U.S. 367 (1969).

12. *Virginia State Board of Pharmacy* v. *Virginia Citizens Consumer Council, Inc.*, 425 U.S. 748 (1976).

13. *United States* v. *Richardson, supra* note 4.

14. *Id.* at 201.

15. *Pell* v. *Procunier*, 417 U.S. 817 (1974).

16. *Id.* at 841.

17. *United States* v. *Nixon*, 418 U.S. 683 (1974).

18. *Kleindienst* v. *Mandel*, 408 U.S. 753 (1972).

19. See, e.g., *Columbia Broadcasting System* v. *Democratic National Committee*, 412 U.S. 94, 162 (1974).

20. *Kleindienst* v. *Mandel, supra* note 18 at 772.

21. *Columbia Broadcasting System* v. *Democratic National Committee, supra* note 19.

22. *Id.* at 148.

23. *Branzburg* v. *Hayes, supra* note 1 at 665.

24. *Id.* at 722.

25. *New York Times Co.* v. *United States, supra* note 5 at 713.

26. *Secretary of the Navy* v. *Avrech*, 418 U.S. 676, 680 (1974).

"Journalistic Autonomy" 3 as a First Amendment Concept

VINCENT A. BLASI_____

William O. Douglas' fundamental social goals were to achieve world peace, to preserve the natural environment, and to expand and enforce the First Amendment. The Symposium touched on the topic of international law in speeches by Jay Murphy and Arthur Hicks. Environmental conflicts were discussed in workshops devoted to all-terrain vehicles, nuclear power in the Skagit Valley, government regulation, and in a speech by Superior Court Judge Norman Ackley on "How Justice Douglas' Position on 'Standing' Reveals His Soul." The First Amendment received attention in this paper on the freedom of the press by Professor Blasi.

Blasi renders a needed service in trying to move our discussion of press freedoms away from protracted battles over obscenity to the question of political power. Those who read the First Amendment as a license to self-fulfillment not only may be historically inaccurate, as Blasi insisted in his response to Thomas Emerson, but also socially inexpedient. Professor Blasi suggests that we would do well to consider press rights institutionally instead of individually—as powers of a fourth branch necessary for democratic government, and not simply the personal prerogatives of reporters, writers, and editors. His paper raises many issues for study and thought: How did the Framers of the Constitution define "the press"? How did they define individual expression? Is freedom of the press a means or an end? What are the historical as well as the legal precedents for press autonomy? Are a few words in the First Amendment sufficient to create press sovereignty? Are the media primarily crafts, bulwarks against tyranny, or businesses in a capitalistic society? This paper also outlines several First Amendment dilemmas, especially the one of press autonomy versus access to effective means of mass communication. The reader may wish to consult Blasi's "Newsman's Privilege: An Empirical Study," *Michigan Law Review* (1971), and his book on *Press Subpoenas* (1972).

> The standards of TV, radio, newspapers, or magazines—whether of excellence or mediocrity—are beyond the reach of Government. Government—acting through courts—disciplines lawyers. Government makes criminal some acts of doctors and of engineers. But the First Amendment puts beyond the Government federal regulation of news agencies save only business and financial practices which do not involve First Amendment rights.
>
> Justice Douglas, concurring in
> *CBS* v. *Democratic National Committee*

Traditionally, litigants invoking the First Amendment have cast their claims either in terms of certain specific interests of individuals—to express oneself, to hear the opinions of others, to choose one's own reading fare—or in terms of the interest of society as a whole in phenomena such as a marketplace of ideas, a free flow of information, and an enlightened electorate. In the last few years, however, a new type of interest has achieved some prominence in our First Amendment discourse. It seems neither fish nor fowl: not individual, not societal, but rather institutional. This is the interest, variously phrased, in "journalistic independence," "journalistic freedom," "journalistic discretion," or "institutional autonomy" for the press.

In this writing, I first explore how the interest denoted by these interchangeably invoked labels has figured in recent Supreme Court decisions interpreting the First Amendment, and then inquire whether there is any basis in our traditional theory of freedom of expression for ascribing constitutional value to this interest. I think the phrase "journalistic autonomy" best captures the basic concept suggested by the Court's use of these labels; so I will employ that phrase exclusively in the analysis that follows.

I

The Supreme Court's use of the concept of journalistic autonomy is perhaps best illustrated by the decision three years ago in *Miami Herald Publishing Co.* v. *Tornillo*.[1] In that case, Chief Justice Burger wrote for all nine justices (a rare occurrence in First Amendment adjudication) in holding unconstitutional a Florida law which required a newspaper to grant free reply space to any candidate whose personal character or public record had been assailed in the paper's columns. One reason given by the Chief Justice in support of the decision was the fear that such a right of reply might cause newspapers to blunt or reduce their election coverage, thereby depriving readers of valuable facts and opinions. In addition, however, he offered an independent rationale for the holding, a rationale based on the concept of journalistic autonomy:

Even if a newspaper would face no additional costs to comply with a compulsory access law and would not be forced to forego publication of news or opinion by the inclusion of a reply, the Florida statute fails to clear the barriers of the First Amendment because of its intrusion into the function of editors. A newspaper is more than a passive receptacle or conduit for news, comment, and advertising. The choice of material to go into a newspaper, and the decisions made as to limitations on the size and content of the paper, and treatment of public issues and public officials—whether fair or unfair—constitute the exercise of editorial control and judgment. It has yet to be demonstrated how governmental regulation of this crucial process can be exercised consistent with First Amendment guarantees of a free press as they have evolved to this time.[2]

The essential point here, it seems, is that journalistic autonomy is intrinsically valuable; the interest can be infringed even in the absence of an adverse effect on the flow of information.

A similar solicitude for journalistic autonomy was evinced by several justices in *CBS* v. *Democratic National Committee*,[3] which held that would-be political advertisers have no First Amendment right to purchase broadcast time from stations which adopt a policy of selling advertising time only for commercial messages. The majority opinion, again authored by Chief Justice Burger, set forth two responses to the argument that the viewing and listening public would receive a more diversified fare if all stations were required to accept political ads. First, the opinion questioned whether the information flow would in fact be improved:

> Nor can we accept the Court of Appeals view that every potential speaker is "the best judge" of what the listening public ought to hear or indeed the best judge of the merits of his or her views. All journalistic tradition and experience is to the contrary. For better or worse, editing is what editors are for; and editing is selection and choice of material.[4]

In addition, the majority suggested that even if listeners would benefit from a requirement that political advertisements be accepted, a regime of enforced access would result in a net detriment to First Amendment values because such regulation would infringe journalistic autonomy:

> Under a constitutionally commanded and Government supervised right-of-access system urged by respondents and mandated by the Court of Appeals, the [Federal Communications] Commission would be required to oversee far more of the day-to-day operations of broadcasters' conduct, deciding such questions as whether a particular individual or group has had sufficient opportunity to present its viewpoint and whether a particular viewpoint has already been sufficiently aired. Regimenting broadcasters is too radical a therapy for the ailment respondents complain of.[5]

Justices Stewart and Douglas contributed concurring opinions elaborating on the theme of journalistic autonomy.

A somewhat different claim of autonomy was presented in *Pittsburgh Press* v. *Pittsburgh Commission on Human Relations*[6] when a newspaper challenged a local ordinance which as interpreted prohibited the paper from listing job advertisements under separate columns designating certain jobs as primarily of interest to one or the other sex.[7] The *Pittsburgh Press* argued that the First Amendment prohibits any government interference with journalistic layout decisions. Although four dissenting justices voted to uphold the newspaper's autonomy claim, the majority held that the First Amendment does not guarantee news organizations absolute control over the placement of items submitted by commercial advertisers. Justice Powell's majority opinion warned, however, that the decision did not "authorize any restriction whatever, whether of content or layout, on stories or commentary originated by *Pittsburgh Press*, its columnists, or its contributors."[8] And the majority underscored the importance it attached to journalistic autonomy: ". . . we reaffirm unequivocally the protection afforded editorial judgment. . . ."[9]

The cases I have discussed thus far have involved efforts by government to force news organizations to disseminate items they prefer to exclude from their publications or programs, or to present their information in a format not of their own choosing. But journalistic autonomy can also be implicated when government prohibits certain kinds of new disseminations. For example, ten years ago in *Mills* v. *Alabama*[10] the Court struck down an Alabama law which as interpreted prohibited newspapers from editorializing about candidates or issues on election day. Mr. Justice Black, writing for the majority, treated the issue as a simple one. "It is," he said, "difficult to conceive of a more obvious and flagrant abridgment of the constitutionally guaranteed freedom of the press."[11] The statute in question was not directed specifically at election day campaigning conducted via the mass media, but rather applied to all campaigning on the day of an election. The law thus left open the possibility of unanswerable eleventh-hour smears, and hence seemed to serve no strong regulatory interest. But there would be some point to a law that prohibited mass-media campaigning on election day while leaving candidates free to answer election-eve media smears with pamphlets and other forms of personal campaigning. Justice Black's opinion in *Mills* gives no indication that such a statute would be upheld by the Court, for the essence of the *Mills* decision seems to be that any "news blackout," even for a single special day on a narrow albeit important topic, is unacceptable under the First Amendment because it infringes journalistic autonomy.

A similar notion may lie behind the Court's recent decisions regarding trial publicity. *Cox Broadcasting Corp.* v. *Cohn*[12] held that news organizations cannot be held liable in tort for publishing accurate information they obtained from public records, even when the information involves a matter as sensitive as the identity of a rape victim. True, public records are by definition open to public inspection. But it would be fatuous to contend that a person's privacy cannot be harmed significantly by the publication in the mass media of facts that members of the public could otherwise learn only if they took the initiative to browse through court records. The Court did not purport in *Cox Broadcasting* to balance the gains to public enlightenment by dissemination against the harm to individual privacy. The key to the holding appears, instead, to be the proposition that one element of journalistic autonomy protected by the First Amendment is the prerogative to disseminate all information that is open to public inspection.

The Court's decision last term in *Nebraska Press Association* v. *Stuart*[13] seems also to rest on the premise that there is something especially troublesome about a regulation that prohibits journalists from disseminating information in their possession. In that case, the Supreme Court struck down a state court order forbidding the publication before trial of certain items of information thought likely to jeopardize a criminal defendant's chances of being tried by an impartial jury of his peers. The majority expressed the gravest reservations about all such non-publication orders directed to the press, but implied that the First Amendment might not be violated by other measures designed to reduce pretrial publicity, such as restrictions on "what the contending lawyers, the police, and witnesses may say to anyone," and orders prohibiting journalists and the public from attending pretrial hearings.[14] Now the flow of information to the public is not less impaired if a judicial order aborts a potential story at its source rather than at the point when a journalist has acquired the information and desires to publish it. But the Court in *Nebraska Press Association* appears to have discerned an important difference turning on the point of judicial intervention, for the majority in discussing non-publication orders directed at news organizations invoked the following characterization from its *Tornillo* opinion: "We remain intensely skeptical about those measures that would allow government to insinuate itself into the editorial rooms of this Nation's press."[15] The point seems to be that journalistic autonomy is infringed when the "editorial process" is regulated, but is not violated, or at least is violated to a lesser degree, when the news-gathering process is regulated.

This interpretation gains credence in light of the Supreme Court's decision in *Branzburg* v. *Hayes*,[16] rejecting claims by three journalists to a testimonial privilege immunizing from grand jury inquiry information they acquired in the course of confidential relationships with sources. The journalists contended, buttressed by a most impressive record in one of the cases, that the practice of grand juries sub-poenaing reporters makes news sources self-conscious and unexpan-sive, if not totally uncooperative, to the detriment of the flow of infor-mation to the public. The majority devoted much of its opinion to a refutation of this empirical claim, but also indicated that a free-press claim relating to the news-gathering stage of the journalistic endeavor implicates fewer First Amendment values than claims relating to the editorial or publication stages. On the other hand, Justice Stewart's dissent in *Branzburg* appears to rest in part on the conclusion that journalistic autonomy is indeed violated by this particular form of in-terference with the news-gathering process. For in addition to arguing that the news flow would be adversely affected by an unrestrained power to subpoena reporters, Justice Stewart complained that the ma-jority's holding "invites state and federal authorities to undermine the historic independence of the press by attempting to annex the journal-istic profession as an investigative arm of government."[17]

Finally, I discern a reliance by the Court on some notion of journal-istic autonomy in its recent decision restricting the types of damages that can be recovered in defamation actions. *Gertz* v. *Robert Welch, Inc.* [18] held, among other things, that libel plaintiffs can recover only compensatory damages for actual, proven injuries. Punitive damages and presumed damages cannot be awarded consistent with the First Amendment. The Court's holding regarding presumed damages is not particularly troublesome as a theoretical matter, since it rests on con-siderations relating to the feasibility of proof and the adjustment of presumptions in light of the perceived strength of competing values. But why in the name of theory must punitive damages be disallowed? One reason might be that punitive damages can be assessed in such unpredictable amounts that editors will engage in undesirable "self-censorship" so long as the mere possibility of punitive damage awards exists. But the *Gertz* opinion did not rest solely on this point, a dubious one in any event in light of the widespread use by news organizations of libel insurance, typically in the form of inexpensive policies with high deductibles designed precisely to guard against aberrationally punitive awards. Instead, the opinion invoked an additional argument:

Like the doctrine of presumed damages, jury discretion to award punitive damages unnecessarily exacerbates the danger of media self-censorship but, unlike the former rule, punitive damages are wholly irrelevant to the state interest that justifies a negligence standard for private defamation actions. They are not compensation for injury. Instead, they are private fines levied by civil juries to punish reprehensible conduct and to deter its future occurrence.[19]

But what is wrong with a fine designed to punish and deter "reprehensible conduct" by the media? The most plausible explanation seems to be that government infringes journalistic autonomy when it creates a system of financial disincentives designed to influence editorial judgments. In other words, government can require news organizations to "pay their way" by compensating individuals for harm done by stories, but cannot attempt to alter journalistic practices as a general matter.

These are the various contexts in which the justices have justified their interpretations of the First Amendment in part by reference to the concept of journalistic autonomy. A striking feature of the opinions discussed previously is that virtually all of them invoke the concept as though its contours and significance for constitutional analysis were self-evident. But autonomy is a concept that is notoriously difficult to pin down, and the fact that we are here dealing not with individual autonomy but rather institutional autonomy only serves to complicate matters. What then are the basic intuitions that inform the notion that news organizations are constitutionally entitled to some measure of freedom from governmental scrutiny and regulation concerning certain of their activities? On analysis, does the claim reduce to the contention that traditional individual and societal interests will be served if news organizations are granted such freedom, for example that the flow of information will be enriched or the process of self-government will be facilitated? If so, one would expect the concept of journalistic autonomy to be defined in terms of anticipated consequences to these individual and societal values. As I have demonstrated, however, the Supreme Court has invoked the concept of journalistic autonomy as though it were of independent significance, not simply instrumental to traditional individual and societal values. I now inquire whether there is any basis for such a view of journalistic autonomy.

II

Recently, a few First Amendment scholars, including Justice Potter Stewart,[20] have suggested that contemporary interpretation should perhaps be influenced by the fact that the constitutional text protects the freedom of speech and press under separate clauses rather than under one cognate rubric. Here might be a textual basis for ascribing intrinsic value to journalistic autonomy. For "the press" can be viewed as a constitutionally ordained institution the preservation of which is required by the text of the First Amendment. Under this reading, journalistic autonomy would refer to those attributes which an organization (or profession) must possess in order to qualify for the appellation "press." Thus one might argue that unless a news organization retains the freedom not to publish items which the state desires that it disseminate, the organization can no longer be considered part of "the press." The prerogative to decide what goes into a publication is the very foundation of the concept of "the press."

There are several difficulties with this line of analysis. For one thing, it is probable that the Framers of the First Amendment used the term "press" to refer to the printed medium of expression, which anyone might employ, rather than the journalism profession or any of its constituent parts. Moreover, even if "the press" is given the latter meaning, it seems difficult to argue that such regulations as statutory rights of reply, pretrial non-publication orders, and punitive damages for defamation so undermine the operations of news organizations that the name "press" seems no longer apt as applied to them. One might well conclude that "the freedom of the press" should be interpreted to prohibit the foregoing regulations in light of the history and basic philosophical values that inform the First Amendment, but hardly that the mere presence of the word "press" in the text of the amendment demonstrates the invalidity of such regulations.

A different type of justification for the concept of journalistic autonomy might build from the fact that individual autonomy is sometimes ascribed intrinsic value in First Amendment theory. We consider the net balance of good and bad social consequences to be somehow beside the point when ruling upon certain regulations of speech that go to the heart of our notion of what it means to be an autonomous human being. This is why the Supreme Court decisions two decades ago regarding bar admissions and legislative investigations[21] strike many of us today as abominations: Whether or not knowledge about a person's deepest political beliefs helps us to predict his performance as a lawyer or teacher, and whether or not governmental probing into these matters has a "chilling effect," it is simply dehumanizing to force a person against his will to reveal his fundamental political tenets. Might not the claims of journalists to autonomy in some of their professional endeavors be analogized to these claims of personal autonomy? May not journalists react to government efforts to probe into source relationships or editorial practices with a genuine indignation, a sense that such regulatory efforts are an affront to the dignity of the journalism profession?

I do not believe that this line of argument succeeds. Individual journalists may feel greatly trampled upon by certain governmental intrusions into their professional domains, but so do many business persons who are subjected to often stifling official regimentation. Governmental regulation is almost always frustrating and dehumanizing in one sense; the key to the concept of individual autonomy is the notion that certain official intrusions take away from persons elements of control over their own lives that define their basic, irreducible essence as human beings. Regulations that operate only on specialized, professional activities engaged in by a tiny elite fraction of the population would seem not to qualify under this standard.

One might argue, however, that the autonomy claim relates not to the endeavors of individual journalists qua individuals, but rather to the collective endeavors of news organizations, or even of the entire journalism profession. Do not these groups have an irreducible essence which government must respect? I find this argument troublesome. The intrinsic value ascribed to individual autonomy stems from the individualistic political tradition out of which the Constitution emerged. Several provisions of the Constitution embody a view of the individual as a vital unit in the allocation of political decision-making authority. Some organizations are also designated by the document to enjoy sovereign power, and necessarily therefore to exercise a considerable measure of control over their own internal affairs. The three branches of the federal government, the state governments, and juries come to mind. But news organizations, as well as religious and political groups, seem to me to fall into a different category consisting of units not possessed of any inherent sovereignty but rather deserving of autonomy only to the extent that certain basic constitutional values would be served thereby. In other words, I think the interest in journalistic autonomy has no intrinsic validity; only if the granting of autonomy to news organizations can be shown to forward fundamental First Amendment values can it be considered constitutionally ordained.

In addition to individual autonomy, the two fundamental values that have dominated modern discourse about freedom of expression are (1) diversity and (2) self-government.

"Diversity" is a concept broad enough to embody all the virtues attributed to the mythical marketplace of ideas: social progress by means of a rational dialectic, the personal satisfaction provided by the experience of processing cognitive stimuli, the nurturing of eccentric genius, the promotion of social stability by giving discontented persons an outlet, and many others. The case for the recognition of journalistic autonomy as a constitutional concept is strong if it can be shown to be importantly instrumental to the First Amendment value of diversity.

At this point it is necessary to make an important distinction. It is one thing to say that a particular constitutional protection claimed by news organizations will directly further the value of diversity, quite another to say that a particular protection may or may not enhance diversity in the short run but will in any event promote a structure or ethos in the journalism profession that will redound in the long run to the benefit of diversity. The *Tornillo* decision is a good illustration. Chief Justice Burger argued that the Florida right-of-reply statute would probably have a chilling effect resulting in less vigorous election coverage, a net loss in terms of diversity. But he went on to imply that even if the reply statute resulted in a net gain in diversity by giving wide circulation to the rebuttals of candidates criticized in the mass media, the cost to journalistic autonomy would still require the invalidation of the law. He did not specify why he thought journalistic autonomy has constitutional value, but one reason could be that a government regulation requiring newspapers to print replies could, while not necessarily altering press coverage immediately, erode the sense of craft and purpose in journalists, ultimately to the detriment of diversity. Whether or not one finds this development plausible with regard to a reply law like Florida's, it is important to appreciate the difference between an immediate effect on diversity and a long-run effect linked to the concept of journalistic autonomy. It is only the latter kind of effect that concerns us, for if diversity is immediately impaired by a regulation, there is no need to rest the constitutional challenge on the more controversial concept of journalistic autonomy.

Is the granting of autonomy to news organizations a significant precondition to the maximization of diversity? I find this a difficult question. In some respects, I believe that the recognition of journalistic autonomy could lead to a more responsible, more innovative press simply by engendering in journalists higher standards of self-criticism and self-regulation. Institutions that are already heavily regulated are less likely to develop additional internal regulations that are institutions that are given the responsibility of keeping their own houses in order. Also, the more journalism is treated by the government as a special craft worthy of respect and trust rather than just another business in need of constant policing, the more will journalism seem an attractive career to talented, conscientious persons. On the other hand, autonomy can also lead to arrogance, to a preoccupation with one's own values and desires, to a loss of touch with the needs and standards of others, including other institutions and the society at large. Particularly at the local level does this seem a realistic fear. If granted a great deal of constitutional autonomy, would the news staff of a locally dominant newspaper necessarily feel more obliged to give balanced coverage to hotly contested local issues? Or provide agitators some opportunity to puncture the civic consensus? Or check facts carefully to avoid unwarranted injury to individual reputations? Or refrain from fueling the fires of prejudgment against persons charged with heinous crimes? I do not know. But I am troubled by the possibility that a recognition of journalistic autonomy could in some localities lead to an undesirable ethos. Thus I would be reluctant to strike down, for the sake of long-run diversity, those regulations shown to promote diversity in the short run.

Much the same analysis holds for the contention that journalistic autonomy will in the long run foster the regime of self-government that Alexander Meiklejohn has argued lies at the root of our commitment to freedom of expression.[22] Some government regulations claimed to infringe on journalistic autonomy are in fact designed to promote widespread political participation. An example is the D.C. Court of Appeals order, invalidated by the Supreme Court in *CBS* v. *Democratic National Committee*, which required broadcast stations to sell time to political advertisers.[23] Pretrial non-publication orders imposed in order to make a jury trial a realistic option for the defendant can also be viewed as enhancing the process of self-government. But again, as with diversity, an autonomous press might be more probing, more innovative, more vital, and in these respects more helpful to citizens attempting to perform their political responsibilities as "self-governors." On the other hand, as was also true for diversity, at the local level an arrogant, orthodox, superficial, unresponsive press can have the effect of stifling grass-roots political involvement. Moreover, the recognition of journalistic autonomy would set up the journalism profession as an elite of sorts, and even if this elite would perform better if granted constitutional recognition, there might be a symbolic effect from this recognition that would be to the detriment of the self-government philosophy, with its powerful egalitarian underpinnings. In sum, the long-range gain in terms of self-government to be expected from a constitutional solicitude for journalistic autonomy is speculative at best, and probably not sufficient as a general matter to outweigh the short-run promotion of self-government represented by at least some government regulations of press practices.

The traditional values of individual autonomy, diversity, and self-government thus do not provide a compelling rationale for the recognition of journalistic autonomy as a First Amendment concept. There is, however, another value which I think deserves a prominent place in First Amendment theory for which several manifestations of journalistic autonomy may be instrumental. This is the value of checking the misuse of governmental authority.

The tradition of political thought out of which the First Amendment developed viewed free expression as important primarily as a counterforce to the perceived tendency of government officials to misuse the power entrusted to them.[24] In this respect, free speech was viewed as a right for the powerful opposition forces in society, not simply for the fringe elements. By an accident of history, however, the First Amendment was not really subjected to judicial interpretation and rationalization until just after World War I, and then the principal claimants of First Amendment rights were relatively powerless people—anarchists, socialists, and syndicalists.[25] The theories devised by judges to explain the First Amendment were responsive to the types of claims presented. These theories stressed the importance of everyone's input into social decision making, and they contained a strong undercurrent of respect for the individual autonomy of even the most pitiful, bizarre speakers. The fact that many of the free-speech issues presented in the 1930s and 1940s were initially raised by the Jehovah's Witnesses[26] accentuated this tendency to think about the First Amendment primarily in terms of compassion for unorthodox persons, and not in terms of the struggle for political power among significant social forces. The preoccupation with domestic communism during the McCarthy era, which resulted in numerous Supreme Court cases, only reinforced this phenomenon. One result of this sequence of cases is that the value of free expression in checking official power has not figured as prominently in First Amendment theory as one might have expected, given the original eighteenth-century emphasis on this aspect of the constitutional guarantee.[27]

We seem now to have entered an era in which many of the claims made in the name of the First Amendment are put forth by powerful persons, representatives of movements and institutions which in a realistic sense do serve as counterforces to government. I refer to leaders of the civil rights and antiwar movements, and to the personnel of large media organizations. A remarkable percentage of the First Amendment claimants of the last fifteen years answer to these descriptions.[28] I believe this development will lead to a resurrection in First Amendment theory of the fundamental value of checking the misuse of government power. And I think it is this checking value that provides the most convincing justification for the concept of journalistic autonomy.

Probably the most important way in which journalistic autonomy is instrumental to the checking of official behavior is simply by reinforcing and symbolizing the philosophy of limited government. Particularly in light of the fact that government control of the press is one of the hallmarks of a totalitarian state, a constitutional regime makes a major symbolic statement when it recognizes a zone of autonomy for an institution which has so much potential influence on the struggle for political power as does the press. Moreover, if the philosophy of limited government is seen to grant special privileges to the journalism profession, one can expect the press to reciprocate by feeling a special responsibility to defend and nurture the system of limited government. The temptation is sometimes strong for those who control the major media outlets to view themselves primarily as venture capitalists rather than as guardians of political liberty. The constitutional recognition of journalistic autonomy, itself a statement of faith and idealism, might give those who favor an idealistic view of the journalist's calling a boost in the struggle for the soul of the profession. I think, for example, that the incursion on the autonomy of the broadcast press represented by the extensive system of regulation by the FCC is one reason why broadcast organizations tend to be more profit conscious than their print counterparts.

So far, I have been concerned with the ways in which a grant of autonomy to an institution can encourage that institution to develop an ethos of detachment, of devotion to principles that transcend the partisan desires of those who hold government power. But such a grant might also facilitate a form of counterpartisanship, an attitude of adversariness with regard to government. Thus the recognition of journalistic autonomy can be seen as endorsing the view of the press as a "fourth branch of government," a full-fledged participant in the system of checks and balances, a center of power designed to push against the other constitutionally ordained centers of power. And even if the effect of journalistic autonomy is to promote this counterpartisanship rather than detachment, I think the checking value is well served. Indeed, viewed strictly in terms of the checking value, counterpartisanship is probably the more desirable journalistic ethos.

In addition to the fostering of an ethos, journalistic autonomy can facilitate press counterpartisanship in some important material respects. There may be occasions when a news organization can best serve to check abuses of official power by waging a highly partisan "campaign" against the miscreant officials. The *Washington Post*'s Watergate coverage is the leading example, but the practice is more often significant at the local level. A news organization may be seriously handicapped in waging such a campaign if it is not autonomous in certain respects—not able, for example, to guarantee its news sources confidentiality, or to make charges against officials without having to give them reply space, or to publish "classified" information. Government regulations that are claimed to infringe journalistic autonomy are often designed to forestall or counteract press partisanship, to provide for a "balanced" and "responsible" press. One possible implication of the checking value is that the ideal of an objective, nonpartisan press may be a false ideal.

Finally, the recognition of journalistic autonomy can be considered to serve the checking value by forestalling the establishment of regulatory structures and practices which, though perhaps not objectionable in themselves, may have the potential of doing great harm if controlled by a government intent on discrediting or otherwise incapacitating its press critics. For example, the FCC's power to grant or deny renewals of broadcast licenses based on a highly subjective standard of overall performance might serve the end of improving the quality of programming and might be seldom abused over a long span of time. But the power *could* be invoked to punish critics of government, and the fact that only an administration with a truly totalitarian mentality would use the power for that purpose does not mean this potentiality should not be given great weight in the constitutional calculus. The same reasoning holds for the power to subpoena reporters: The power is almost always employed for the legitimate purpose of obtaining admissible evidence, but a totalitarian government could use the subpoena power to great effect in repressing its opponents. The checking value encourages one to take a pathological view of government structures and powers, in other words to assume the worst. A concept like autonomy, particularly institutional autonomy, gains force when viewed from this perspective rather than in terms of a short-run calculus of benefits and detriments in a fundamentally healthy political environment.

I conclude, therefore, that the concept of journalistic autonomy does after all have a sound basis in First Amendment theory. Certain claims by journalists to control their own activities should be granted because such institutional self-control is instrumental to the fundamental First Amendment value of checking misconduct by government. But the establishment of a basis in theory constitutes only the beginning of inquiry on the subject of the constitutional significance of journalistic autonomy. The contours of the autonomy concept remain to be delineated in light of its theoretical underpinnings. The Supreme Court, it should be noted, has been undiscriminating as well as conclusory in its invocation of journalistic autonomy. I doubt, for example, whether a concept of autonomy derived from the checking value would support the notion, apparently advanced in *Cox Broadcasting* v. *Cohn* and *Nebraska Press Association* v. *Stuart*,[29] that news organizations have the prerogative to publish information in their possession but no special prerogatives regarding the process by which information is acquired in the first place. For reasons of space, however, I leave to another day the task of refining the concept and exploring its specific implications.

Notes

1. *Herald Publishing Company* v. *Tornillo*, 418 U.S. 241 (1974).
2. *Id.* at 258.
3. *CBS* v. *Democratic National Committee*, 412 U.S. 94 (1973).
4. *Id.* at 124.
5. *Id.* at 126–27.
6. *Pittsburgh Press* v. *Pittsburgh Commission on Human Relations*, 413 U.S. 376 (1973).
7. The restriction applied only to jobs for which it would be illegal to employ sex-based criteria in hiring.
8. *Pittsburgh Press* v. *Pittsburgh Commission on Human Relations, supra* note 6 at 391.
9. Ibid.
10. *Mills* v. *Alabama*, 384 U.S. 214 (1966).
11. *Id.* at 219.
12. *Cox Broadcasting Company* v. *Cohn*, 420 U.S. 469 (1974).
13. *Nebraska Press Association* v. *Stuart*, 427 U.S. 539 (1976).
14. *Id.* at 564.
15. *Id.* at 560–61.
16. *Branzburg* v. *Hayes*, 408 U.S. 665 (1972).
17. *Id.* at 725.
18. *Gertz* v. *Robert Welch, Inc.*, 418 U.S. 323 (1974).
19. *Id.* at 350.
20. See Stewart, "Or of the Press," 26 *Hastings L. J.* 631 (1975). See also Nimmer, "Introduction—Is Freedom of the Press a Redundancy: What Does It Add to Freedom of Speech?" 26 *Hastings L. J.* 639 (1975).
21. *Konigsberg* v. *State Bar of California*, 366 U.S. 36 (1961); *In re Anastaplo*, 336 U.S. 82 (1961); *Barenblatt* v. *United States*, 360 U.S. 109 (1959); *Uphaus* v. *Wyman*, 360 U.S. 72 (1959).
22. See Alexander Meiklejohn, *Political Freedom* (New York: Harper & Row, 1960).
23. *CBS* v. *Democratic National Committee*, 450 F.2d 642 (D.C. Cir. 1971), *rev'd*, 412 U.S. 94 (1973).

24. I have developed this thesis at some length in a manuscript to be published later this year. See also Bernard Bailyn, *The Ideological Origins of the American Revolution* (Cambridge, Mass.: Harvard University Press, 1967).

25. See, for example, *Schenck* v. *United States*, 249 U.S. 47 (1919); *Debs* v. *United States*, 249 U.S. 211 (1919); *Abrams* v. *United States*, 250 U.S. 616 (1919); *Whitney* v. *California*, 274 U.S. 357 (1927). See generally Zechariah Chafee, *Free Speech in the United States* (Cambridge, Mass.: Harvard University Press, 1941).

26. See, for example, *Lovell* v. *Griffin*, 303 U.S. 444 (1938); *Cox* v. *New Hampshire*, 312 U.S. 569 (1941); *Chaplinsky* v. *New Hampshire*, 315 U.S. 568 (1942); *Cantwell* v. *Connecticut*, 310 U.S. 296 (1940).

27. See, for example, *Dennis* v. *United States*, 341 U.S. 494 (1951); *Yates* v. *United States*, 354 U.S. 298 (1957); *Communist Party* v. *Subversive Activities Control Board*, 367 U.S. 1 (1961); *Barenblatt* v. *United States*, 360 U.S. 109 (1959); *Watkins* v. *United States*, 354 U.S. 178 (1957).

28. See, for example, *NAACP* v. *Alabama*, 357 U.S. 449 (1958); *NAACP* v. *Button*, 371 U.S. 415 (1963); *Cox* v. *Louisiana*, 379 U.S. 559 (1965); *Bond* v. *Floyd*, 385 U.S. 116 (1966); *Tinker* v. *Des Moines School District*, 393 U.S. 503 (1969); *United States* v. *O'Brien*, 391 U.S. 367 (1968); *Cohen* v. *California*, 403 U.S. 15 (1971); *Watts* v. *United States*, 394 U.S. 705 (1969); *New York Times* v. *Sullivan*, 376 U.S. 254 (1964); *Time, Inc.* v. *Hill*, 385 U.S. 374 (1967); *Saxbe* v. *Washington Post*, 417 U.S. 843 (1974); *CBS* v. *Democratic National Committee*, 412 U.S. 94 (1973).

29. *Cox Broadcasting Company* v. *Cohn, supra* note 12; *Nebraska Press Association* v. *Stuart, supra* note 13.

The Nature and 4
Source of Constitutional
Law: The Supreme Court
Decisions on Race and
the Schools
LINO A. GRAGLIA_____

Nathan Glazer's laudatory review of *Disaster by Decree: The Supreme Court Decisions on Race and the Schools* (Ithaca, N.Y.: Cornell University Press, 1976) brought Lino Graglia to our attention; a short phone conversation convinced us that he could make a challenging contribution to a symposium honoring William O. Douglas. To ask unpopular questions and not offer comfortable answers, to provoke emotional opposition without causing rancor, to excite other minds without inspiring pedantry, these are qualities of outstanding teachers. Undoubtedly, they are the qualities that earned Professor Graglia a Distinguished Faculty Award at the University of Texas in 1976. As a speaker he revels in the bold, the blunt, the flamboyant. No one at the Symposium, whether stunned by his ideas or stung by his delivery, could ignore what he had to say. "Graglia's statements illustrated with painful clarity," one participant later wrote, "the frightening rationale behind many of the [Court's] oppressive rulings," and another person said that Graglia required her to rethink the desirability of judicial review by the Supreme Court. Graglia went beyond merely "holding a position" to stridently and skillfully attacking ideas and institutions that to him appeared contradictory, self-defeating, and foolish. Admirers of William O. Douglas have long relished such an abrasive voice speaking in clear, colorful language for judicial activism; Douglas would be quick to champion the right of a forceful personality to speak for the other side.

Professor Graglia's speech was delivered without notes and has been transcribed from tape; citations have been added. In our editing we have endeavored to retain his spontaneity.

From where does it come? How is it formulated? That is the essential question if we want to understand the subject of constitutional law. It really is the only central question or thread question that runs through the subject. Constitutional law is not really a subject. In constitutional law when you look at a casebook in law school you see a chapter on the regulation of interstate commerce. You see a chapter on state taxation of business. Then you'll see a chapter on pornography, and a chapter on religion. You say, "What do these things have to do with one another?" They have nothing to do with one another except that the Supreme Court has decided to intervene in those areas, has decided to lay down the requirements or limitations. That's all that ties them together. When you talk about constitutional law, the central question, the basic question, should be, "What part should the Supreme Court play in the resolution of these problems?"

Now the most essential fact to begin with, startling as it seems, and as difficult as it is to believe, and I know it's difficult to believe because I can preach it for months to a class of students and at the end they won't believe it—because I'm talking about religion here. I'm attacking the most fundamental religion. I'd have a better chance of going to India and convincing Hindus that throwing widows on the burning pyre is not necessary. I'm talking about fundamental religious beliefs. We do have sacred scripture in this system. It's the Constitution. It's not long enough to make a good short story. It's only about 7,000 words, the vast bulk of which are clearly obsolete.

Being a very short document, it's rather remarkable that one can find in it answers to specific questions the way Mr. Emerson can. He apparently has a remarkable copy. He can peer in there and find the answers to almost anything. The shocking thing that I would tell you and have you believe, even though you won't, is that the Constitution has nothing to do with constitutional law. It's irrelevant. The constitutional decisions that are made by the Supreme Court are in no way related to or relevant to the Constitution. I can conceive of questions to which the Constitution would be relevant, but those questions don't arise. If, for example, the federal government passed a law saying you can't publish a book without getting a federal license, that would violate the First Amendment. The Constitution really would bear upon that question. But Congress hasn't passed such a law and won't. To all the questions that do arise, the Constitution is irrelevant. It provides no guidance as to how those questions should be answered. None! It not only doesn't answer the questions, it doesn't help. Now that's startling! I can sooner tell a fundamentalist preacher that the Bible is not the Word of God, than sell this to Mr. Emerson—or your average law student, your average law professor. But I can demonstrate, even prove it empirically, logically, that the Constitution is irrelevant. The purpose of *Disaster by Decree* is, in essence, to demonstrate this, to explain the nature and source of constitutional law. That's the only question, and it's not even talked about in constitutional law. It doesn't matter if students know anything about the law of obscenity, or of school segregation, or of state taxation of interstate commerce, no— they don't need information about any of those things. But it is rather interesting, and possibly useful, to have some understanding of the role of the Supreme Court. So my book means to describe the nature of constitutional law, and it uses the busing cases and the school segregation cases as a vehicle. I could do the same thing with speech or any other significant area.

At one time the Constitution permitted the assignment of children to school according to race in order to keep them apart. How do we know the Constitution permitted that? Because it says so? No! It doesn't say that. But we know that because the Supreme Court said so. Charles Evans Hughes, Chief Justice, in one of his most famous remarks said that we live under the Constitution, but the Constitution is what the judges say it is. That is literally true. It's often thought of as a clever saying, fancy, hyperbolic, exaggerated, but it's *literally true*. The Constitution is what judges say it is and that means, of course, that we live under the judges. The Constitution has nothing to do with it. They could say that black is white, and it would be. Jackson added to that once, the great Justice [Robert] Jackson: "We're not final because we're infallible, but we are infallible because we're final."[1] That's true too! If nobody can say you're wrong, you're right!

The race area illustrates it. The Supreme Court held that the Constitution permitted the assignment of children to school according to race in order to keep them apart. Fifty years later the Court determined that the Constitution prohibited the assignment of children according to race to keep them apart. Some fifteen or so years after that, the situation at the present time is that the Constitution *requires* the assignment of children to school according to race. First they permit racial assignment, then it is prohibited, and now they require it. All the possibilities. All that time the Constitution was never changed. Not one word relevant to any of this. By all reports the Constitution continued to lie happily in the Archives all through it—with never a protest or a moan. The Constitution obviously did not make those decisions. It's not even relevant to them.

It is easy to illustrate my point with the famous *Brown* v. *Board of Education*[2] case of 1954, in which the Court held that the Constitution prohibited school segregation by the states. Why? Because the equal protection clause in the Fourteenth Amendment says "no state shall deny any person equal protection of the law." The Court says school segregation violates that! That's why it is unconstitutional. Well, a rational person or a scientific type of person or a person who is engaging in an intellectually respectable endeavor, and not law, would think, "Well, it violates the Constitution. It's unconstitutional because it violates the equal protection clause." But at the very same time that *Brown* was decided, on the very same day, the Court decided another case involving segregation in the District of Columbia.

You have to know a certain constitutional technicality here—the Fourteenth Amendment does not apply to the federal government. The Fourteenth Amendment says *no state*, so it clearly doesn't apply to the federal government. The District of Columbia is the federal government and is ruled by Congress. So the Fourteenth Amendment doesn't apply, the equal protection clause couldn't possibly apply to the District of Columbia. I shouldn't say possibly. Anything is possible with the Supreme Court; but it had always been understood that the Fourteenth Amendment does not apply to the federal government and therefore it could not prohibit segregation in the District of Columbia. Did that make a difference? It did not! It did not at all. The Supreme Court says it now violates something else called the due process clause. If there were no due process clause, it would have violated something else. It could have violated the provision that Congress can't discriminate among ports.[3] You think that it is humorous or it's clever. But think about it. If you apply the kind of reasonable, logical thinking that you apply to any subject except law and religion, you would realize that it just doesn't make sense. The Constitution has nothing to do with the Court's decisions. They have to be evaluated, criticized, approved in some other way.

Now my position is that *Brown* is one of the easiest constitutional decisions ever made by the Supreme Court. One of the easiest to support and to justify. Why? Because the Constitution really does prohibit school segregation? Of course the Court did say in 1896, in *Plessy* v. *Ferguson*,[4] that segregation was fine. Well, you can say maybe *Plessy* was wrong and *Brown* was right. In what sense do you mean wrong or right? Do you mean that *Brown* is more in keeping with the meaning or the intent of the Constitution than *Plessy*? No, that's not so. *Plessy* was more in keeping with the meaning of the Fourteenth Amendment as understood by the people who adopted it. It was not meant to prohibit school segregation because the very same Congress that adopted the Fourteenth Amendment at the same time passed laws providing for racial segregation in the District of Columbia. Indeed you may recall that we have the Fifteenth Amendment, which says you can't keep blacks from voting. Well, hell, if the Fourteenth Amendment didn't even give blacks the right to vote, if it did not prohibit racial discrimination against them in deciding who could vote, it surely didn't prohibit school discrimination. It surely didn't create a right to go to racially mixed schools. As a matter of historical fact, the Fourteenth Amendment did not prohibit segregation.

The *Brown* decision is correct not because the Fourteenth Amendment, or anything else in the Constitution, mandates desegregation. I think it's correct because it can be based on what could be called a constitutional principle. It could be called a moral principle, if "moral" means something to you. It doesn't to me. It could be said there are principles with which no one will disagree, that have wide acceptance. I put to you the principle that no person should be disadvantaged by government because of his race. That "sells." No one questions it.

Very few people questioned it openly at the time of *Brown*. It's a principle which seems to have a lot to commend it. It is general, very appealing, rarely challenged, almost never challenged persuasively. And there is a feeling that it is part of the American ideal and therefore can be considered to be in the Constitution somehow. No discrimination, no disadvantaging of people because of race. With a good principle, as broad a principle as any we have, that's all it takes to justify the *Brown* decision. Very few Supreme Court decisions can be justified so well or so easily.

But what happened? We begin with the *Brown* decision, which I totally support and justify and which meant that government could not assign children to school on the basis of race. . . . How did it happen that we got from that principle to the present situation where government *must* deal with people on the basis of race, *must* assign children racially, *must* undertake to ascertain the race of people, categorize them as belonging to one race or another, *must* ask and investigate and ascertain the race of children so that they may be excluded from their neighborhood school when it is decided that the school already has enough of their race? How did we move from *Brown* prohibiting racial assignment to requiring racial assignment? . . .

Emerson worries about government secrecy, and he's entirely right. Government institutions bear watching and are not to be trusted. Do you know why? Because they are run by people. People bear watching and are not to be trusted. But the judiciary bears at least as much watching and is less to be trusted, because there's less you can do about it even when you spot impropriety or corruption. In 1964 the federal government by statute, in effect, ratified *Brown* when Congress passed the great 1964 Civil Rights Act—the greatest piece of civil rights legislation in the history of the country. It said that *Brown* is the law of the land to be enforced by all branches, the legislative and the executive, not just the courts. Now the attorney general could sue to prevent the assignment of children to schools on the basis of race. HEW [Department of Health, Education, and Welfare] could deny funds. Segregation was entirely gone by 1967 or 1968.

The only resistance to the 1964 Civil Rights Act by most southerners was from people who said, "You know this '64 Act is going to be perverted, abused." These southerners said, "What the courts and the administrative agencies are going to do is start *requiring* racial assignment under this act!" Proponents of the act said, "You guys are crazy. This is obviously typical southern paranoia! You dream up fantasies!" Hubert Humphrey said, "Boogeymen! Fantasies! Nightmares! The act says you can't discriminate. How are you going to change it so you can? But you're worried, so we'll say it again." So they amended the act. Then it said it again. The southerners were still not satisfied. They said it again! The act says it four times! A most redundant piece of legislation. Neighborhood schools are all right, it says. Assignment to neighborhoods is okay. You cannot require assignment according to race. It's just race discrimination that's prohibited, four times repeated. It made no difference.

Under the prodding of the Civil Rights Commission, HEW started requiring that kids be assigned to schools according to race despite the 1964 act because HEW was unhappy with the results of *Brown*. *Brown* brought on a great moral fervor. This great evil was stopped. We were going to try to have racial equality. For the first time in our history the law stopped being anti-black. Great fervor resulted, we were going to end segregation, and indeed we did. But these crusaders, these fighters who struggled so long, looked around and were dissatisfied. They said, "You know, we're not assigning kids to schools on the basis of race anymore, but the schools are still all black or all white, or very heavily black or very heavily white." They were dissatisfied. They were unhappy. They had fought so hard, the victory was unsatisfying, and they felt the losers should suffer more and winners cheer more. So the idea occurred to them that we had to start assigning according to race again, this time to mix races up.

Well, as I said, the 1964 act prohibited racial assignment explicitly and repeatedly. But the Civil Rights Commission totally, wrongfully, and with gross abuse of authority, recommended it anyhow. HEW, also with a total abuse of authority, started to do it. Indeed, that's in the debates on the '64 Civil Rights Act. Somebody said, "Suppose HEW tries to have racial balance despite the act." Senator Javits, the great liberal leader, said "They'd get thrown out on their ear! The courts will laugh at them. They'd be fools!" Unfortunately, they didn't get thrown out on their ear. The courts didn't laugh. The courts said, "You're right, we've got to start racial balancing." The issue reached the Supreme Court in the *Green* case of 1968, a case more important than *Brown*.[5] *Green* made the move from prohibiting segregation, which is easy enough to justify, to requiring integration, which is very difficult to justify. Prohibiting segregation means that government can't treat people differently on the basis of race. Requiring integration means that government *has* to treat them differently on the basis of race. If we want schools more integrated, more racially mixed than the neighborhoods are, we do not get that racial mix until we bus kids. The *Swann* case of 1971 said we have to bus the kids.[6]

The Supreme Court never said that integration was required. The Court could have said, "In *Brown* we said the Constitution prohibited segregation; now we say the Constitution requires integration. The Constitution now requires that you ascertain the race of kids and assign by race in order to mix." I think they would have done a very foolish thing. I think it was a very foolish social policy, but at least they would be honest! The Court never said that; the Court has never said we have to integrate the schools. The Court couldn't say it. My God! For the Court to announce that the Constitution now required racial discrimination after twenty years of insisting that it prohibits racial discrimination was impossible. So the Court said to desegregate, not integrate, and this is what confuses the understanding of what's involved, with enormous advantages to the Court.

By calling it desegregation, everybody in the North thought, "Well, this applies to the South! You desegregate." The North said "What do we care? It's the good old moral Supreme Court stopping those redneck bastards again. They undoubtedly more than deserve it. Why should we worry?" So, under this divide-and-conquer policy, it looked like it applied only to the South. Now, when northerners come crying to the South, the South says "Where were you when we were steamrolled?"

In *Swann*, the basic busing case, the Court said that no child can be excluded from school because of his or her race. That's the constitutional requirement. Then they constitutionally required that children *must* be excluded from schools and transported elsewhere on the basis of race. Isn't that interesting—exactly the opposite! How can they do that, you say? Nobody can say they're wrong. They are the final appeal. They can do it! It's not less enforceable because it's dishonest. It's not of less impact or less valid because it's illogical. There's no requirement of logic or honesty. For those interested in constitutional law, it shows you where constitutional law comes from: from the courts, from the judges. Nowhere else.

Are these men of unusually high integrity, honesty, and meticulous accuracy? No, the opposite is true. Don't rest in any such hopes if you opt as Thomas Emerson does for government by judges instead of government by mere politicians. Politicians are people, subject to temptation and corruption. Unfortunately, judges are much more dangerous. To watch politicians closely is certainly the course of wisdom. But at least you can watch them, at least you can do something when their crimes become too obvious.

Now let's get to that other question which Emerson doesn't distinguish from the Constitution. Apart from the question of whether something is constitutionally required, is it a good thing to do? Is it good social policy to assign children to schools by race to achieve integration? If you do it, you have mandatory racial discrimination by government. We have to ask, as with any social policy, what do we expect to gain and what will we lose?

In the sixties some people thought the blacks would learn better in white schools. They also argued, usually as an afterthought, that somehow this would improve race relations. Mixed together more in the schools, they'd come to like one another better. I would say that if either of those ideas was true, you'd have a strong case for compulsory racial mixing. Certainly blacks do not generally do as well academically as whites, and this is a grave social concern. If anything alleviates that, I think it's worth a great deal of cost and energy to alleviate it. Unfortunately, it appears that creating racially mixed majority white schools does not . . . aid anybody's academic achievement. It doesn't seem to aid race relations either. It seems to promote racial animosity.

Finally, something clearly has to be mistaken social policy if it's self-defeating. The idea of busing was to achieve racially mixed schools. Racially mixed schools may be a good thing or a bad thing, but a policy which seeks to achieve racially mixed schools and does not achieve them, that creates greater separation, is simply a mistake. That happens because whites leave. When busing requirements arrive, whites depart. Whites depart from city schools for many reasons, but busing accelerates the exodus. Today when we look at our biggest cities in the country, the majority have black school systems. Atlanta's, for example, was 85 percent white in 1955. It's now 92 percent black. Philadelphia's is over 65 percent black; Wilmington's is over 85 percent black; Detroit's is over 85 percent black. That's the way it is. The busing requirement is counterproductive. It doesn't even produce the racial mixing. At that, I'll throw it open to discussion.

AUDIENCE PARTICIPANT: You've dealt with the problem in a very articulate way, but you haven't solved the problem of Court power.

GRAGLIA: Your question deals with the problem of judicial power. I'm afraid I have to say I don't know the solution. You can't fight religion. Emerson proposes greater judicial power and he gets the applause. The movement's his way. All the ERA [Equal Rights Amendment] means is a further transference of power to judges. On busing, the polls show 80–85 percent disapprove of it, but it doesn't stop. Isn't that remarkable? These are our innocent, lovely judges according to Emerson. No legislature can require busing. Any school board would be voted out at the next election. But you can't do anything about the judges. Why don't we pass a constitutional amendment saying "judges may not order busing." That will do it. Yet we don't even need that. Constitutional amendments are hard to get. Proper legislation would do it. Why have we never passed that legislation? Obviously, the Supreme Court, the Constitution, have a momentum of prestige, a true sacredness. . . . The Supreme Court practically prohibited the control of pornography. The Supreme Court required reapportionment. The Supreme Court made it practically impossible to convict and prosecute people effectively. None of these is changed by constitutional amendment. Groups get outraged by them. I don't get outraged by all of them. I *like* some of those results.

So what can you do about judicial power? I don't know. Some people thought that two Republican Presidents appointing so-called conservatives would turn the Court around. It hasn't happened. It hasn't happened. We had these Republican Presidents and now the states can't prohibit abortion. That came from the Burger Court. And just last week the Burger court with five Republican appointees freed a man who murdered and raped a ten-year-old child. No question that he did it. He showed them where the body was. The Supreme Court *reversed* the conviction. Nothing has happened. It hasn't turned around. Douglas is not there anymore, happily, but what difference does it make? [Justice John Paul] Stevens is there.

I was sent to this conference, by the way, to cause trouble. It was going to be an orgy of love for Douglas.

AUDIENCE PARTICIPANT: I want to return to the principle that would justify the *Brown* decision. Where did you get that principle?

GRAGLIA: Basically, all I really come down to is something that sells, that is very acceptable. No one contests it. What do we mean by justifying? How do we justify? The Court can take a principle which you accept and show that a decision follows from that principle. When a court does that, it has justified about all it can justify. When a court announces that government, neither state nor federal, should never disadvantage any person because of that person's race, I offer that as a principle, almost an axiom of the good. Not only is it acceptable, but the consequences are very good. It makes for a stabler, more secure, happier society if government does not disadvantage people on the basis of race. That is as broad and as solid a general rule as I know.

AUDIENCE PARTICIPANT: So it [the Supreme Court] should have some sort of a Nielson rating to determine when a principle is fundamental enough to impose upon the society?

GRAGLIA: That is not as critical and as piercing as you make it sound. If the Court can say "This is a principle which very few people combat, and this is an essential part of the American ideal and tradition"— the sort of thing Douglas always said—in that case it could be imposed. You could even trace it to the Constitution in a certain roundabout way. Not in any historically accurate way, but in a roundabout way. After all, the Thirteenth, Fourteenth, and Fifteenth amendments do protect blacks. The Thirteenth did abolish slavery. The Fourteenth meant that blacks could not be punished more severely than whites, that blacks could own property, that blacks could sue and make contracts. The Fifteenth gave them the right to vote. So one could say of those three amendments that came out of the Civil War, the basic central purpose was to protect blacks, at least in some ways. I can't do better than that. If that's unsatisfying, that's it.

AUDIENCE PARTICIPANT: I challenge you to level with us about the courts, because I think you're playing a game. I think you're a better lawyer than you indicate to us. You say you don't trust the courts. You like politicians, you like legislatures, but judges are by nature tyrants, autocrats, answerable to no one. Yet there are states where, as in our state, judges have to be elected. For some reason you place the legislature on a higher plane. And you must know that before *Gideon*[7] the Sixth Amendment was largely a dead letter; that when people were put on trial for their lives, if they didn't have money for a lawyer, they had to rely on their own resources. Now you say we should have appealed to state legislatures and convinced them to do what ultimately the courts did. Well, there is an important difference. I suspect you know it. Legislatures, whether they be federal or state, represent the majority. Criminals at this point, I hope, are not the majority in this country, and the majority doesn't give a damn about criminals and how they get into prison. A legislature is not interested in protecting the rights of minorities. The courts, precisely because they are not easily attacked by the passion of the majority at any given moment, have that responsibility and they carry it out. That's a critically important function.

You're surely not serious that the United States Supreme Court ought to read the words of the Constitution and say "Well, there's nothing in the Sixth Amendment about the right to counsel at public expense, therefore there should be no right to counsel." You don't mean that. I know you don't.

GRAGLIA: I started out by saying that many of you would never believe me. You're surely one. . . . You figure out what the Sixth Amendment means. It's a bunch of words. What do words mean? Ordinarily we know what words mean by seeing how they are used. It was very clear that, under general Anglo-American common law, the Bill of Rights was intended to establish some minimal protections. A person had to be permitted counsel if he could pay for it. Common law prior to that said you could not have counsel, even if you could pay for it. Common law was a very hardheaded sensible system. With reasonable expedition and reasonable cost criminal laws could be effectively enforced. But if you put a bunch of lawyers in there to yell at the judge, you will have a circus. That was the position of the common law. Under the Sixth Amendment it was understood that the federal government would permit lawyers *if* the accused could afford one. Go beyond that, and you're not applying the Sixth Amendment. You're making social policy.

Now is it a good social policy? Should a society not try people for serious crimes unless it gives them a lawyer? That's a difficult question. *The issue is who should answer it.* You say the courts should answer it because criminals are a minority, at least let's hope they remain a minority. Minority interests will not be protected by the majority. It certainly is a frequent justification for judicial power that courts protect minority rights. It certainly also is the case in Great Britain that courts do not have power to do any such thing. What comes out of *Parliament* is the law of Great Britain. Can anyone say their society is less free, more abusive, more repressive, than ours? In terms of race discrimination, they had a Jewish prime minister fifty-six years ago.

It's difficult for people to realize that our problem really is a conflict of interests—a conflict of legitimate principles, of desired objectives. It's hard to live in a world without absolutes and make difficult policy decisions. Should the accused be allowed a lawyer? In what kind of crimes? Should the accused be allowed just a lawyer, or should he be allowed a fingerprint expert, a document expert? Psychiatric help might be useful. How much help? Twelve lawyers led by Edward Bennett Williams? That's what Jimmy Hoffa always had.

There's no denying that it is a difficult policy question requiring a resolution of conflicting interests. The issue is: Who should make it? I think that the system would work better, be more stable and safe, if virtually all decisions were made by people controlled by the ballot. If you want an uncontrolled judge, I think that's dangerous. . . . Give a lawyer to an illiterate capital defendant in one case, and now we've got to let this child murderer-rapist free for no apparent reason at all.[8] A policeman was driving him to the jail and the policeman remarked, "You know it's Christmas Eve, I'll bet the mother of that little girl would like to have the body so they could bury it by Christmas." That's all he said. He didn't even ask him a question. The criminal said, "It's buried over there." The Supreme Court decided that's improper coercion and he cannot be convicted, he must be set free. Well, that's a resolution of conflicting interests. Is it a sensible one? The tendency for ideological positions in a judge is vastly more dangerous than from elected bodies.

AUDIENCE PARTICIPANT: Your faith in democracy astounds me, especially when it comes to problems of protecting minority groups, the disadvantaged, and people who do not control the political system. That's the role the Court has played at its best. It's easy to take pot shots at the Court and point to individual cases . . . and make them sound outrageous. But the fact is that the legislative branch of our government has not been responsive to the needs of minorities until the Court acted.

I think that it makes very good sense in a country which is not homogeneous to have a body of people that does in a sense act as the conscience of the nation, that does stand up for people not in the majority. And you're simply wrong to say there are no checks on the Court. The Nielson rating is not a myth. The Court obviously is aware of what happens in society. You said yourself that the Court is backing away from busing. They're backing away because there is a check, social pressure.

GRAGLIA: If Stalin was powerful, it was because when he gave orders people obeyed. If everybody in Russia lay down and said to hell with it, we quit, presumably it'd be all over. So where does power come from? Everybody's powerful if other people obey. Power ultimately, I agree with Mao Tse-tung, comes out of physical force, the mouth of a gun. What physical force does the Supreme Court control? Two or three marshals who throw out noisy people. It's a perfectly powerless institution. It's a marvelous system. They are the American equivalent of the military junta. Democracy works as long as the junta likes it. If the junta doesn't like it, they reverse the results. The courts do the same thing for us. You can vote. If the courts like the result, it's okay. If they don't, they reverse it. When the Supreme Court says, "Let the tanks roll," the tanks roll. There was resistance in Little Rock, do you remember? When the Supreme Court said "Let bayonets be unsheathed," bayonets appeared. Eisenhower didn't like the *Brown* decision, and he was not prepared to enforce it; he wished it would go away. He personally opposed it. But he enforced it! Stalin tells the general roll the tanks, the general tells the tank commander roll the tanks, and the tanks roll. That's all power is. If the Supreme Court says roll the tanks and they roll, they have power.

AUDIENCE PARTICIPANT: But you're ignoring the question of why tanks do roll when the Supreme Court tells its three marshals to. . . .

GRAGLIA: It's religion, largely it's religion. It's God speaking from the temple.

AUDIENCE PARTICIPANT: It's exactly because of the position of moral suasion that the Supreme Court occupies, even amongst people who are most hostile to the Court, that there is a sense of a certain rightness in what the Court does. You point to the consequences of the Court's imperialism, but you failed to point to the consequences of failure in state legislatures and the failure of Congress to respond to vast and great social problems and to the suffering of people. If there is disaster by decree by the Supreme Court, I can point to much larger disaster by the unwillingness of democratically controlled legislatures to act. I agree with your analysis that we can pull almost anything out of the Constitution; but that is not a sufficient answer. You have to go beyond your textbooks and ask what's happening in the real world to real human beings. The political scientist may agree with your theoretical definitions of the division of power, but ultimately the ends may justify the means.

GRAGLIA: I won't dispute that the ends justify the means. We might disagree when you talk about social needs, or failures in the legislature. Well, what is an unmet need, or how do we decide there is a need to be met? You apparently have some standard for deciding. If, for example, the people of an area decide that the prisons do not have to be improved, but you look and you say those prison conditions aren't very good, "These prisoners should be treated better. I see a great and pressing need for improvement," how did you establish that need? The people do not see that need; they think conditions are fine. "We're not trying to create a country club; they're in a prison." The legislature thinks they're fine. Well, there are conflicting interests. That's why you and Emerson go to the Constitution when you want your views to become authoritative. Emerson's views do not prevail except upon courts. . . .

Where does the Court get this "moral suasion"? Because obviously they *are* moral, you tell me. They're so right! Everybody can look at the lovely things they can do! That's angelic, that's holy, it's moral. Everybody gets a new barrel of rights every time they meet. It's a cornucopia. That's what students are taught throughout this country, particularly at this institution. The Court acts and lots of people are better off, and nobody's worse off. Isn't that marvelous! But unfortunately that's not the case. Whenever some things improve, others worsen. There is a trade-off in every social choice. To create more rights of speech, you risk more dangers of disorder. If you give rights to parades, it's less easy to walk the streets. However you make those choices, there are choices.

What has the Court done for us? The ends justify the means. They gave us *Dred Scott*,[9] which brought on the Civil War. In 1875 Congress prohibited racial discrimination in public places. The good old Supreme Court, in there pitching morality, held it unconstitutional[10]—so we could have racial discrimination for another hundred years. Congress prohibited child labor; the Supreme Court held it unconstitutional.[11] It's a wonderful record. That's why everybody loves it so much. Look at the great things they do. While they're busing your children, this child rapist-murderer goes free. Everybody realizes that's the voice of God. You can't quarrel with that. It's such obviously marvelous stuff, is it not? It is not! They didn't start being a disaster last month, they have been a disaster from the beginning! . . .

You say, "What would I substitute?" Personally I do have a great deal of faith in democracy. Not because I think it's so great. No, no! Nothing is great. All that you can say for anything is—compared to what? Churchill said "Democracy obviously stinks, except compared to the next best form of government." That's all you can say. . . .

What the Supreme Court amounts to is rule by philosopher kings. Is that crazy? Well, Plato liked it, and he wasn't crazy. Plato said to find a society's best and wisest people, and make them kings. Philosopher kings! Maybe you can justify it. I have no faith at all in my ability to pick kings. But even if that is what we want, that is not what we have. If we were looking for philosopher kings, I don't think Harry Blackmun would be anybody's choice. We've picked a bunch of crummy lawyers who avoided education by going to law school. If you want philosopher kings, let's have it openly. I don't want it, but at least we should have it openly instead of philosopher kings under guise of constitutional law, under the ruse of interpreting a document that in fact has nothing to do with the decisions the Court reaches.

Notes

1. *Brown* v. *Allen*, 344 U.S. 443, 540 (1953), (concurring opinion).
2. *Brown* v. *Board of Education*, 347 U.S. 483 (1954).
3. U.S., *Constitution*, Article I, Section 9.
4. *Plessy* v. *Ferguson*, 163 U.S. 537 (1896).
5. *Green* v. *County School Board*, 391 U.S. 430 (1968).
6. *Swann* v. *Charlotte-Mecklenburg*, 402 U.S. 1 (1971).
7. *Gideon* v. *Wainwright*, 372 U.S. 335 (1963).
8. *Brewer* v. *Williams*, 97 S. Ct. 1232 (1977).
9. *Dred Scott* v. *Sanford*, 60 U.S. (19 How.) 393 (1857).
10. *Civil Rights Cases*, 109 U.S. 3 (1883).
11. *Hammer* v. *Dagenhart*, 247 U.S. 251 (1918).

Citizen Access to the Federal Courts: Douglas v. The Burger Court

5

ARVAL A. MORRIS

When the Supreme Court ended its 1976 term, Justice William Brennan was openly distressed over recent decisions that he felt had restricted public access to the federal judiciary. Professor Arval Morris shares that concern, arguing here that the Supreme Court since 1970 has become inaccessible to the public and an active agent for counter-reform in America. Although Morris and Lino Graglia would agree on little else, they concur in questioning the Supreme Court's proper role in government. Incensed at an ever-expanding federal system interfering with the daily lives of children and parents, Graglia described the judiciary as "riding on the backs of the people ... the most dangerous and the most irresponsible form of government." Morris likewise becomes alarmed at government intrusion into private lives, as does William O. Douglas, except Morris and Douglas fear the CIA, Army Intelligence, and the FBI. Who abuses whom, for what reasons, and to what end? Has the Court shifted to the right, is it an uncertain trumpet, or is it still an instrument of reform?

Morris gave his answer at the Douglas Symposium in this summary of jurisdictional decisions since 1969. His concerns have been shared by Alan M. Dershowitz and John Hart Ely in "*Harris* v. *New York*: Some Anxious Observations on the Candor and Logic of the Emerging Nixon Majority," *Yale Law Journal* (May 1971). Archibald Cox's *The Role of the Supreme Court in American Government* (New York: Oxford University Press, 1976) offers a moderate viewpoint and places the Burger Court in historical context. A relevant article by Morris is "Equal Education Opportunity, Constitutional Uniformity, and the *DeFunis* Remand," *Washington Law Review* (June 1975).

In June of 1969 when Warren Burger appeared before the Senate confirmation committee that was considering his nomination as chief justice, the late Everett McKinley Dirkson said that Burger "looks like a Chief Justice, he speaks like a Chief Justice, and he acts like a Chief Justice." Burger's appearance and impression no doubt expedited the Senate's approval. Warren Burger, fifteenth chief justice of the United States, like many of his predecessors, has given his name to a Court, and today we have the Burger Court. Article III of the Constitution establishes only "one supreme court"; nevertheless, we speak of many—a Marshall, a Taney, a Taft, a Hughes, a Warren Court. Thus we segment the Supreme Court's history into discrete periods of time as though the periods of service marked off by the tenures of chief justices are relevant divisions. They aren't. Generally speaking, the practice is harmless enough; yet there is debate in the case of the Burger Court because many people believe it is misnamed. Behind the Burger Court there was Richard M. Nixon.

Richard M. Nixon had an opportunity accorded few presidents. Supreme Court justices generally vacate their offices at the rate of one vacancy every two and one-half years; thus the usual four-year president may appoint one justice to the Supreme Court during his four-year term, and over a span of eight years he may appoint three justices. But, because of unusual circumstances, Richard M. Nixon appointed four justices to the Supreme Court in less than two terms as president.

The basic outlook of President Nixon's appointees can be gleaned from the fact that in 1968 Nixon campaigned on a promise "to reform" the Supreme Court; that is, the Warren Court, which, he said, had been "soft on crime." That this charge was untrue did not bother him. After his election, Nixon's next move was to have his minion, Gerald R. Ford, then in the House of Representatives, lead a campaign to impeach William O. Douglas. This unsuccessful venture was followed by four vacancies on the Supreme Court. Richard Nixon vowed "to balance" the Supreme Court by appointing "strict constructionists'' who would lead the Court away from judicial activism. He appointed Warren Burger as chief justice and Harry Blackmun, Lewis Powell, and William Rehnquist as associate justices. The last—William Rehnquist—was a clerk for Mr. Justice Jackson when *Brown* v. *Board of Education*[1] was before the Court, and Rehnquist at the time wrote a memorandum asserting that the Court, under the Fourteenth Amendment, had no legitimate power to overrule the ''separate but equal doctrine'' of *Plessy* v. *Ferguson*[2] or to declare racial segregation unconstitutional. Nixon ''balanced'' the Supreme Court, and thus many people claim that, in reality, we have the Nixon Court, misnamed the ''Burger Court,'' in control today.

Before the Burger Court existed, there was the Warren Court. The Warren Court consistently ruled unconstitutional all aspects of intentional racial discriminations by any branch of government anywhere. It ruled that each person eligible to vote shall have a vote equal in power to any other person's vote; it ruled that state as well as federal criminal trials must be fairly conducted and that all branches of law enforcement must abide by and respect the law. Because of these, and other decisions, the Warren Court was labeled the ''conscience of our society'' by *New York Times* columnist Anthony Lewis.

But, in hindsight, the most valuable contribution of the Warren Court may not turn out to be its specific decisions in particular civil liberty areas, important as these have been. Rather, the Warren Court's greatest impact may lie in its rulings that made the federal courts more available and more responsive to the claims of persons wronged by governmental and private misconduct—women, minorities, environmentalists, victims of malapportionment, mental patients, prisoners, poor people—all, in varying degrees, found a forum in which to vent their complaints. The Warren Court breathed new life into the idea that federal courts ought to be vigilant agencies of protection for the rights guaranteed by the Constitution and the laws of the United States.

Chief Justice Warren E. Burger has frequently deplored the humanistic activism of the Warren Court. For example, in July 1971, he cautioned young people against becoming lawyers in order to accomplish social change through the courts, saying ''that is not the route by which basic changes in a country like ours should be made.'' One way to stop such attempts is to close the courthouse doors. Today, the Supreme

Court, under the chief justiceship of Warren Burger, is making it much more difficult for a person to get a federal court to hear claims to a constitutional right.

The techniques used by the Supreme Court in closing doors to the federal courthouses have been technical. Decisions of the Warren Court have been narrowed or otherwise restricted, sometimes without explicitly recognizing the previous decisions: In some instances, prior cases have been overruled. Moreover, the Burger Court has been active in highly technical areas of the law involving subjects such as class actions, standing to sue, attorneys' fees, the scope of federal court review over state civil and criminal cases, abstention, and a range of meaningful remedies available to redress constitutional wrongs. The decisions are highly technical, newspapers do not discuss them, and citizens generally are ignorant of them. Thus the Court's decisions avoid "sunlight," which Louis D. Brandeis said "is the best of all disinfectants."

The counterrevolution against the protection of human rights fostered by the Warren Court began just as soon as the Nixonites joined the Court. The process has been evolutionary; two steps forward and one backward. Its course is not marked by a straight-line development because, occasionally, the Warren Court holdovers—William Brennan, Thurgood Marshall, and William O. Douglas—could convince the centrist wafflers—Potter Stewart and Byron White—to join them, thus making a majority of five.

Overall, however, the Supreme Court today has become the bastion of counterrevolution. In major ways Richard Nixon has succeeded. But it should be understood that in one respect he failed "to balance the Court." The Burger Court is not quiescent; it is just as "activist" a court as the Warren Court. The difference between the two lies in the direction of the activism. A few specific examples:

The Burger Court's activism is shown in its reformulation of the technical legal rules of jurisdiction and procedure to make it much harder to move civil liberty cases into federal courts in general and into the Supreme Court in particular. "Class actions"—lawsuits in which one person sues in the name of many others, a "class"—have been made difficult to sustain.

There are cases usually involving business or governmental abuse in which the harm to an individual may be much less than $10,000, making it financially impractical for that person to sue. This state of affairs exists when excessive utility rates are charged, in consumer frauds, harm from pollution, or harm from antitrust violations. To remedy this, "class actions" have been developed which permit people with similar claims to band together, thereby making a lawsuit possible. Otherwise, the wrongdoer may escape liability completely.

Starting in 1969 with *Synder* v. *Harris,*[3] the Supreme Court has set up almost insuperable barriers to the maintenance of class actions by a large number of people each having only a small claim. In 1974, the Burger Court decided *Eisen* v. *Carlisle & Jacquelin.*[4] A purchaser of odd lots of stock on the New York Stock Exchange brought a class action against two brokerage firms under the antitrust laws for monopolizing the business and for charging excessive fees. The class consisted of himself and about 6 million others. The lower federal court found that 2,250,000 members of the class could be identified and that it would cost $225,000 to notify them individually. The federal trial court thought that requiring a plaintiff to spend $225,000 to notify 2,250,000 members of the class would defeat the purpose of class actions. Therefore, the lower court devised a scheme to notify the members of the class by publication in the *Wall Street Journal* and other newspapers and to send individual notices to over 7,000 key individuals and groups. This scheme would have cost $21,750. The federal court also ruled that 90 percent of this cost should be paid by the defendants because it was "more than likely" that they were guilty of violating antitrust laws and that the plaintiffs would win. The federal court's scheme was appealed to the Supreme Court.

By a 6–3 decision, the Burger Court ruled that the lower federal court's scheme could not be used and that personal notification of all the 2.25 million people had to be made by the plaintiff, that he had to bear the entire cost, and that he had to do all of this before the federal court could decide his case. This decision effectively killed class actions in situations where a great number of average citizens have been wronged. The only people who can now afford to bring class actions are those who don't need to bring them. Mr. Justice Douglas dissented, saying:

I agree with Professor Chafee that a class action serves not only the convenience of the parties but also prompt, efficient judicial administration. I think in our society that is growing in complexity there are bound to be innumerable people in common disasters, calamities, or ventures who would go begging for justice without the class action but who could with all regard to due process be protected by it. Some of these are consumers whose claims may seem *de minimis* but who alone have no practical recourse for either remuneration or injunctive relief. Some may be environmentalists who have no photographic development plant about to be ruined because of air pollution by radiation but who suffer perceptibly by smoke, noxious gases, or radiation. Or the unnamed individual may be only a ratepayer being excessively charged by a utility, or a homeowner whose assessment is slowly rising beyond his ability to pay.

The class action is one of the few legal remedies the small claimant has against those who command the status quo. I would strengthen his hand with the view of creating a system of law that dispenses justice to the lowly as well as to those liberally endowed with power and wealth.[5]

To take another example, if the parties to a lawsuit are citizens of different states, they can only litigate in the federal courts if the "matter in controversy" exceeds the value of $10,000. This amount is required in order to avoid wasting the federal courts' time on minor disputes. In some cases no single plaintiff has been injured that much, but a group has. In 1969, the Burger Court ruled that if no plaintiff, individually, claimed more than $10,000, then it was not enough that their claims totaled more than $10,000 in the aggregate, and they could not sue in federal court.[6] In 1973, the Burger Court followed up on this ruling. In *Zahn* v. *International Paper Co.*[7] two hundred people who owned lakefront land sued the International Paper Company for polluting Lake Champlain in Vermont. Four of the lakefront owners clearly had claims of more than $10,000, but many others did not. Nevertheless, through a doctrine known as "ancillary jurisdiction," the lakefront owners with claims of less than $10,000 thought they would be able to join the same lawsuit with lakefront owners having claims of more than $10,000, especially since the same issue was presented in all of the claims. But the Burger Court ignored a long line of ancillary jurisdiction cases which would have permitted the suits in federal court and, by the same 6–3 majority that decided *Eisen*, ruled that each member bringing suit must validly claim the jurisdictional amount of $10,000. The Burger Court refused to allow a class action, thereby leaving the lakefront owners having smaller claims without a viable and inexpensive remedy.

The Burger Court has extended its restrictive approach to ancillary jurisdiction in public interest cases to other contexts. For example, in *Aldinger* v. *Howard*,[8] decided in 1976, a schoolteacher was dismissed from her job without a hearing because, allegedly, she was "living with [her] boyfriend." Her work was "excellent." She brought a federal civil rights action in a federal court against the county treasurer, and she also tried to include in her lawsuit a claim, based on a state law, against the county itself. She thought the federal court would decide both claims, because they arose out of the same set of facts and because of the doctrine of ancillary jurisdiction. The federal Civil Rights Act has been interpreted to prohibit federal lawsuits against governmental agencies, including counties, but state law apparently allowed a suit against the county. Her purpose in putting her two claims together in one lawsuit was to resolve everything in one proceeding and thereby avoid the expense and duplication of two separate suits in federal and state courts. The Supreme Court has allowed plaintiffs to do this and to add state law claims to federal suits when they grew out of a "common nucleus of operative fact."[9] Nevertheless, by a 6–3 majority, the Burger Court forced the plaintiff to split her federal lawsuit in two, requiring her to litigate in a separate state court proceeding against the county. Because state courts can decide claims under the federal Civil Rights Act, the net result of their decision will be to force people having both state and federal claims to litigate their federal constitutional claim in state courts rather than in the more sympathetic federal courts. Now the only way a person can simultaneously sue both the official state agency and the individual who violated civil rights is by staying out of federal court.

"Standing" is a technical legal term that refers to the legal interest that a plaintiff must assert before he can litigate in federal courts. Almost always a plaintiff's standing interest must be his own, and it must be substantial. Obviously, the Supreme Court can eliminate lawsuits from the federal courts by requiring stricter "standing" standards. Technical rules of "standing" govern the legal interest a plaintiff must present in order to invoke the power of a federal court to grant a remedy. These "standing" rules have been made much stricter by the Burger Court, thereby eliminating many types of civil liberty lawsuits. *Laird* v. *Tatum*[10] is an example.

Intelligence units of the U.S. Army had established a data-gathering system with field offices staffed with approximately a thousand agents, 94 percent of whose time was devoted to this purpose. Attending demonstrations and meetings, the agents took pictures of people at political rallies and gatherings and gathered information, including names. This information was fed into a computer data bank located at Fort Holabird, Maryland. Tatum, a person photographed at political rallies, brought a class action lawsuit seeking to enjoin the entire data-gathering system on the ground that its existence has a chilling effect on his, and other persons', free exercise of First Amendment freedoms of expression. The lawsuit failed when the Supreme Court could not identify any injury to Tatum or to his class who failed to present the requisite standing interest. In a 5-to-4 decision, Chief Justice Burger held that Tatum and others like him who had been photographed and identified by the U.S. Army lacked the legal interest to invoke federal court power. Chief Justice Burger stated in his opinion for the Court that "absent [a showing] of actual present or immediately threatened injury resulting from unlawful governmental action" that Tatum and his class "have not presented a case for resolution by the courts." Mr. Justice Douglas dissented, saying:

One need not wait to sue until he loses his job or until his reputation is defamed. To withhold standing to sue until that time arrives would in practical effect immunize from judicial scrutiny all surveillance activities, regardless of their misuse and their deterrent effect.

The present controversy is not a remote, imaginary conflict. Respondents were targets of the Army's surveillance. First, the surveillance was not casual but massive and comprehensive. Second, the intelligence reports were regularly and widely circulated and were exchanged with reports of the FBI, state and municipal police departments, and the CIA. Third, the Army's surveillance was not collecting material in public records but staking out teams of agents, infiltrating undercover agents, creating command posts inside meetings, posing as press photographers and newsmen, posing as TV newsmen, posing as students, and shadowing public figures.

Surveillance of civilians is none of the Army's constitutional business and Congress has not undertaken to entrust it with any such function. The fact that since this litigation started the Army's surveillance may have been cut back is not an end of the matter. Whether there has been an actual cutback or whether the announcements are merely a ruse can be determined only after a hearing in the District Court. . . . We are advised by an *amicus curiae* brief filed by a group of former Army Intelligence Agents that Army surveillance of civilians is rooted in secret programs of long standing:

> Army intelligence has been maintaining an unauthorized watch over civilian political activity for nearly 30 years. Nor is this the first time that Army intelligence has, without notice to its civilian superiors, over-stepped its mission. From 1917 to 1924, the Corps of Intelligence Police maintained a massive surveillance of civilian political activity which involved the use of hundreds of civilian informants, the infiltration of civilian organizations and the seizure of dissenters and unionists, sometimes without charges. That activity was opposed—then as now—by civilian officials on those occasions when they found out about it, but it continued unabated until postwar disarmament and economies finally eliminated the bureaucracy that conducted it.

This case involves a cancer in our body politic. It is a measure of the disease which afflicts us. Army surveillance, like Army regimentation, is at war with the principles of the First Amendment. Those who already walk submissively will say there is no cause for alarm. But submissiveness is not our heritage. The First Amendment was designed to allow rebellion to remain as our heritage. The Constitution was designed to keep government off the backs of the people. The Bill of Rights was added to keep the precincts of belief and expression, of the press, of political and social activities free from surveillance. The Bill of Rights was designed to keep agents of government and official eavesdroppers away from assemblies of people. The aim was to allow men to be free and independent and to assert their rights against government. There can be no influence more paralyzing of that objective than Army surveillance. When an intelligence officer looks over every nonconformist's shoulder in the library or walks invisibly by his side in a picket line, or infiltrates his club, the America once extolled as the voice of liberty heard around the world no longer is cast in the image which Jefferson and Madison designed, but more in the Russian image. . . .[11]

United States v *Richardson*[12] presents another example of standing. The Burger Court held that a federal taxpayer did not have a sufficient interest and therefore did not have standing to bring a lawsuit demanding that the budget of the CIA be made public. Article I, Section 9 of the Constitution expressly provides that "no money shall be drawn from the Treasury, but in consequence of an appropriation made by law; and a regular statement and account of the receipts and the expenditures of all public money shall be published from time to time." The CIA budget has never been revealed, and a citizen-voter-taxpayer, according to the Burger Court, does not have a sufficient interest to invoke federal court power to make government obey the Constitution. This constitutional provision joins several others rendered judicially nonenforceable. Burger's opinion in *United States* v. *Richardson* recognizes as much, for he wrote: "In a very real sense, the absence of any particular individual or class to litigate these [types of] claims gives support to the argument that the subject matter is committed to . . . Congress, and ultimately to the political process." A taxpayer's redress, Burger further wrote, is "in the political forum or at the polls" and not in our federal courts. Thus all that can be done is to vote for a different congressman who may or may not obey the Constitution. That is the way in which the Supreme Court has been "balanced." Again Mr. Justice Douglas dissented, saying:

History shows that the curse of government is not always venality; secrecy is one of the most tempting coverups to save regimes from criticism. As the Court of Appeals said:

> The Framers of the Constitution deemed fiscal information essential if the electorate was to exercise any control over its representatives and meet their new responsibilities as citizens of the Republic; and they mandated publication, although stated in general terms, of the Government's receipts and expenditures. Whatever the ultimate scope and extent of that obligation, its elimination generates a sufficient, adverse interest in a taxpayer.

Whatever may be the merits of the underlying claim, it seems clear that the taxpayer in the present case is not making a generalized complaint about the operation of Government. He does not even challenge the constitutionality of the Central Intelligence Agency Act. He only wants to know the amount of tax money exacted from him that goes into CIA activities. Secrecy of the Government acquires new sanctity when his claim is denied. . . . Secrecy was the evil at which Art I, § 9, cl. 7, was aimed.

From the history of the clause it is apparent that the Framers inserted it in the Constitution to give the public knowledge of the way public funds are expended. No one has a greater "personal stake" in policing this protective measure than a taxpayer. Indeed, if a taxpayer may not raise the question, who may do so? The Court states that discretion to release information is in the first instance, "committed to the surveillance of Congress," and that the right of the citizenry to information under Art. I, § 9, cl. 7, cannot be enforced directly, but only through the "[s]low, cumbersome, and unresponsive" electoral process. One has only to read constitutional history to realize that statement would shock Mason and Madison. Congress of course has discretion; but to say that it has the power to read the clause out of the Constitution when it comes to one or two or three agencies is astounding. That is the barebones issue in the present case.

The sovereign in this Nation is the people, not the bureaucracy. The statement of accounts of public expenditures goes to the heart of the problem of sovereignty. If taxpayers may not ask that rudimentary question, their sovereignty becomes an empty symbol and a secret bureaucracy is allowed to run our affairs. . . .

The public cannot intelligently know how to exercise the franchise unless it has a basic knowledge concerning at least the generality of the accounts under every head of government. No greater crisis in confidence can be generated than today's decision. Its consequences are grave because it relegates to secrecy vast operations of government and keeps the public from knowing what secret plans concerning his Nation or other nations are afoot. The fact that the result is serious does not, of course, make the issue "justifiable." But resolutions of any doubts or ambiguities should be toward protecting an individual's stake in the integrity of constitutional guarantees rather than turning him away without even a chance to be heard.[13]

Two more cases involving standing deserve passing mention. In *Warth* v. *Seldin*[14] the Burger Court ruled that minority citizens did not have "standing" with respect to exclusionary zoning codes of suburbs, codes which prohibited low-income housing that minorities could afford. Thus minority members were effectively confined to the cores of cities, and ghettos perpetuated.

In *Paul* v. *Davis*[15] the Court, through an opinion by Mr. Justice Rehnquist, ruled that a person's reputation alone, apart from some more tangible interest such as employment, does not fall under the liberty provisions of the Fourteenth Amendment. Edward Davis III, a newspaper photographer, had been arrested on a charge of shoplifting. He pled not guilty, but his case was never tried. We do not know if he was guilty or innocent because the prosecutor failed to prosecute. Later the police chief included Davis' picture among others in a sheaf that was circulated to businessmen and others in the city of Louisville. Each page of the sheaf of pictures was labeled "Active Shoplifters." Davis sued. Justice Rehnquist said for the Court that Davis had an insufficient standing to invoke the liberty or property clauses of the Fourteenth Amendment's due process clause, and therefore his lawsuit against the police chief should be dismissed. By manipulating and restricting the standing doctrine, the Court controls the flow of cases and the role of the federal courts in American government.

In addition to being strict-construction activists in class actions and standing, the Burger Court has resurrected the long-buried "states' rights" doctrine in order to bar civil rights suits in federal courts. *Rizzo* v. *Goode*[16] is an example. Black citizens in Philadelphia claimed numerous indignities and the denial of their constitutional rights by the police. These facts were expressly recognized by Mr. Justice Rehnquist's opinion for the Court. He wrote that Philadelphia's "police department received complaints but ultimately took no action against the offending officers." Because there was no effective redress, Goode and others brought a lawsuit against Mayor Rizzo and various police officers of Philadelphia in a federal court under the federal Civil Rights Act, alleging that their constitutional rights had been denied by the officials. Violations of constitutional rights were clearly described, and the federal district court then had to consider what relief to grant. It ordered Goode and others to submit a proposed "comprehensive program for improving the handling of citizen complaints alleging police misconduct." A proposed program was actually negotiated between the parties to the lawsuit. The plan was submitted to the district court, which incorporated it into the final judgment. Rizzo appealed, and the federal court of appeals upheld the district court's finding and it also affirmed the relief. The Supreme Court reversed everything. Mr. Justice Rehnquist argued that Goode (and the others) lacked "standing" because his claim to "real and immediate" injury rested not on what Rizzo did, or might do, but on what a small, unnamed number of policemen did. Rizzo merely failed to control them. Thus, according to the Court, Goode and others lacked standing to obtain an order overhauling police disciplinary procedures. Secondly, Rehnquist said, states' rights principles of federalism required that the federal district court's overhaul of police disciplinary procedures constituted an unwarranted federal intrusion into state and local matters. The federal court was chastised, and a citizen lost even when his constitutional rights had been invaded.

Is it a mere coincidence that *Rizzo*, *Warth*, and *Paul* all involved attempts by black Americans to secure judicial relief? Or is the Supreme Court telling black Americans not to look to it for relief in the seventies as they looked to the Warren Court in the fifties and sixties? Consider two school desegregation cases. In a 1971 case—*Swann* v. *Charlotte-*

Mecklenberg School District[17]—the Burger Court expressly approved of busing as a technique to achieve desegregation. However, three years later, in 1974, in *Milliken* v. *Bradley*,[18] the Court held that busing across political boundaries that separated Detroit from its suburbs was constitutionally prohibited unless acts of *de jure* segregation could be proved in each suburb as well as in the central city. Given the total black population of Detroit, the central schools cannot be desegregated below a mix of 65 percent black and 35 percent others. *Brown* v. *Board of Education*, is effectively nullified in such cities. This decision, plus *Warth* v. *Selden* and *Arlington Heights* on exclusionary zoning, have slowed the pace of desegregation in the North considerably.

In the area of criminal procedure the Burger Court has been particularly active. The opinions of the Warren and Burger Courts are completely opposed. One criminal law development will illustrate. "Harmless error" doctrine allows courts to ignore "small" errors made during criminal prosecution. The Burger Court has allowed so many items to qualify as "small" or harmless errors that criminal trials today have almost reverted to their status prior to the Warren Court. The Burger Court has also sharply curtailed the rights of prisoners, so much so that Justice Stevens has recently moved to say that the Court had almost reduced prisoners to a "slave" status. Finally, in the area of criminal law, there were the death penalty cases of the Burger Court.

One must evaluate the Burger Court's contributions to civil liberties against this background. They lie in two areas. First, in 1973 the Court held that a right to privacy protected a pregnant woman's and her doctor's decision to terminate her pregnancy by abortion during either of the first two trimesters. The Court then ruled that poor women have no right to an abortion at governmental expense, thereby making abortions available only to those women who can pay. Secondly, there has been a consistent set of opinions on freedom of the press. In 1971 the Court, in the Pentagon Papers Case,[19] invalidated the government's claims to secrecy based on the doctrine of national security and allowed the papers to be published. It also has overturned gag orders on newspapermen by trial court judges. Standing against these decisions is *Branzburg* v. *Hayes*,[20] in which the Court rejected a reporter's refusal to tell a grand jury his sources of information.

In summary, it can be stated that, with a few cases to the contrary, the Burger Court is turning back the hands of the civil liberty clock. Moreover, nearly everything the Burger Court does seems calculated to keep people out of court. When it rules on procedural or substantive issues, it consistently restricts individual rights and liberties. The future seems to be moving backward at full speed, with a reduction in constitutional protection and freedom for all of us. We can hope that President Carter will make from two to four appointments. Justices Brennan and Marshall will probably leave the Court within the next four years—Brennan is seventy-two and Marshall is seventy and in ill health. Powell, Blackmun, and perhaps Burger may depart—Powell is seventy-one and Blackmun, like Burger, is seventy. Rehnquist is fifty-five and White is sixty-one. But the conservative, anticivil libertarian bias of the Court will change only if the new appointees are different. Until then, the trend launched by Richard M. Nixon continues. Justices Brennan and Marshall, joined occasionally by Stewart and Stevens, will be an embattled and sometimes an embittered minority. Richard M. Nixon, alive and well, reigns as the Imperial President from the Marble Palace of the Supreme Court of the United States.

Standing against the work of the Burger Court is the rich legacy of William O. Douglas. If President Carter replaces the Nixon appointees with people of a more humane focus and an intellectually liberal approach, then the dissenting opinions of Mr. Justice Douglas can serve as a rich vein of ore. They are ready for mining. Once again our federal courts can be opened to all citizens, whether they are minorities, women, victims of consumer fraud, poor people, environmentalists, prisoners, mental patients, victims of governmental irregularities, or just ordinary people. When this occurs, the Supreme Court of the United States once again will be the conscience of our society and resume its rightful role in American government as an agent of social change in the service of humanity. That was the vision of Mr. Justice Douglas.

Notes

1. *Brown* v. *Board of Education*, 347 U.S. 483 (1954).
2. *Plessy* v. *Ferguson*, 163 U.S. 537 (1896).

3. *Snyder* v. *Harris*, 394 U.S. 332 (1969).
4. *Eisen* v. *Carlisle & Jacquelin*, 417 U.S. 156 (1974).
5. *Id.* at 185–6.
6. *Snyder* v. *Harris*, *supra* note 3.
7. *Zahn* v. *International Paper Co.*, 414 U.S. 291 (1973).
8. *Aldinger* v. *Howard*, 427 U.S. 1 (1976).
9. *United Mine Workers* v. *Gibbs*, 383 U.S. 715 (1966).
10. *Laird* v. *Tatum*, 408 U.S. 1 (1972).
11. *Id.* at 26–7.
12. *United States* v. *Richardson*, 418 U.S. 166 (1974).
13. *Id.* at 198–202.
14. *Warth* v. *Seldin*, 422 U.S. 490 (1975).
15. *Paul* v. *Davis*, 424 U.S. 693 (1976).
16. *Rizzo* v. *Goode*, 423 U.S. 362 (1976).
17. *Swann* v. *Charlotte-Mecklenburg School District*, 402 U.S. 1 (1971).
18. *Milliken* v. *Bradley*, 418 U.S. 717 (1974).
19. *New York Times Co.* v. *United States*, 403 U.S. 713 (1971).
20. *Branzburg* v. *Hayes*, 408 U.S. 665 (1972).

To Sit in Judgment: 6
Sex Discrimination and
the Courts
ANITA M. MILLER⎯⎯⎯⎯⎯⎯

William O. Douglas steadfastly attacked sex discrimination in American society during his last five years on the bench, as evidenced in the following cases: *Alexander* v. *Louisiana*, 405 U.S. 625 (1972); *Cleveland Board of Education* v. *LaFleur*, 414 U.S. 632 (1974); *Schlesinger* v. *Ballard*, 419 U.S. 498 (1975). As usual, a break with precedent, a rejection of conventional wisdom on sex differences, and a departure from what constitutes the Court's proper business did not perturb Douglas. If his instincts prove correct, the Court and legal historians will enlarge this area of constitutional discussion. The women's movement of the 1970s promises to have a revolutionary influence on how we explain our past and on what scholars select to study in constitutional history.

Anita M. Miller's address at the Douglas Symposium demonstrates the revisionist function of new perspectives. She stresses the role of subjectivity and of unacknowledged cultural stereotypes in determining what is legal and constitutionally allowable. Miller has served since 1972 as chairwoman of the California Commission on the Status of Women; she has been a member of the state's Republican Central Committee, and she created the National Equal Rights Amendment Project. An articulate activist, she lectures throughout the country on the topics of humanism, the ERA, marriage, and the mythologies of sex differentiation.

The great legal scholar Samuel E. Stumpf said that modern man's life is controlled more effectively, forcefully, and in greater detail by law than by any other agency of social control.[1] The same can be said of modern woman! But when we examine the law in terms of women, we can see that it has not always had those judicial virtues of detachment, reflection, and critical analysis which are usually applied to laws governing men. In fact, the *New York University Law Review* recently described the performance of American judges in the area of sex discrimination as "ranging from poor to abominable."[2]

We can best "get at" this problematic legal approach to women by looking first at the symbolic nature of law, what it purports to do for us all. Then we should examine the mystical symbol in terms of the factual reality. We should look at some specific cases, the decisions arising therefrom, and the effect of those decisions on the lives of American women everywhere.

Consider for a moment the mystification of the courtroom. Its operation is, among other things, great and consuming theater, a fact to which television, Hollywood, and Broadway have testified for years. All the actors, save one, face in the same direction. All the learned dialogue is directed toward the same audience of one. And at the center, both literally and figuratively, sits the judge: a figure robed in black; one for whom everyone rises in a show of respect, an individual placed on a raised platform who towers over all during the course of litigation, the symbol of ultimate arbitration. The mandate under which this person serves is society's "terms for order," ideas such as justice, equality, right and wrong. All of these terms are abstract human constructs that must be personified, made real—if you will—by the judge and his decisions. Given the trappings, is it any wonder that we acquiesce in the judge's pronouncements?

We choose to believe that a wrongheaded person would never become a judge. We choose to believe that wisdom and concern for the common good inform every decision. But even a cursory examination of judicial history shows extraordinary contradictions. For example, the concept of separate but equal school facilities was judged "right, just and fair" for decades until the *Brown* decision said it was "wrong, unjust and not fair." The point here must be that judges, no less than other persons, are influenced by the social pressures of the moment. They may join them or fight against them. But they must respond.

Judges, no less than others, react to political factors, to customs, and to the sum total of their own principles, prejudices, and individual persuasions. To be a human is to be fallible, and this applies no less to judges than to you and me.

I will turn now to a brief examination of several decisions concerning women. Has detachment been the principal informing agent, or has a measure of the patriarchal tradition crept into the decisions?

In 1873 an Illinois woman by the name of Bradwell was denied her application to practice law solely because she was female.[3] The Supreme Court denied her appeal and based its decision on the traditional assumptions regarding the proper role of women. It ignored the fact that Bradwell was as fully qualified and as completely trained to practice law as any male. Mr. Justice Bradley, writing for the majority, said: "The paramount destiny and mission of women is to fulfill the noble and benign offices of wife and mother. This is the law of the creator. And the rules of civil society must be adapted to the general constitution of things, and cannot be based upon exceptional cases." Sounds familiar, doesn't it? In fact, we are so used to this "natural-order-of-things" argument that we seldom stop to analyze it. Nor have we, until recently, come to understand its insidious effect on the lives of women.

As we look at the very beginnings of political and legal philosophy, we recognize that the concept of natural law exercises enormous influence. Mankind—and I use that term advisedly—has held the belief that basic laws of the universe govern human conduct as they govern physical nature. The order of nature, at least as perceived and interpreted by men, has served as grounds for social order. As a result, sexual differentiation receives meaning in the legal realm that it does not possess in nature. As Professor Charles Elkins has observed: "What does the male–female difference signify in nature? Nothing: It simply exists. But *we* have made much of the difference."[4] We have transformed the male–female "biological" distinction perceived in natural order into a man–woman polarity circumscribed by human law. Bradwell was denied the right to practice law because of her femaleness; that reproductive capacity has nothing to do with mental power was discounted as irrelevant. So much for judicial detachment in 1873.

Nor had things noticeably improved by the turn of the century. At the tag-end of the Gilded Age, in a time of enormous technological progress, America moved smoothly toward Model-T Fords and Ragtime. The working class now began its historic march toward full partnership with management. The *male* working class, that is. In 1905, the Supreme Court declared unconstitutional a law which regulated the maximum work hours for all bakery employees.[5] *Lockner* v. *New York* (1905) decided that the worker's constitutional right to freedom of contract held precedence over all other considerations. Now this law applied to both men and women—for exactly three years. In *Muller* v. *Oregon* (1908), the Supreme Court upheld an Oregon statute restricting the work hours of women.[6] Suddenly, men could work any number of hours because of the hallowed constitutional freedom of contract. Women, however, were denied that right. Why? Because of potential motherhood, of course. That, and the implicit inferiority of women acknowledged in the decision. Mr. Justice Louis Brandeis, writing for the majority, said:

Woman's physical structure and *the performance of maternal function* places her at a disadvantage in the struggle for subsistence . . . history discloses the fact that woman has always been dependent upon man. He established his control at the outset by superior physical strength, and this control in various forms . . . has continued to the present. [Therefore, woman] has been looked upon in the courts as needing especial care that her rights may be preserved. [The Court recognizes] that a proper discharge of her maternal functions . . . justifies legislation to protect her from the greed as well as the passion of man.

I have always been amused that, insisting upon woman's special right to motherhood, the Court effectively stripped her of every other legal consideration. Surely, maternity is the one role women have always managed somehow, with or without the Court's blessing. So much for legal detachment at the turn of the century.

Jumping ahead by several decades, there is one more example before we concentrate on the 1970s. By 1948, America had been involved in two world wars, and the women of this country had performed admirably in both efforts. For the duration of World War II the protective laws circumscribing female labor had been lifted. Women were needed in the factories for the war effort, and, as a consequence, their so-called special needs were put aside in order to work overtime producing military matériel. At the end of the war, the laws came back in effect and the women had to step aside for returning soldiers. The courts went right along. In 1948, for example, a woman challenged a Michigan statute which denied a bartending license to a female unless she was the wife or daughter of the owner.[7] Now this law prior to its passage had been intensely lobbied by an all-male union seeking to get and to keep jobs for its members. But the Supreme Court upheld the law. Mr. Justice Felix Frankfurter wrote:

The fact that women may now have achieved the virtues that men have long claimed as their prerogatives and now indulge in vices that men have long practiced does not preclude ... drawing a sharp line between the sexes ... the Constitution does not require (state) legislatures to reflect sociological insight, or shifting social standards, any more than it requires them to keep abreast of the latest scientific standards.[8]

Mr. Justice Frankfurter acknowledges social change only to discount its relevance to the court or to legislative lawmaking bodies. Women had accomplished extraordinary tasks during the years of the war; women had not only survived the freedom accorded them during the war, but actually *thrived* on it. It made no difference to the Court. The judicial opinion gives credence *only* to the "hazardous moral and social problems" that may confront a barmaid without "protecting oversight" by a male. And what of the claim that the law's only purpose was to enforce the union's effort to keep the occupation all male? Mr. Justice Frankfurter dismissed it with the smug complacency. He wrote: "We cannot give ear to the suggestion that the impulse behind this legislation was an unchivalrous desire of male bartenders to try to monopolize the calling." Unchivalrous, indeed! The fact of the matter was that Michigan was swamped with returning veterans and this decision is just one of many successful attempts to keep the women out of the work force. More importantly, perhaps, this decision is but one example of the separate legal and constitutional place accorded women by the courts throughout our history.

We might do well to pause for a moment and talk of Felix Frankfurter, to look briefly at the man beneath the flowing black robe. Frankfurter was a renowned liberal and a celebrated intellectual. His impassioned defenses of Sacco and Vanzetti, of the Scotsboro boys, are legendary. He had a lifelong interest in social welfare. As Mary Dunlap has written, Justice Frankfurter had an intense "dedication to the ideals of economic fairness and active governmental regulation of the greedy, the landed gentry, and the corrupt." Yet this celebrated liberal, like so many others, had a blind spot concerning women while insisting on the rights of everyone else; he could declare that the states may "draw a sharp line between the sexes." While condemning racial and religious prejudice, Frankfurter saw no reason to advance the cause of sexual equality. In fact he—and millions living today—illustrate the point that sexual prejudice is the only remaining socially acceptable bias. We must treat everyone fairly in this land, but women are somehow different. Women, somehow, won't mind. Women, somehow, will adjust.

The proof of my accusation may be found in a strange hesitation on the part of the Supreme Court in the past fifteen years to declare sex a suspect classification. Put simply, a classification is deemed suspect, and therefore illegal, when there is no legitimate reason for it. Race was declared a suspect classification years ago, and laws which distinguished between blacks and whites purely on the basis of color were declared unconstitutional and thrown out. But, even today, laws which distinguish between men and women purely on the basis of gender remain in force. Laws having to do with education, criminal sentencing, family relationships, and countless other things say that women must be treated differently simply because they are women.

This is not to say that sex discrimination laws have not been struck down. In 1971, the Supreme Court declared unconstitutional an Idaho statute that said males must be preferred over females in the administration of estates.[9] The Court failed, however, to apply the "strict scrutiny test" necessary to declaring sex a suspect classification. The same held true in 1975 when the Court struck down a Utah law which said females were to be supported to eighteen, males to twenty-one.[10] The only court which held sex to be a suspect classification is the California High Court in *Sail'er Inn* v. *Kirby.*[11] The California opinion lacks the weight of a Supreme Court decision, of course, but it might serve as a shining example for cases pending on the Supreme Court docket. Justice Raymond Peters said:

Sex, like race and lineage, is an immutable trait, a status into which the class members are locked by accident of birth. What differentiates sex from nonsuspect statuses, such as intelligence or physical disability, and aligns it with the recognized suspect classification is that the characteristic frequently bears no relation to ability to perform or contribute to society ... the result is that the whole class is relegated to an inferior legal status without regard to the capabilities or characteristics of its individual members.

And here we come to the heart of the matter—the thesis of my talk. Peters' opinion for the California court goes on:

Laws which disable women from full participation in the political, business and economic arenas are often characterized as "protective" and beneficial. Those same laws applied to racial or ethnic minorities would readily be recognized as invidious and impermissible. The pedestal upon which women have been placed has all too often, upon closer inspection, been revealed as a cage. We conclude that the sexual classifications are properly treated as suspect.[12]

I agree. I'm sure that most of you in this room agree. But the Supreme Court has yet to join with us. In recent years, in fact, the Court has refused to hear cases in which state laws perpetuating sex-based discrimination were challenged. In 1974 and 1975, for example, the Court denied hearings to cases dealing with child custody,[13] alimony,[14] and statutory shares[15] in decedents' estates. Any of these would have provided an opportunity to test the legality of sex as a classification, but the Court dismissed all of these opportunities. As Professor Charles Johnson has observed, this hesitation has tended "to compress the sweep and retard the impact of the other decisions invalidating gender-based state laws."

As the women of America approach the men in black who "sit in judgment," they often find the dice loaded. The rules under which they live are often informed more by stereotypic assumptions than by justice and equality. And the same can sometimes be said of the officials who enforce those rules.

We have recently seen ironic testimony to this pattern. In *Califano v. Goldfarb*, the Supreme Court ruled that widowers were entitled to their wives' social security benefits without having to prove prior dependency.[16] Although the ruling applied to men, fair-minded women all over the country applauded the decision. It is only right and just that men be accorded the same benefits as women. Gender, here as elsewhere, should have no bearing on the issue. The same detachment did *not* apply, however, in the recent *General Electric* v. *Gilbert* decision.[17] In a 6-to-3 majority, the Supreme Court ruled that employers are free to exclude pregnancy-related conditions from employee benefit programs. It held that such exclusion did not violate Title VII of the Civil Rights Act of 1964. Now we must put this ruling in context; we must examine it in terms of the other conditions covered in employee benefit plans. General Electric's benefit plans cover such "voluntary" disabilities as venereal disease, sports injuries, hair transplants, and elective cosmetic surgery. Moreover, it also includes such single-sex conditions as prostate surgery, vasectomies, and circumcision. We cannot conclude, therefore, that the plan denies *all* specialized or single-sex conditions. We must conclude that the denial applies only to women.

Writing in dissent, Mr. Justice Stevens said: "The rule of issue places the risk of absence caused by pregnancy in a class by itself. By definition, such a rule discriminates on account of sex; for it is the capacity to become pregnant which primarily differentiates the female from the male."[18] I might add that this historical insistence on that difference is, and has been, the main motivation behind disparate court rulings as applied to men and women. But there is more than pregnancy benefits at issue here. We must also understand what this ruling says about the position of women generally in American society.

Writing in the *New York Times*, December 13, 1976, Clayton Fritchey put the matter succinctly:

The U.S. Supreme Court has just confirmed what everybody else already knows—the need for women justices on our highest bench. If there had been even one woman on the Supreme Court, it is doubtful if the other justices would have dared look her in the eye and then render their decision that employers may legally exclude pregnancy benefits . . . one even wonders how the justices can even look in the eye the judges on six U.S. Court of Appeals, *all* of which ruled precisely the opposite.

While I agree with Fritchey's assessment, I also have an abiding faith in the concept of law, and I believe that it can be made to work for women as well as for men. It will work when women share equally in the lawmaking process. And, finally, it will work when women share equally in the judicial decision making which affects us all. Put simply, when women are completely involved in the process of public policy, then we will see more evenhanded justice applied to both genders.

I would like to leave you with my favorite definition of law. It is by Samuel Stumpf. Traditionally, the law "has frequently been considered as playing the role of an umpire, watching the race only to insure that nobody is pushed off the track. Or tripped. It is not the function of law to make sure that everybody wins the race but only that the lanes are kept clear."[19] That really is all I ask for women: that the lanes are kept clear.

Notes

1. Samuel Enoch Stumpf, *Morality and the Law* (Nashville, Tenn.: Vanderbilt University Press, 1966).

2. J. D. Johnston, Jr. and C. L. Knapp, "Sex Discrimination by Law: A Study in Judicial Perspective," *New York University Law Review*, 46:675 (October 1971).

3. *Bradwell* v. *Illinois*, 83 U.S. 130 (1873).

4. Charles L. Elkins, "Social Impact," *Impact ERA: Limitations and Possibilities* (Millbrae, Calif.: Les Femmes Publishing, 1976), p. 222.

5. *Lochner* v. *New York*, 198 U.S. 45 (1905).

6. *Muller* v. *Oregon*, 208 U.S. 412 (1908).

7. *Goesaert* v. *Cleary*, 335 U.S. 464 (1948).

8. *Id*. at 466.

9. *Reed* v. *Reed*, 404 U.S. 71 (1971).

10. *Stanton* v. *Stanton*, 421 U.S. 7 (1975).

11. *Sail'er Inn* v. *Kirby*, 485 P. 2d 529 (1971).

12. *Id*, at 540–1.

13. *Arends* v. *Arends*, 517 P. 2d 458 (1974).

14. *Murphy* v. *Murphy*, 206 S.E. 2d 458 (1975).

15. *Humphreys* v. *Humphreys*, 520 P. 2d 193 (1974).

16. *Califano* v. *Goldfarb*, 97 S.Ct. 1021 (1977).

17. *General Electric* v. *Gilbert*, 97 S.Ct. 401 (1976).

18. *Id*. at 421.

19. Stumpf, *Morality and the Law*, p. 231.

The Equal Rights Amendment: A Debate

7

THOMAS EMERSON,
ANITA MILLER,
LINO GRAGLIA

AMENDMENT XXVII (Proposed)

SECTION 1. Equality of rights under the law shall not be denied or abridged by the United States or by any State on account of sex.

SECTION 2. The Congress shall have the power to enforce, by appropriate legislation, the provisions of this article.

SECTION 3. This amendment shall take effect two years after the date of ratification.

Congress submitted the Twenty-seventh Amendment to the states on March 22, 1972. Within three months nearly twenty state legislatures had approved it, but by April 1977 the number of ratifying states was stalled at thirty-five, or three short of the required thirty-eight. The following impromptu debate occurred late in the second day of the Douglas Symposium.

EMERSON: I became involved with the ERA in 1962 when a graduate student was working as a member of the task force of the President's Commission on the Status of Women. She was making a study of the question whether or not equal rights should be achieved through the Equal Protection Clause or through a constitutional amendment. That woman, by the way, was Pauli Murray, who later became the first black woman priest in the Episcopal Church. In 1970 I testified before the House Judiciary Committee and Senate Judiciary Committee on the ERA. I then undertook to write a rather long article for the April 1971 issue of the *Yale Law Journal* with three coauthors who were third-year law students. The article was distributed to all members of Congress by Martha Griffiths, who sponsored the Equal Rights Amendment in the House.

Since the Senate and the House passed it, I've been active in the ratification process, and have testified before legislative committees in Connecticut, Indiana, Missouri, Nevada, and Florida—unsuccessfully, except in Connecticut.

MILLER: I got into the ERA back in the late sixties and early seventies when it was current before the congressional committees. I tried to organize and rally support for its passage, primarily through women's organizations at that point in time.

In 1973 we received funding from the Rockefeller Foundation to do a special study on the impact of the ERA on state laws. For the past four years my institute has been involved quite intensively in looking at that particular aspect. We produced four publications as a result of the grant. Two of the books looked at state codes, and the changes that would have to be made in order to comply with the principle of legal equality. One book titled *Impact ERA: Limitations and Possibilities* is a compilation of works done by people from several social science disciplines, as well as law, to determine how society would look if we ever really did have egalitarian principles in force. We have also done a bibliography on the ERA: There are 6,000 articles that have been written on the issue.

My work has also involved going to industry and being in contact with the various state legislatures.

GRAGLIA: For me, fighting ERA is just a sideline; it's not a vocation, so I don't have a very lengthy impressive list of activities to report. I gather the main reason for the expression of my views on this subject is so there would be somebody to fight with. I've done very little except appear about every two years before the Texas legislature to recommend that their ratification be rescinded. I do that because about a dozen law professors from all over Texas appear to say that ratification ought to be affirmed. And it seems to me that the majority of the people of the state who oppose it should have at least one representative. I do oppose it. I think it would be a very bad thing socially. That's all I've done with it.

The main thing about the ERA is that its apparent simplicity is deceptive. I think this could be said about most of these proposals to settle complex and varied problems by some verbal formula that makes it appropriate that they be settled by courts, as Mr. Emerson has strongly recommended.

Unfortunately, the world and its problems are not that simple. The problems of sex discrimination involve a wide range of issues. They are very difficult problems. They cannot be settled by a slogan, which is all the ERA is. It's an appealing slogan, and it's very difficult to seem to be against equal rights which, of course, I'm not. I've established my credentials. I have three daughters and no sons, three sisters and no brothers. I love them all, and their interests are my interests. But this is a slogan, it does not help resolve any problems, and to the extent that it indicates a resolution, it will resolve problems in a way that most people consider intolerable.

ERA can be given a meaning, certain and definite. It can be understood to mean that all discrimination, differentiation, classification by government, state or federal, on the basis of sex is prohibited. It can simply prohibit all sex discrimination; or it might be given a flexible, you might call it a more reasonable, interpretation. The effect of the first absolute interpretation would be to produce results that are clearly so intolerable that even proponents of the amendment find them embarrassing and look for ways to escape. The result of a flexible amendment, on the other hand, would be to transfer the decision-making power on these questions from local elected representatives to centralized federal control, and indeed, most importantly to judicial control. A whole new area will be opened up for judicial regulation from Washington.

Take the absolute interpretation first: No sex discrimination at any time. I maintain that this would mean that, for example, Congress would not be able to draft men for military service unless it provided for the compulsory enlistment of women in exactly the same way. Similarly, they would not be able to allow voluntary enlistment of males unless they provided for the enlistment of women in exactly the same way. In another area, the law in the great majority of states still holds that a man must support his wife, even if she is able to support herself. Some changes in the law have created new obligations. The wife must now support the husband when she is able to do so and he is unable to support himself. That's been a change, clearly a good one. But it remains the case that the male spouse has an additional or primary obligation of support—an obligation to support even when the woman can support herself. The ERA would change that.

I don't think that to achieve equality it is necessary to do this. I debated with another law professor just before I left Texas. The result was as amazing to our students as it was to me, because my opponent, a woman, wound up saying the amendment would protect men, as I'm sure it will. Defending the need of *men* for protection, she looked like the male chauvinist and I was the feminist.

The amendment in absolute interpretation will require, and I think if properly interpreted ought to require, unisexuality. This is not a myth, this is not something silly people are making up. If you're not going to discriminate on the basis of sex, you can't discriminate among restrooms, athletic facilities, dressing rooms. Discrimination in restrooms was a major area of combat in race discrimination. I would maintain that the ERA would make sex discrimination at least as unfavored as race discrimination. In its legislative history every attempt to introduce an exemption or an escape was defeated, opposed by the proponents. The argument that any legal status granted to parties of different sexes would also have to be granted to homosexuals also seems to me an unanswerable argument.

Let me wrap it up. Decisions will have to be made by judges. What will follow in ERA's wake, and this is a very important point, is what has happened in the area of race. The attempt to prohibit race discrimination has developed into a *requirement* of racial discrimination. What is known euphemistically as affirmative action is a legal requirement *to* discriminate, and that presumably will happen here. You will get demands for quotas, demand for ratios, for equal representation of the sexes in all fields and all institutions. The Civil Rights Commission will conduct investigations and issue reports. HEW will issue regulations. The Department of Justice will enhance its enforcement arm. The federal bureaucracy will proliferate into one of the very few areas—domestic relations, child rearing—still left primarily to domestic control.

EMERSON: I'm not going to try to answer my friend at this time, because I want to establish some affirmative propositions. When he says that the ERA's apparent simplicity is deceptive, I think it's not deceptive although he tries to make it so. It really is a simple, fundamental proposition: namely, that rights under the law shall not be determined on the basis of whether a person is a member of one sex or another. They must be determined on the basis of various characteristics, individual traits, functions performed, and any other relevant factor of that sort, but sex cannot be the factor. Primarily and ultimately there are two moral reasons for the ERA. One is that in our society today we cannot tolerate an entire group having inequality of rights under the law. The other is that women, as all other persons in our society, are entitled to develop their own potentiality, to be treated on the basis of their own characteristics, and not to be treated on the basis of classification by sex.

Two general limitations apply. The ERA applies only to rights under the law. It does not apply to social relations, to personal relations, or to matters of that sort. Secondly, it applies only to state actions, not to the private sector. Two further qualifications should be made. It is said the ERA does not recognize physical differences between the sexes. That is not true. Insofar as there are physical differences which are unique to one sex and do not appear in the other sex, that factor can be taken into account. It does recognize, insofar as it's proper to do so, physical differences.

The second limitation is that the ERA does not abrogate other constitutional rights. The constitutional right of privacy established in *Griswold* v. *Connecticut* remains in effect, and that is the complete answer to bathroom questions and all other arguments about coeducational dressing rooms and the like that have been brought up. It does not abrogate the First Amendment or freedom of religion. That is the answer to the charges that are frequently made about the churches having to change their rules about admission to the priesthood or the ministry. Fundamental constitutional rights remain in effect. All the

ERA does is to put men and women on the same basis so far as the law is concerned. That's a very simple proposition.

MILLER: It's true that in the entire experience I have had with the ERA, I have never heard a white male deny that he had a good mother, a nice wife, a nice daughter: He couldn't possibly be against ERA for discriminatory reasons. The interesting thing about that thinking is they will then deny that mother, that wife, that daughter, equal opportunity in the society. Should anything happen to that white male and he is not, in fact, present to look after their welfare, the results are considerable. I do not for a moment consider the ERA just a slogan. It means absolutely one thing to me. It addresses the words over the Supreme Court, up above the marble stairs, that say "Justice, Equality Under the Law." That is all we're talking about. As far as saying the Equal Rights Amendment shouldn't be passed because it will involve court cases, I could care less about the process by which we finally achieve equal opportunity and equal rights under the law for all the people, including those who are females. Frankly, I don't care what the system has to do to bring that about. We want our citizenship. We have not had it.

Assuming that we can get there by electing right-minded legislators, and if they don't do your bidding then you elect someone else the next time around, is unsatisfactory. We've been at that point for *two hundred* years. . . .

So the reason for the ERA is as simple as the twenty-four words that comprise its text. "Equality of rights under the law shall not be denied nor abridged on the account of sex." The ERA will declare sex a suspect classification and when the cases go to court, we will have a different situation. . . .

Far from downgrading women in society, the ERA recognizes that a woman who marries should not sacrifice her legal rights just because she becomes a wife. We might, in fact, someday reach the point where we recognize the role that the wife and mother plays in the home, other than simply congratulating her for subscribing to the society's values on that point. When a marriage breaks up after twenty years, we presently say, "you've been sitting around for the last twenty years, now go out and make it on your own." There may be other answers.

MODERATOR: Professor Graglia may take five minutes to continue his argument or to offer a rebuttal.

GRAGLIA: I don't think that the privacy argument or the religious freedom argument Mr. Emerson offers is entirely sound. The unisex bathroom/dressing room idea is an embarrassment to the ERA. You may argue that unisex bathrooms aren't so bad or that homosexual marriages aren't so bad. I don't know. I have nothing personally against homosexuals. But it sure is a winning point in political debate to point out that if the ERA means what it says—no legal sex discrimination— it will make homosexual marriages legal. That switched my mother-in-law. She thought she was a women's-libber, but she wasn't for that.

The answer given is, "Wait, there are other constitutional rights, the right to privacy." Well, the right to privacy is rather weakly established. But in any event, somebody will have to decide that the so-called right of privacy overrides this later and apparently absolute principle of no sex discrimination. You know, there's also a right of freedom of association, as Mr. Emerson was telling us this morning about the First Amendment. But the right of freedom of association doesn't override the principle of no race discrimination. A lot of people didn't want to go to school with blacks, didn't want their children to associate with them. It didn't sell, as it shouldn't have. And will the ERA only apply to state action? That means the state has to be involved in some way. But the state, as a practical matter, is always involved in everything.

For example, can private schools sexually discriminate? Suppose you want to have a private school for girls, and a private school for boys. You cannot, I take it, if the school is receiving federal or state funds. Maybe even if it merely receives a tax exemption. These are difficult questions. The ERA does not involve a single, simple question. Read the marble above the Supreme Court, is all Mrs. Miller has to do. And that has great appeal; we love to simplify life. Here is a simple formula to remove all our problems. To argue against that is to argue against the times. But think of the specifics! There is, for example, a fine special high school in Boston called Girls' Latin. And there's a fine special high school called Boys' Latin. And there are co-ed schools that are also very good. Now, presumably under the ERA this will be no more, a Boys' Latin and a Girls' Latin even though there's a co-ed school. Now why? Is that necessary, is that important? Must it be the same in Boston as in Kansas City? Must it be decided by Harry Blackmun for all of us? I don't know why! What will we gain?

Now if there is oppression of women, if there is denial of rights and these people are being denied opportunity then, indeed, drastic strong measures are called for. I agree! But where are these denials? Now I'm not female, maybe I'm not sensitive to them. My wife became a lawyer twenty years ago. I assume she's fairly alert to them. It's not easy to come up with precisely what these inequalities are. Do we need another federal apparatus? Is that not killing a flea with an elephant gun? And why can't a public school experiment with an all-girl kindergarten and another one all-boy? Is that bad?

EMERSON: I will talk for a minute about the legal question of privacy and homosexual marriage. I think it's quite irresponsible to keep saying over and over that the ERA will legitimize homosexual marriage. It is not within the range of possibility that any court in this land would make that decision. The ERA requires equality on the basis of gender, not on the basis of sexual orientation. The legislative history makes perfectly clear, in answer to the same charge by Senator Ervin, the ERA will not legitimize homosexual marriages. This argument has been made throughout the country. It's a complete red herring, with no substantial basis whatsoever. The same can be said about integrated bathrooms . . . the right of privacy still prevails. Nothing in the ERA eliminates the right of privacy anymore than it eliminates the First Amendment or the due process clause. It is quite clear that the right of privacy applies to bodily functions, disrobing, and sleeping quarters, questions of that sort. That was also made clear in the legislative history. In fact, Senator Bayh put the whole *Griswold* v. *Connecticut* decision of the Supreme Court in the record to emphasize the point. I think those arguments should not be made. This ought to be debated on a higher level than that.

As to the main argument which is made, that we do not know how these things will come out or that there are many problems, that picture is totally overdrawn. For two years after ratification the states have an opportunity to revise their laws. Ninety-nine percent of the issues will be settled by legislation dealing with marriage, property, criminal law, and other areas not now sex neutral. There are model laws in existence. It is not a very difficult job. The resulting doubtful cases can easily be disposed of by the Supreme Court. Seven states now have ERAs in the identical language of the federal amendment, and none of these problems has arisen. The state of Washington has itself said that homosexual marriage is not permitted by the ERA. What my friend is asking for is a degree of certainty which he cannot have in this world. You cannot expect to figure out everything in advance. The ERA is a basic principle of our civilization which should be embodied in constitutional law, and to ask for more certainty is the equivalent of saying we shouldn't have the First Amendment, we shouldn't have the due process clause, we shouldn't have the equal protection clause, because nobody knows what they mean.

MILLER: I want to give one answer to my friend over here [Graglia]. There is absolutely no such thing as provisional equality. You either have equality or you don't. I think that has been proven over and over again. . . . No matter how we might like to do so, we will not achieve equality if we hang on to the beneficial discriminations that we have learned to enjoy as women.

On the school question which you brought up, we're talking about public funding. Men and women both pay money for the public schools. There is no reason to suppose that any kind of separation of schools makes sense under equal opportunity for education. We settled the question of separate not being equal on the school question. Private schools operating for separate sexes simply does not come under this provision, unless they are receiving public finance, so that's a moot point.

MODERATOR: Okay, we'll now have questions from the audience.

AUDIENCE: I have a technical question which I think has some practical relevance. As I understand it, certain states having once passed the ERA have taken steps to rescind that decision. There is some question as to the validity of doing that. I'm sure that each of you may have different perspectives on that legal technicality, and I'd appreciate knowing your positions.

GRAGLIA: I happen to be somewhat informed because of the Texas situation. They have ratified, but these not quite perennial but biennial proposals came up to rescind. The question arises, would rescission be effective, or would rescission itself be constitutionally prohibited? I hope that my colleagues here will agree that there is no danger of a Supreme Court decision against rescission. That is, the Supreme Court would say that there is no constitutional question for them to consider. There might well be a constitutional question, but it would be a constitutional question to be considered by Congress.

So the question becomes, interestingly, not what the Supreme Court will or is likely to do, but what will Congress do? That's more difficult to say. My prediction is that Congress will accept rescission, because it's just silly not to. We'd be making the serious process of constitutional amendment into some kind of game, a lobster trap. You can try to ratify any number of times; if you fail, you can try it again. Once you've ratified, you're trapped and you can't get out. You can imagine the extreme you could reach in a situation with thirty-seven states that have ratified and rescinded, then a thirty-eighth state ratifies, and as of that moment it's the only state in the country that wants it, yet it comes into effect! Congress clearly will not do it.

EMERSON: I agree that the Supreme Court has held a similar question to be a question for Congress. They will probably rule the same way this time. Where I balk, however, is on what Congress will do. Congress has considered this question three times in the past, and in every case they have said that states cannot rescind. It came up when Ohio and New Jersey attempted to rescind the Fourteenth Amendment. Secretary of State Seward sent the information to Congress, and both houses passed a resolution saying that the amendment had been ratified despite the attempt at rescission, and those votes were necessary for the three-quarters ratification. New York attempted to rescind the Fifteenth Amendment. Congress reacted the same way. They would not recognize the attempts to rescind, except in that case there were enough votes for the three-quarters without counting New York. When women's suffrage, the Nineteenth Amendment, came up, Tennessee unsuccessfully attempted to rescind. . . . Historical precedent has been consistent in three cases. You can't say it doesn't make sense either. A salesman for the *Encyclopaedia Britannica* comes around to see you, and asks you to buy the *Britannica*, and you turn him down. He comes back the next day and you turn him down. He comes back again and you turn him down. He comes back a fourth day and you say, "yes," and you sign up—you are stuck.

AUDIENCE: Professor Emerson, could you explain, please, specifically what new rights would accrue to women if the ERA were ratified?

EMERSON: To a certain extent that depends on state law. But there are, at the latest computer printout, 800 federal laws, some in the Social Security system, others in the criminal system, that treat women differently from men, in most cases to the detriment of women. There are practices in all government institutions, federal, state, local, school districts, which are discriminatory. It would simply wipe those out. By legislation, it can be done piecemeal if you want to wait a hundred years. If you're going to do it immediately, it takes a constitutional amendment.

MODERATOR: [to Graglia] Would you like to say anything to that?

GRAGLIA: Well, no, I think that answer is an excellent one. It shows there's nothing to be done. He tells you there's hundreds of laws. He can't point to anything. That's what his answer amounts to. The question goes to the heart of the matter. *What is the need?* If there are hundreds of ordinances, those ordinances presumably deal with hundreds of topics. Should every one of them say that we cannot have sex discrimination—either in favor of the male or in favor of the female? I certainly don't see why! I suspect there are 150 questions here and if we investigated each one, we would come to very different conclusions as to many of them.

Now you can illustrate this. Congress adopted the ERA proposal by the necessary two-thirds vote. Sailed right through! But Congress at the same time enacts some sex classification in connection with Social Security, allowing for *more* regulations discriminating by sex, different provisions for widows and widowers, for example. The discriminatory law also goes through. Why is it, if more than two-thirds of each house has voted against sex discrimination in the ERA, Congress then sex discriminates when all it takes is a majority vote to defeat any specific sex discrimination? Do you know why that is? It's because equal rights is just a slogan. As Mrs. Miller loves to say, it's written in stone. So if you tell Congress everyone should have equal rights, they say yes! "I don't want to be put down as being against equal rights, for goodness sakes!" But then they face a specific proposal where maybe it makes sense in this circumstance to treat a widow differently than a widower. Reasonable people think about it and say, "Yes, maybe it makes sense."

AUDIENCE: If the amendment is passed, will there be an affirmative action requirement as we now have for race?

EMERSON: It would not be the same as racial affirmative action. Under the present doctrines of the Supreme Court, race is only a suspect classification. If the government can show compelling reasons, it may discriminate on account of race. Consequently, in affirmative action race cases you have to show there are compelling reasons and that the objectives cannot be achieved by other means. That is not true under the ERA as I interpret it. The ERA says no discrimination, no matter how plausible the reasons may be. Affirmative action would be tied to a theory of remedy, and it would not be the same as the race cases.

GRAGLIA: Mr. Emerson's confidence just could not be more misplaced. Affirmative action *will* follow. It almost certainly will. Look at the examples in legislative history. Look at the legislative history of the great 1964 Civil Rights Act, as I said to the people in my seminar today, which states and restates redundantly four times that the act was *prohibiting* racial discrimination. Neighborhood schools were okay. You could not assign on the basis of race for any purpose. That has now become a *requirement* for racial assignment in order to integrate, although it was insisted many times in Congress that that is exactly what was *not* to be done. Your dean here described to me in some detail the difficulties, the absolute impossibilities, he faces under affirmative action requirements. The ERA will surely multiply them.

MILLER: I want to comment on the earlier question about what laws would in fact have to be changed. The reason why we cite figures like 800 federal laws is because we don't know what kind of laws will have to change.
　Integrated into the American legal system is the cultural assump-

tion that every man is a breadwinner, is in charge of the family, and that every woman is cared for from the time she is born until old age. Those assumptions simply do not prevail anymore, but laws in the area of family, property, pensions, retirement, in criminal justice, contain that kind of assumption. A specific law will in fact have to be changed when a woman, who happens to be the breadwinner and in charge of children, has needs separate from the husband.

AUDIENCE: Mr. Emerson made a comment that under the ERA there would be no discrimination. Mr. Graglia brought up the case of drafting men and women. Now if the draft were reinstituted and I as a male was drafted, wouldn't I have a perfect legal right to complain that women should be drafted in equal proportion? Or in the case of the all-boy kindergarten, or the all-girl kindergarten that Mr. Graglia brought up—couldn't I as a father say I do not want my son in an all-male kindergarten and I demand that he be integrated?

EMERSON: You're quite right. If the draft were reinstituted, we would have to draft women as well as men and use women in combat also. There is no question about that. I think that's justified. Would the army then the 50 percent men and 50 percent women? That's ridiculous! Persons qualified would be drafted regardless of sex, but qualifications would still exist: exemptions for ministers, for persons who care for children, for homemakers, whatever exceptions Congress decided to create, but not on the basis of sex, that's true. Now let me say one thing about that. . . . I do not think there is any difference between drafting sons and drafting daughters. I do not think there should be. It would have been possible to get the ERA through the Senate at least a year earlier if the women had agreed to make an exception on the draft. They refused to do that, and I think they were absolutely right because once you make an exception of that sort, women are second-class citizens. If women are ever going to maintain themselves on the same level as men, they have to accept the same obligations no matter how terrible those obligations are.

AUDIENCE: I'd like to make a comment about some of the things that have been said. I, as a woman, have felt discrimination for a long time, and I come from the same state as you do, Mr. Graglia. There is no worse state in the United States.

If my daughter were going to be drafted or my son, if they were equally prepared and the country said "You're going to go," my daughter would be as pleased to go as my son. . . . I think most women, most free-thinking women in the United States today, are willing to accept the risks equally with the advantages. When I say no discrimination, and I am placed in a position of authority, I accept the same risks that men do, but I also want the same money, the same privileges.

AUDIENCE: Mr. Emerson, I was not satisfied with your first answer to Mr. Graglia. Once the ERA passes, why will I have a right to be in a bathroom without women any more than I have a right to be in a bathroom without blacks? Why should a woman have more right to marry a man than I have to marry a man?

EMERSON: Those are two different questions. The point about the bathrooms depends upon the right of privacy. The Supreme Court in *Griswold* v. *Connecticut* in 1965 held that various provisions of the Constitution guaranteed against government infringement upon an individual's privacy. There is no question of that: Although not explicit in the Constitution, it is for all practical purposes now a part of the Constitution. The question of the scope of privacy is not entirely clear. The *Griswold* case involved birth control; *Roe* v. *Wade* involved abortion; another case involved viewing obscenity in the privacy of your home. It is perfectly clear that privacy extends to intimate association, sexual relations, dressing, exposure, body searches by police, and so on. That would remain in effect. . . .

Homosexuality is different. The homosexual argument is false because homosexuality is a question of sexual preferences—sexual actions. I don't think my friend Mr. Graglia would say that the ERA eliminates all laws prohibiting homosexual actions. They would remain valid laws. Perhaps they should be changed, I'm not arguing that . . . [but] it was not intended that states would be forced by the ERA to create relationships which violated the law. That doesn't make any sense. So unless he's arguing that the ERA would eliminate all laws relating to sexual acts between the same sexes, it's clear that the ERA will not authorize a marriage relationship which involved criminal acts. The wording is "on account of sex," and that doesn't mean sexual orientation. It means gender. There's no discrimination in terms of gender with respect to laws prohibiting homosexual marriages. That is perfectly clear from the legislative history. I cannot imagine a court taking that position. The whole thing is a total red herring. There is no basis for it.

GRAGLIA: You know, Mr. Emerson finds so many things perfectly clear. And what is perfectly clear about constitutional law is that almost nothing is perfectly clear. He finds this nonexplicit but well-developed (it's not well-developed) right of privacy. To say there is a right of privacy merely recognizes there is a problem. That's all it presents, a conflict of interests. Different interests are in conflict in every situation. You cannot decide the restroom problem on this slogan—you don't want to. It's too embarrassing to even want to. Certainly there is no assurance of what different courts, different federal judges will do, completely apart from what the Supreme Court will do. I personally would predict that no court is going to hold that unisex bathrooms are required under the ERA. You're afraid that's going to happen? I can't imagine it. It seems so far out that even in Congress this was the only element on which the women would make a concession. The right of privacy is not an adequate basis for the concession, however. The right to privacy is not absolute.

Mr. Emerson says that my talk about the need for judicial decisions under the ERA [is invalid] because 97 percent of the laws would be voluntarily changed within two years after the ERA. That itself is not valid. That's a lot like saying you won't be hanged next week if you commit suicide this week. Yes, there will be no need for judicial decisions *if* we abolish all sex discrimination from the books! There will then be very few disputes. But legislators are not going to abolish all sex discrimination and, more importantly, they shouldn't. Some of the laws are quite defensible. I can only sympathize with the woman who has lived in Texas and has felt sex discrimination. But we do have federal laws on equal employment now, and equal pay, and nondenial of jobs. We do have those laws! What are some of the consequences? What has happened? You look around, read the newspapers! I don't know how accurate all the stories are, but one thing that seemed to cause some fuss is female guards in male prisons, and male guards in female prisons. Can there even be female and male prisons? You know they will be getting around the law. There will be some exceptions. It won't be the right to privacy. It will be the right of prisoners, or something, to escape from this foolish attempt to lay down an absolute. Now in the case of prisons, there have been women guards molested. Well, does it make sense to put men in prison and then have women parade in front of them? Is it that necessary or desirable in order to eliminate job discrimination in Texas? Women have complained in prison that they do not want to perform their sanitary and their excretory functions in their cells with male guards. I, for one, sympathize with that. I do indeed! I want to know what is being gained to make that necessary. How about the trenches? Must women be in the trenches? That would be effective too, wouldn't it? . . . That should make for an effective trench line, some female running around in the trenches.

MODERATOR: I'm sorry, we have to adjourn. The participants of the panel will be at the banquet tonight and I hope that you'll continue the discussion.

GRAGLIA: I don't.

The Ultimate Sources 8
of Legal Authority
THOMAS EMERSON,
LINO GRAGLIA,
MARSHALL FORREST,
DONALD HOROWITZ

Any law infringes. From capital punishment to leash laws to building codes, legal decrees by definition restrict or redirect human behavior. In this sense all regulations are moral and all involve ethical presuppositions. A Watcom County political group, the Concerned Christian Citizens for Political Action, organized a Douglas Symposium workshop on "Relegislating Morality" aimed at debunking those who preach the axiom of value-free law. But if morality inevitably is legislated, we also rightly assume that restrictions on our conduct must be justified. By what authority? Some answers to this question satisfy many, and some persons are satisfied with none. Others obey or break the laws, pay their taxes, and ignore philosophical questions. To avoid the problem of authority, however, is not a luxury given to judges and others responsible for law enforcement, or to those who reflect on the world of legal entanglements.

The four panelists in this discussion were asked to share their convictions about the theoretical bases for law. Professors Graglia and Emerson need no introduction. Judge Marshall Forrest attended the University of Chicago during the Hutchins era and now presides in the Whatcom County Superior Court. Donald J. Horowitz, a former King County judge, practices in Seattle and has lectured on the relationship between the social sciences and law.

EMERSON: To me it's very clear that the ultimate source of legal authority must be morality, from whatever source that may be derived. In my own case the source is part intuition and part reason, a combination of the two hemispheres of my brain. It seems to me quite clear that law is not an end in itself, but rather a means of achieving certain social ends. Law is not in itself a basis for building the good society.

It follows from that, I think, that the law must be attuned to, shaped by, and constantly in touch with the value system. It cannot exist totally on its own.

Nor is law synonymous with a system of morality. That is so for a number of reasons. For one thing, law must be expressed in terms of general principles. Therefore, it's not as easily applied to concrete situations and is more inflexible than a system of morals would be. Law is more rigid in the sense that one of the main attributes of a good legal system is certainty, one ought to know *what* the law requires. Moreover, as conditions change, as facts shift, the law stays the same, and therefore grows out of date. The law certainly changes to a certain extent, but it often doesn't fit the situation where values or morals have adjusted more rapidly to social needs.

So the problems that I'm interested in are the relationships of law to the value system. There are many aspects of that; let me discuss several of them.

How far can the law be an objective system of principles? It has certain values of its own, but to what extent is it a separate system that runs only under its own rules? One discovers two tendencies. There can be a great reliance put upon abstract legal reasoning. The law is viewed as a brooding omnipresence in the sky. One discovers truth by virtue of a logical deductive process, from immutable legal principles. This mechanical process is very easy to overdo, and can produce quite sterile results. Similar approaches view law as primarily a process, as a series of procedures with emphasis on form, the implication being that if the forms are honored, justice is done. Again, one must remember that law is an instrument for achieving social purposes.

On the other hand, one can go to the extreme of saying that legal reasoning is totally illusory, that it's strung out to make people believe that it operates on principle when really it's nothing but a way of stating a conclusion. I don't agree with that position either. Somewhere in between there has to be a balance.

What role can law play in social control? Western society places great emphasis on law as social control. We start from the theory of almost complete individualism, anyone can do whatever they wish. Then we try to control the result by a system of due process, by a system of statutes and regulations, of courts and administrative tribunals, jails and penalties. We may be reaching the limits of this approach as there are signs that the system is somewhat breaking down. There are other alternatives. I spent two weeks in China not long ago. The Chinese rely very little on formal rules and law. Instead, there is almost complete reliance on small-group controls. A basic line is laid down by the national government, but within that occurs a considerable amount of community participation and discussion. I saw very few signs of criminal process or jails. I don't think that we will or should reach that point, but I wonder if we ought not be looking somewhat more in that direction, and less upon formal legal controls.

Finally, the essential problem is how to achieve a better balance between individualism and collectivism. I question whether we can do that under our present value system. To a large extent our value system is based on private property as compared with a value system based on what the Chinese would call serving the people. In other words, ours is a value system based on personal gain as compared with social service. We may have come to the end of our rope in trying to maintain a system based on personal gain. We have a densely populated country, a highly organized, extremely complex society, and dwindling natural resources. To make the law work better, we may have to change our values.

GRAGLIA: I couldn't disagree more, as usual, with Professor Emerson.

The ultimate source of all authority quite apparently, quite obviously, although we want to resist it and deny it, is simply force, physical force. We live in a world with physical forces, and that's the ultimate basis of everything. By what authority or right does a bird eat a worm or a frog eat a fly, or one man kill another? Force! The ability to do so.

It doesn't make sense to say, "By what right did you eat the worm, bird?" "I was hungry and the worm was there. My interest was to eat it to live, and I had the superior force. My interests prevailed."

In a society, an organization, or a cooperative group, the same is true. It's physical force that counts, ultimately. We're talking about the *ultimate*! It's all that counts. The only thing that becomes different is that groups have force. The question no longer is: "Is the frog faster or stronger than the fly?" The question now is: "Are you part of a group?" Your interests depend not on your capabilities as an individual, your force as an individual, but the force of the group that supports your interests . . . saying, "Does he have the right to do it?" cannot be meaningful except to say, "Can they (his group) do it; are they physically able to do it?"

The man on the island has the right, the authority, to eat the rabbit, the tiger has the right to eat the man. Each can do those things. To ask any other question about that situation is to mystify yourself. But it becomes more complex in a social situation. Groups must make it known that they are somehow carrying out group power, so you get rules. Then it becomes possible to ask, "Did he do it in accordance with the rules?" And that (presumably) will determine whether the group will exert the superior force. That's what happens when you have rules, and of course you get complexities and difficulties with as many laws as we (unfortunately) have.

One example. We might ask if the Supreme Court has authority, the "right." No word is more confusing, as Justice Holmes said, than the word "right." Rights are enforceable interests. If it's an enforceable interest, it's a right. Otherwise there is no right. Does the Supreme Court have the "right" to reverse the conviction of an admitted murderer-rapist of a child as it did a few weeks ago? Does it have the right to prohibit states from regulating abortion? To prohibit the states from regulating pornography? Prohibit the states from refusing to hire Communist teachers? Prohibit the states from permitting prayer in the schools? These are some of the benefits the Supreme Court has bestowed upon us.

You might ask, "Do they have the right to do that?" Of course they do; they did. It's happening. What more are you asking?

A second question can arise when you have groups, "Are they doing it according to the rules?" That question gets very complex with the Supreme Court. Who makes the rules and how do you determine what the rules are? It's nice, as Leon Jaworski[1] said, that even President Nixon is subject to the rule of law. That is a highly desirable state. But the Supreme Court is not subject to any rule of law. The Supreme Court makes the law. It is a totally lawless institution.

We could look for examples. Do they have the right to bus children? That's of particular interest to me. It happens, incredibly enough it seems to me, that children do get bused with all the disastrous consequences that follow. It happens. They have the same "right" Joe Stalin had to kill five million peasants. When he ordered it done, it was done. How can you say the Court doesn't have a right to do it? Well, you say, not according to the rules. We think we have a rule that says they can do it only if the Constitution requires it. The fact is the Constitution doesn't require anything the Supreme Court has done. In no way could it be said that the Constitution requires these things. In a sense they are deceptive, doing it by trickery, if anyone believes the Constitution requires it.

You might say, there are certain requirements, are there not, of logic and honesty and factual accuracy. Are these requirements for the Supreme Court? They are not! No, it's just like Justice Jackson said, "We're not final because we're infallible, but we are infallible because we're final." If when you say something is right, and no one is authorized or permitted to say it's wrong, then it *is* right for all practical purposes. Supreme Court decrees are not less enforceable or of less impact because they are illogical, because the reasoning is totally false, or because they're factually inaccurate.

Take the busing decree for example. . . . The actual requirement is exactly the opposite of what the Court states the requirement to be. That doesn't matter! It doesn't make it less enforceable! It doesn't make it of less impact! There's no requirement at all that the Supreme Court be logical or honest. There is not! That's the nice thing about supremacy, the whole point of being supreme.

The Court said, for example, that Charlotte-Mecklenburg had not been complying with the *Brown* decision. Simply not true! Demonstrably, factually not true. Five years earlier the courts told Charlotte what it had to do. That case went to the Fourth Circuit Court of Appeals. The decree was handed down, and the Court said, "This is what you have to do, Charlotte, in order to comply with the Constitution." And Charlotte did everything it was told to do, as the lower courts found. But the Supreme Court said Charlotte hadn't complied.[2] That's just not so. It makes no difference. The Supreme Court also said that the circuit court had found the Charlotte school board uncooperative. Not so! The circuit court didn't say that. The Supreme Court said the circuit court chided the board for noncooperation. In fact, the circuit court's opinion actually *praises* the board. Exactly the opposite. Well who knows that, and who cares. What difference does it make? None!

FORREST: One advantage of following these two speakers is that you're almost bound to have one of them on your side at any point. They also have a great advantage. They can make their pronouncements and go away, and I have to stay in Bellingham and face you, so mine will perhaps be a little more tempered.

As one who feels that American society in general, and the legal profession in particular, suffers from a great lack of historical knowledge and historical orientation, in answering what was posed as a personal question, perhaps it is not inappropriate to take a very brief glance at some of the traditions that I think help us answer the question as to the ultimate sources.

I might say, parenthetically, that the opening part of Professor Graglia's speech is really a rather eloquent restatement of the argument of Thrasymachus that Plato made many, many years ago, that might is right and the courts and legal systems are really nothing more than agents for the powers that be. However, there is a tradition that I suppose can loosely be called the Positive Law tradition, which states, "law is command of the sovereign." Sovereign is here used in this sense to mean not only the sovereign in the sense of king, but whatever group rules. In other words, it's the central authority of any political subdivision that has an independent existence in the world and whose statutes, decrees, or administrative orders are enforced as law. In one sense, when we say "law," that's what we mean. In more recent times, I suppose that's the view that Holmes espoused when he said that "law is the prediction of what the courts will do in fact," very much as we just heard. Law is what we do, what decrees and orders and verdicts and executions actually take place.

Another strand in our tradition is the so-called Natural Law tradition. It would be beyond my competence as well as the time allowed to give a detailed exposition of it. Suffice it to say, natural law takes the view that independent of any particular legal or political system, there is out there somewhere a standard to which we can appeal, something that grows out of, and is inherent in, our own human nature. I thought I'd take the liberty of just reading a very short selection from St. Thomas Aquinas. It's a brief statement that reflects this view of the world. St. Thomas was dealing with the question of whether every human law is derived from natural law. And he says this:

> That which is not just seems to be no law at all, wherefore the force of law depends on the extent of its justice. Now in human affairs a thing is said to be just, from being right, according to the rule of reason. But the first rule of reason is the law of nature, as is clear from what has been stated above.... Consequently every human law has just so much of the nature of law as it is derived from the law of nature. But if at any point it deflects from the law of nature, it is no longer a law but a perversion of law.[3]

And in one form or other this is a tradition by which people appeal to some higher law, to some other authority. It has some obvious affinities with, although I think it's distinct from, the Thoreau approach that says this is an unjust law, and I will protest it by being civilly disobedient.

I think the force in Thoreau, the force in Ghandi, is that they say "granted this is the law in the everyday sense, we will persuade you people that this is wrong by our refusal to comply and in our peaceful defiance of it." The idea is to bring about a change of heart. It's not just to win by revolution or rebellion. The idea that Ghandi expressed many times was that you could do this by being good enough and self-sacrificing enough to somehow form a common human bond that would make the other person, the oppressor, see that you were right.

Now it seems to me that Justice Douglas and a number of other great members of the Supreme Court who shared his views are in a sense exponents of natural law. Under our system of government the power of the Supreme Court is really a means of putting great constitutional principles into practical everyday law, into what police do, into what government does. We all know that the great phrases in the Constitution—"due process," "equal protection"—are not self-explanatory. The Court develops a series of cases, rightly or wrongly. The men who enunciate these decisions are doing exactly what St. Thomas would have done. In other words, they appeal to certain values they hold dear, which they find to exist, which they then make actual through their interpretation of our Constitution.

I have often thought that students could gain a philosophical and yet practical sense of law in law school by starting with the Nuremberg

Trials. The little exposure I had came at the end of my law school and I found it a rather trying experience. In the Nuremberg situation the victors convened a court and tried the vanquished, and the German defense tended to be "well, I was acting under orders," or "this was the law" in the narrow sense of Nazi statutes or directives from Hitler. The tribunal said in effect "that isn't law; that's no defense. We're going to hold you responsible. There are certain things, certain values that transcend any of this. And if you're called upon to perform such acts, it's your duty to refuse." And philosophers say that should apply to the United States, to Russia, and to everybody else. Of course the practicality of applying it to those who are still strong is not very great, but it does pose the problem of the ultimate source of legal authority in a very dramatic way, coming after one of the most horrible regimes and the most horrible perversions of law we've ever known, the rule of Nazi Germany.

How does all this relate to the Superior Court in Bellingham that has to decide a case? Fortunately, it doesn't relate day by day as much as you may think. I am glad of that for two reasons. One, the most important one, is it's too hard to think about. And secondly, less facetiously, one of the strengths of our legal system is that it is a shared responsibility and that it grows out of a tradition in which the responsibilities of the individual judge, and even of the Supreme Court, are for incremental change. We have a chance to back off and review and modify after we see how things go. There are not many pronouncements of law, any more than of science, that look as self-evident and as certainly true and just a hundred years later as they do at the time they are made.

It also seems to me there is a reconciliation of these two traditions, that we use "authority" in two senses. One is that we obey when the Supreme Court speaks. The winners are gratified, maybe partially; the losers may be dissatisfied, but they accept that. They feel there's a certain moral authority not derived from the judge, but from a system which they generally feel is just and aims to give a fair hearing for their contentions. That is one sense of authority.

Another sense of authority is that if people really become disenchanted with the law, if, for example, they won't accept prohibition, the law becomes practically unenforceable. We see this now with drugs, particularly marijuana. The repeal drive is a result of public attitudes. We all know that there are times in history when laws become so unpopular that they produce rebellion.

All these values, all these systems—religious systems in my view—grow out of a cultural matrix. Law is only one aspect of culture, religion is another, art is another, philosophy is another. Whether it is St. Thomas' views of a just law or unjust law, whether it is Justice Douglas' interpretation of the Constitution, they have their roots in a cultural tradition. These same cultural underpinnings produce different results; we don't agree, and that's what makes lawsuits and ultimately that's what makes different systems of government in China and here.

To conclude, I would like to recall to your mind one of the most famous trials in history. This one is the trial of Socrates. What he says at the end of the *Crito* is quite apropos to the whole question of the ultimate source of authority for law.

Let me set the scene. Socrates has been convicted, he's in prison, and he's awaiting the day of his execution by a drink of hemlock that would be brought to him. His friends urge that he escape. And he says, essentially, "If you can persuade me that it is right to escape, I will let you help me escape." In this particular passage he pretends that the laws are addressing him. So the laws are saying to Socrates:

> Tell us Socrates, what have you in mind to do? What do you mean by trying to escape but to destroy us, the laws and the whole state, so far as you are able? Do you think that a state can exist and not be overthrown when decisions of law have no force, are disregarded and undermined by private individuals? In war and in the court of justice and everywhere, you must do whatever your state and your country tell you to do, or you must persuade them that their commands are unjust.

The debate continues and Socrates finds himself unpersuaded that he should escape, partly because he says that he cannot return injustice for injustice, and that it is his obligation to obey the law. So finally in the last paragraph the laws implore Socrates:

> No, Socrates, be persuaded by us who have reared you. Think neither of children, nor of life, nor of any other thing before justice so that when you come to the other world you may be able to make your defense before the rulers who sit in judgment there. It is clear that neither you nor any of

your friends will be happier or more just or more pious in this life if you do this thing, nor will you be happier after you are dead. Now you will go away a victim of injustice, not of the laws but of men. But if you repay evil with evil, and injustice with injustice in this shameful way, and break your agreements and covenants with us, and injure those whom you should least injure—yourself and your friends and your country and us—and so escape, then we shall be angry with you while you live: and when you die our brothers, the laws of Hades, will not receive you kindly for they will know that on earth you did all that you could to destroy us. Listen then to us, let not Crito oversuade you to do as he says.[4]

Socrates responds: "Be sure my dear friend Crito, that this is just. The sound of these arguments ring so loudly in my ears that I cannot hear any other arguments." And he does not escape.

HOROWITZ: Perhaps it's appropriate that I would speak last. This panel, each one of these gentlemen, is part of my history. Mr. Graglia doesn't know it, but Mr. Graglia's accent takes me back to my childhood in Brooklyn. I spent my early years in Brooklyn, and then I went to the Yale Law School where Professor Emerson was one of my teachers. He said much the same thing as he said today on the first day of class. We found out how relevant it was as the years went on. And, of course, like Judge Forrest, my most recent incarnation was as a Superior Court judge, in King County.

I do not consider justice a principle. I consider it to be a condition. It's an ultimately and eminently practical condition. It is as practical as bread. This is how I see it from my point of view as a lawyer, a former judge, a worker in the vineyards, and as an adjunct professor of law. It is a condition of reasonable comfort among people. That's all it is. It's how you can live together reasonably, comfortably, get along well with each other. The law should simply be a facilitator of that condition.

Mr. Graglia says that the ultimate source of legal authority is force, and he talks of animal analogies. But the earth is not a rotating pet-shop. What kinds of force? Of course there is physical force which is ultimate, but there is also legal force and moral force, persuasive force. What law presumes to do is create counterforces. It's a mediator.

Once, if you hurt my friend, I would hurt you. But now the law has interposed itself between you and me to create a condition whereby we can live comfortably and not in chaos. It allows people and society, the state and the individual, individual and individual, corporation and individual, to find some reasonable comfort with each other. That's the goal.

There are myths too. One of the myths, and it continues to persist because it's a nice myth, is that we are a government of laws. Well, we are indeed rather a government of men and women and not of laws because men and women administer and apply the laws, each in our own way, and we each do it a bit differently.

A practical example would be if I'm driving down the freeway and I'm stopped by a state trooper. My car has a bumper sticker that says "Support Your Local Police." The odds are I'm going to be treated courteously, a little differently than if my bumper sticker said "Off the Pigs." I don't mean just to hit state patrolmen. When I was a judge, I found that I had a prejudice too, against people with short haircuts. None of us is without prejudice.

We are a government, then, of people who apply the law, and the law is simply a tool to reach the goal of justice that I described. And a tool is only as good as the people who use the tool.

Now when I use a hammer I often end up with a swollen thumb. But if a master carpenter uses a hammer, he can build something very beautiful. We have come to celebrate during these three days a master carpenter. William O. Douglas certainly was that in his use of the law as a tool. I suspect that past all the rhetoric he would say the law is a tool to achieve certain social goals, to achieve practical social justice, to balance various interests and values in our society.

Where it rises from, its ultimate source, is within the people. We too often hear from judges or politicians or leaders, "We rise from the people." Rather it should be, "We rise *within* the people." When I became a judge, a friend said to me, "Don't forget the people." I looked at him and said, "I'm part of the people. How can I forget myself." But I can tell you it becomes easy to forget, because a lot goes on when one becomes a leader, a judge, a politician, or a priest, who has power to make decisions that substantially affect other people's lives. Something called isolation happens, isolation imposed not only by the person himself or herself, but imposed by the people. We somehow need to have our important figures a little larger than life. When that happens, the individual frequently begins to believe that he or she is indeed better than the people being served.

When Marshall Forrest said a few minutes ago that respect was not due to him, but to the institution, he was absolutely correct. But the ultimate source of legal authority, the people, frequently became self-destructive when they isolate the powerful decision makers who interpret and apply and create the laws. I'm giving you a very personal view. The most difficult part of my three years as a judge was the isolation and the desire to relate my own personhood to the symbol which a judge often needs to be.

A judge has a great deal of power, as does a president or a priest. But that power is ultimately derived, and only derived, from the people of whom he is a part. That power must serve the people in a very practical way. That practical sense, that daily practical relationship among people, is what I would call justice.

AUDIENCE: Mr. Graglia, if you feel so strongly about busing, why don't you work for a constitutional amendment to stop it?

GRAGLIA: Suppose we do get a busing amendment saying "courts can't require busing." Well, they might still continue to require it.

For example, the very first amendment really was the Eleventh. The first ten, the so-called Bill of Rights, practically came with the Constitution. The first occasion for amendment was when the Court made a decision which people didn't like, or some people didn't like. The Court had held that Georgia could be sued. The Eleventh Amendment was then adopted saying that a state couldn't be sued. It reversed the Court. Fine, you can tolerate a Supreme Court if you get quick responses of that kind! Unfortunately, for various mystical, theological reasons you can't get anymore. But what happened to the Eleventh Amendment? Well, it was made meaningless. A cynic could say, "Look, you get an amendment which says you can't sue the state. They sue them all the time now!" Public officials are sued all the time. The Eleventh Amendment is just ignored, disregarded. The Supreme Court likes the Fourteenth; it doesn't like the Eleventh. This is really interesting because under the Fourteenth . . . you don't have a basis for a suit unless the state acts. And yet it would seem if the state acts you can't sue by reason of the Eleventh. As I say, logic has nothing to do with it, neither logic, nor fact, nor anything. It is a question of what you can get away with. Douglas told his colleagues for thirty-five years that they can really get away with almost anything. They would say,

"Douglas, if we really do this, boy, somebody is going to stop us some-day." He could say, "I've been here for thirty-five years; I've been hearing that for thirty-five years. I used to hear that from Felix. He kept saying they'll stop us. I said, Felix, you're a worrywart. Let's do it, we'll get away with it."

AUDIENCE: You can see why they brought Mr. Graglia.

HOROWITZ: To follow the animal analogy . . . a quote from Ogden Nash: "In the land of mules there are no rules."

I'm afraid that Mr. Graglia, early in his legal career, opened some closet door and was scared by the ghost of Felix Frankfurter.

The problem is this, as I see it. If we don't have judicial review, the world won't come to an end. We'll be like England. Laws passed by the Congress will be supreme regardless of a written constitution. That's not a terrible thing to happen. The difference, however, is that we have a different tradition. The English tradition grew over hundreds of years, and mostly the English don't react too quickly. . . .

We can survive that way, but given our traditions, it will be difficult. We have relied upon a written Constitution and the judicial interpretation of that Constitution. Mr. Graglia and Justice Frankfurter are indeed brilliant persons—who should have been judges in nineteenth-century England and not in twentieth-century America. . . .

AUDIENCE: Mr. Graglia, which rules are just, and which rules are un-just? You still must ask if these are good rules if you force people to obey them.

GRAGLIA: That opens up a whole world of ethics, philosophy, an enormous seminar of some kind.

People ask not only if the rules are being followed, but if the rules are *good*. That's certainly a relevant question. Unfortunately, it's hardly possible to change the rules when you live under a dictatorship-theocracy, when you have government by the Supreme Court. You cannot change the rules on busing, for example: Eighty percent of the people oppose busing, many of them violently, but it doesn't get changed.

What people want should determine what the rules are. Should the rules be changed, be made better, as you say? That raises the question, "By what criterion are you judging the better? the good? the just?" I would suggest to you that justice is the result of a cost/benefit analysis. To face life cold-eyed and hardheaded is more than most people can tolerate. I admire Justice [Oliver Wendell] Holmes so much because he was one of the very few human beings that could do that. He looked at life and he said man is no more significant in any cosmic sense than a baboon or a grain of sand. To me that is obviously true, but for many it is also obviously intolerable. We came to accept very reluctantly that the earth is not the center of the physical universe. It's a blow to the ego! This isn't the way it ought to be. It damn well *ought to be* the center of the universe. Then we learned that we have descended from apes, from an insignificant amoeba. That isn't the way it ought to be either. Are we subject to the same forces as frogs, and flies, and birds, and worms? Do we have to put up with that?

It's true, but you don't have to put up with it; if it makes you happier to play games and quote poetry, that's lovely. But if you have the stamina and courage to face what justice is, it's obviously a question of cost/benefit analysis. Now what makes it very difficult is that there's no way to determine costs and benefits. I've heard it said during this symposium that we need greater knowledge for these decisions. Sure, we need knowledge and information. The fact is, however, that the needed knowledge is unavailable. It's not even theoretically available. How much less protection for the criminally accused is worthwhile in order to afford sufficient security to people walking the streets, so that in the Bronx the elderly do not have to live behind barred doors? What's the proper exchange there? With no exchange involved, with no conflicting interests, we wouldn't even have a problem. There is no formal or scientific way to determine the proper exchange. You're dealing with imponderables. What is the proper trade-off, for example, between freedom and order? There's no way to know. That's one of the best reasons, among many others, why these decisions should be left to the sense of the people, to our whole experience as a race, as a civilization. Is pornography a good thing or a bad thing? I sure as hell don't know, except that personally I like it. If someone came to me and said "Do you want to see a picture book of rocks?" maybe later I'd look at it. A picture book of naked women, I'll look at right now.

AUDIENCE: Can you answer that question about pornography by cost/benefit analysis?

GRAGLIA: No, no. I'm saying . . . there is no way to answer it. We can investigate if someone says, "Well, where pornography is available, sex crimes increase." That's an assertion about an empirical matter. It might be difficult to investigate, but it's at least possible to try. Maybe they decrease, maybe they increase. That certainly would be relevant in a cost/benefit analysis. But more likely you'll find assertions that "pornography will sap the moral fiber and corrode the character of people." You sophisticates and deep intellectuals can snicker, but I don't know. I do know that lots of people have felt that. Most people in most areas at most times, and I don't know. Where I differ from Justice Douglas is that I'm not so sure that I'm so smart and so intellectual that I can say they are wrong. "If those dummies, if those clods, just had my insight and my good will and good heart, they'd know they are wrong, and therefore I'll tell them they are wrong and make them do otherwise." That's your activist Supreme Court of which Douglas is the paragon.

I don't know what the answer is. What's the right amount of freedom of speech? . . . These things grow out of the whole experience of the race or civilization. Certain arrangements seem to be workable, to be felt necessary. We can investigate, we can think, we can study, we can suggest that something is not necessarily the best. But we must be very slow to convince ourselves that our ancestors were irrational. How did they ever get ideas like it's appropriate to encourage women to stay home and take care of children? How did a nonsense notion like that ever arise, when all good-hearted and sensible people like us see how foolish that is? That society should encourage the female to stay home with the children. I don't know. Maybe it's a nonsense notion, but I'm not sure. . . .

AUDIENCE: Could you give us an example of a law which you would disobey, and why you wouldn't obey? Then we can focus on what your ultimate source of value is.

GRAGLIA: Yes. I'll obey any law. Even if I were on the Supreme Court, I wouldn't be making these kinds of decisions, decisions I'm not authorized to make. I obey all laws because I consider it in my self-interest to do so.

AUDIENCE: All right, give us an example not in your self-interest.

GRAGLIA: Well, if a law said that I, my wife, and my children had to report to a gas chamber tomorrow, I would not consider that in my self-interest.

AUDIENCE: Now what would be your ultimate source of authority in not obeying that law?

GRAGLIA: My survival.

AUDIENCE: Survival?

GRAGLIA: That's right, me and the amoeba and the worm and the bird are all trying to survive. Right, I'll give you that.

AUDIENCE: Are you relying on the concept of natural law which Judge Forrest told us about?

GRAGLIA: It does seem to be part of the natural order of things that living organisms try to survive.

EMERSON: Why would you disobey? Because your wife is involved? That's not you.

GRAGLIA: You are entirely right in your usual perceptive way, that would get to be a difficult question. Maybe it's one I haven't had to think much about, fortunately. Maybe when it really comes down, I'll say, "Gee, I don't know."

AUDIENCE: It seemed to me that you were saying law is derived, as Judge Forrest said, culturally, a cultural expression, not merely an expression of force.

GRAGLIA: I don't know. That's an odd formulation. We're being, of course, so brief and so cryptic here. Bertrand Russell said the choice was between saying nothing and saying something inaccurately. . . .

AUDIENCE: Professor Emerson yesterday mentioned the case of *Richardson* v. the *United States*,[5] a case involving a Pennsylvania resident who as a taxpayer filed suit to have the CIA budget released to the public in accordance with rather clear wording of the Constitution. This case was thrown out on the grounds that he had "no legal standing to bring suit." Since we heard from Mr. Horowitz that the ultimate source of power is the people, why didn't he have standing? It seems a clear case. What is the notion of standing, and how do we determine it if the ultimate source of power is the people and the Constitution?

EMERSON: I said the Court was wrong in Richardson's case when it ruled that a taxpayer did not have standing. The concept of standing is far-reaching. It goes to some of the problems that we've been talking about. It determines what the limits of the courts are. The courts are peculiar institutions that have special procedures and consider themselves bound by the principles in the law. Some things are just not considered suitable for a court to do. One of those is to simply give advice, to set policy, to make speeches, to arouse public opinion. They have to operate within a framework of legal decision. And to do that you have to have a legal controversy: A legal controversy has to involve two people who have opposing legal interests. Therefore, parties must have what is called "standing" to raise legal questions. The Court in effect said: "Just because you are a taxpayer, you can't come to us and ask us for our advice on whether this is legal or not. You must have a more specific interest than that." I think they were wrong, that *Richardson* does present a clear legal problem, but what the Court is trying to say is that any ordinary citizen just can't come and ask for advice.

Let me just say one thing about another problem. My friend Professor Graglia may be operating in the nineteenth century, but I have a feeling that sometime he will see the light. You will notice that, although he starts out saying everything is sheer power, sheer force, when he starts talking about more specific matters he moves to a cost/benefit analysis. Now that's an improvement; not very far, but that's an improvement. Analyze it. Benefit for whom, what is cost? It's a value system. He's operating, not in terms of force, but in terms of a value system. It's quite clear what the law ultimately rests on, and you can't press the idea of sheer force very far. Otherwise you're not back to the eighteenth century, but you're back 10,000 years when force was force and we were animals. The whole development of civilization, as I see it, is a substitution of persuasion for sheer raw physical force. That's what civilization is. The law in its best aspects reflects that and pushes that forward, and creates a society that is a community and not a society that is barbarous and based on force.

MODERATOR: I'd like to thank you all for coming.

GRAGLIA: I'm going to get a picture book of naked rocks.

Notes

1. Leon Jaworski was the special prosecutor in the Watergate investigation.
2. *Brown* v. *Board of Education*, 347 U.S. 483 (1954); *Swann* v. *Charlotte-Mecklenburg School Dist.*, 402 U.S. 1 (1971).
3. St. Thomas Aquinas, "Treatise on Law," *Summa Theologica*, Book II, Question 95.
4. *Euthyphro, Apology, Crito, Phaedo*, translated by F. J. Church and R. D. Cummings (Indianapolis, Ind.: Bobbs-Merrill Co., 1956).
5. *United States* v. *Richardson*, 418 U.S. 166 (1974).

An Interview with William O. Douglas

ERIC SEVAREID _____

9

Eric Sevareid spoke with William O. Douglas during the summer of 1972 at Goose Prairie, Washington. His interview, which was broadcast by CBS that September, comes close to capturing the essence of Douglas as a jurist and human being. The film was shown several times at the Douglas Symposium, including the final session.

We appreciate Edith Tiger's permission to reprint the written text from the *Bill of Rights Journal* (December 1972), a publication of the National Emergency Civil Liberties Committee. The film "Mr. Justice Douglas" is available for rental from Carousel Films, Inc., 1501 Broadway, New York City, 10036.

Eric Sevareid begins the interview:

SEVAREID: I wanted to ask you, Mr. Justice, about some of the well-known people in the last generation you've known very well. After all, you've been around a long time now—thirty-three years on the Court, since you were forty years old. Did you get really intimate with Franklin Roosevelt, who appointed you?

DOUGLAS: Yes, I got to know him pretty well.

SEVAREID: Why do you think he appointed you? You were just forty years old, and had that brief experience with SEC, the Securities and Exchange Commission, at that time, as I remember.

DOUGLAS: I have no idea. I was not a candidate. I had no ambition to be on the Court; I had no ambition for any public office. As a matter of fact, I had been elected dean of the Yale Law School. I was going back there in a few months.... I often wonder what would have happened to Yale if I'd been dean of the Law School.

SEVAREID: Well, I suppose Roosevelt just liked your general approach to things. Your general cast of mind. You made quite a record on the SEC. Wasn't it Joseph Kennedy who brought you into the Securities Exchange?

DOUGLAS: Yes, Joe Kennedy brought me down . . . in 1934. I didn't know him, but he'd heard about me. I'd been active in the field, and he brought me down to head up the reorganization.

SEVAREID: You were out to reorganize business. You didn't like big business. He was a business operator. He took over companies, and he got out of them, and then another one.

DOUGLAS: I was talking to him one night and he said, "You know, I must be nuts." And I said, "What is your evidence?" He said, "The only two people in the world that I really like and enjoy being with are my son Jack and you. And you're utterly different—I disagree with everything you stand for. Now how do you explain it?" I said, "I guess maybe you're nuts." But he was Irish, and he was a great outgoing man. And a great friend.

SEVAREID: And why would a man like that want you in on reorganizing finance?

DOUGLAS: 'Cause he knew I knew something about it.

SEVAREID: Talk about the Kennedys a minute: I remember you went off on a long trip through Russia with Bobby Kennedy, who was pretty young then. He'd been with the McCarthy Committee and all that and in the Congress. Now I've heard people say that it was Bobby Kennedy's being with you all that summer that changed him from a kind of Joe McCarthy-ite type, in his political thinking, to a much more liberal humanitarian type. Do you put any credence in that?

DOUGLAS: Well, I don't know. I knew Bobby for some years prior to that. And Joe called me and said, "You're going to Russia?" And I said, "Yes." "Could you take Bobby?" I said I'd be delighted. He said, "I think Bobby needs some education in the world." So Bobby went, and he learned a lot. He was rather antagonistic. He wanted to argue the merits of communism with everybody he met. He wore himself out. He carried a Bible in his left hand.

SEVAREID: He did? In Russia?

DOUGLAS: And I said, "Bobby, you can't convert anybody. This is the time to find out how they live and how much they make, and the status of women, and the condition of prisons and so on." And by the end of the trip he'd passed off this more or less aggressive, antagonistic role and was beginning to see this civilization, the Slavic civilization, in a different perspective. But he grew. Bobby had a great factor of growth in him, and I think he was on his way to the White House when he was assassinated.

SEVAREID: Well you're now seventy-three as of today [June 29]. You had a horse roll over you and crush your chest once. I well remember that. And you've got a pacemaker in your heart, and you're still hiking and riding. Do you get a feeling you're living on borrowed time?

DOUGLAS: No, no.

SEVAREID: Or you don't think about it?

DOUGLAS: No, no, I don't—I have no worries and concerns. I early adopted a theory that the most dangerous thing a person can do at any time is to be alive.

SEVAREID: So you just go through the same way of living?

DOUGLAS: I don't do exactly the same. I used to walk on Saturday or Sunday in Washington, twenty-five miles. But, I confess to you that I've cut it down to fifteen.

SEVAREID: The whole court situation now would be somewhat, considerably different if Justice Abe Fortas hadn't resigned over this [Louis] Wolfson business.

DOUGLAS: Yes, I was sorry to see Abe resign. I spent two nights with him practically all night talking to him—urging him not to resign, because he hadn't done anything that was unethical. He was associated with a foundation which Wolfson had founded. But on all the Wolfson cases before the Court, he'd always withdraw and never participated. The Court's been very meticulous about not sitting in cases where they have a direct or indirect influence.

SEVAREID: You didn't feel then what Abe Fortas did in the Wolfson case was even an impropriety? Of course, this is an area that everyone makes their own judgments.

DOUGLAS: Well, it depends on what you do with your spare time. And I don't think it's anybody's business as long as it doesn't interfere with court work or collide with court duties or create conflicts of interest.

SEVAREID: You think he could have fought that out?

DOUGLAS: Well, I urged him to because it was purely a political maneuver and there was no substance to that claim at all. I think the sad part of it was that Abe, who I think would have been one of our great judges of all time, didn't want to be on the Court at the beginning. And Lyndon B. Johnson twisted his arm and put him on. So there was a pressure there to get off. I mean that was the natural impulse.

SEVAREID: You've been around the fringes of party politics a lot. And some people who know you have felt that you really at one time— really did want to be President. That you did want the nomination. Were you serious about it at any time?

DOUGLAS: No, I never wanted to run for anything. In Yakima, in the state of Washington, or in the country.

SEVAREID: Now back in '44 when there was a question of the vice presidency coming—Democratic convention. Roosevelt wrote that letter to Bob Hannegan, the party chairman of St. Louis, listing two men as acceptable to him for the second spot—Douglas and Harry Truman.

DOUGLAS: It was in that order, yes.

SEVAREID: I understand there's a letter in existence, the original Roosevelt letter, and I think Grace Tully [Roosevelt's personal secretary] has it or had it.

DOUGLAS: Grace Tully took the dictation.

SEVAREID: That listed your name above Truman's name, but that Hennegan, when he sent out copies to the party leaders. . .

DOUGLAS: Had it mimeographed and turned the names around.

SEVAREID: . . . turned the names around because he wanted his fellow Missourian Harry Truman. Is this actually the case?

DOUGLAS: That's the whole story, I think. It was unknown to me at the time. I'm happy that it happened that way. I didn't have any desire for the office. I would have taken it, I suppose, if I'd been drafted.

SEVAREID: You'd have been President instead of Harry Truman.

DOUGLAS: Well, a lot of different things would have happened. There would have been no bomb dropped on Hiroshima.

SEVAREID: What else do you think you'd have done?

DOUGLAS: I have no idea.

SEVAREID: I guess there's never been any Supreme Court Justice as outspoken about a lot of things off the Court as you've been. Including foreign policy. And you criticize American foreign policy quite often publicly. And the objection to that by a lot of people, as you well know, is that a Justice shouldn't do this. This somehow affects the separation-of-powers principle and you really mustn't cross that line. You find no merit to this argument?

DOUGLAS: Well, I grew up in that tradition, and getting it from college and law schools and getting to know some of the justices like Brandeis. But something happened that changed my view. This happened on the first week or two in Court. One of the first cases argued was whether or not [justices'] salaries were taxable. . . . And the old Court had held that they were not, because there's a provision in the Constitution that says Congress may not—shall not—reduce a salary during term of office. And the old Court held that when Uncle Sam pays you $10,000 and then takes $5,000 back in a tax, that's a reduction. That was, I think, a 6-to-3 decision. Holmes dissented, and Brandeis dissented, and I thought that they were right and so I voted to tax myself. And I remember in conference (each of us has a sheet—a docket sheet for every case), and the youngest after the discussion, the youngest justice in service votes first. And Hughes turned to me and he said, "Douglas, how do you vote?" And I said, "I vote to reverse." And that's the way the Court went. And as I made the little entry in the docket sheet, I said to myself, "Young man, you've just voted yourself first-class citizenship." And I decided that if you're going to pay taxes like everybody else, that you should be a citizen like everybody else, except and unless the thing that you're doing interferes with the work of the Court.

SEVAREID: You've traveled an awful lot. More, I think, than any other justice ever. And a lot in the so-called Third World. What do you find in terms of the reputation of this country because of the Vietnam War?

DOUGLAS: Well, I'm afraid as a result of the Vietnam War that in the eyes of many people in the underdeveloped nations we're the new Genghis Khan, a great destroyer, which is very, very unfortunate.

SEVAREID: There was an effort to have the Court decide the constitutionality of the Vietnam War. And I think you and Potter Stewart wanted to hear the case.

DOUGLAS: We've had three votes at various times, Potter Stewart, Bill Brennan, and myself. I wrote some opinions on this.

SEVAREID: You made a public statement calling it a presidential war. Sounds as though you really made your mind up. That this is unconstitutional.

DOUGLAS: Well, as you read the Constitution, it says that Congress has the power to declare war. And it doesn't say Congress and/or the President, or the Congress and/or the President and/or the Supreme Court. It just says Congress shall have the power to declare war. And historically that has been the case. This is not just a little episode like Jefferson sending the fleet off Africa after some pirates. This is an all-out effort.

SEVAREID: Well obviously we're not going to get a judicial ruling on the war, but you, Justice Douglas, a private person sitting here, believe this is unconstitutional.

DOUGLAS: Well, I'm inclined to think so. I haven't heard argument. I might change my mind.

SEVAREID: Fascinating speculation: If the Supreme Court said Vietnam, while it's going on, is unconstitutional—what would happen?

DOUGLAS: Well it would mean, practically, that the boy who didn't want to go wouldn't have to go.

SEVAREID: The war would still go on.

DOUGLAS: The war would probably go on with volunteers. . . .

SEVAREID: Couldn't draft on that basis?

DOUGLAS: Wouldn't be able to draft on that basis.

SEVAREID: Mr. Justice, you wrote once that we're losing so much privacy to government intrusion that unless there's some kind of rebellion against this, we're going to be suffocated. What kind of rebellion; what did you really mean?

DOUGLAS: Well—protest. I mean people, instead of succumbing and assuming everything the government does is right, should object and protest and write letters to the editor. Or make a speech or form a committee. The greatness of this country is reflected in the Constitution, which, as I said, was designed to take government off the backs of people. Make it difficult for government to do anything to the individual. And the electronic age makes it easy.

SEVAREID: You must feel good about the recent decision that they can't wiretap or bug domestic dissidents without a court order now.

DOUGLAS: I voted with Justice Powell on that side of the case, yes, as might be expected.

SEVAREID: The Army surveillance of domestic dissidents has got thrown back to the Congress. You wanted that decided, didn't you?

DOUGLAS: Right, because the Army has no business, in our system, of fooling around with political ideas. I mean the Army should be on its base marching men up and down, and on the firing range, and so on.

SEVAREID: Can I wheel back to ask you [about] that impeachment effort two years ago, and this Parvin Foundation, of which you were an officer, I think? You were cleared by the [House] Judiciary Committee of anything illegal or wrong. But why did you resign from the Parvin Foundation if you had won the argument that you hadn't done anything wrong?

DOUGLAS: Well, you see the idea of the Foundation came out of a book I wrote called *America Challenged*. And I was proposing in that book that we not send jet planes to Ethiopia (the only thing they could use them for would be to put down the peasants), but spend the money bringing people here and giving them courses in government—First Amendment and fair trials, and so on. And sending them back to their country as a leader—as a new leader. And that our effort should be educational. And so the Foundation was formed to effectuate that. And we established, at Princeton, ten fellowships that brought men from Africa [and] the Middle East. And it was a great success, I thought, because many of the men on their return ended up in jail, which meant that they were doing a good job. . . . That part was finished and running smoothly, and we were expanding to South America, and it was going to take a lot of time. Well, I realized then that somebody would have to take over who could travel a lot; spend a lot of time searching out these people. So I decided, long before this episode happened, that [in] about another year I'd have to get out. So I just did.

SEVAREID: A lot of the criticism of your behavior, speeches, and activities has been that you've really not been and really should be sensitive to the public sense of reverence about the Court. There was a story somebody told me of some man saying at a cocktail party that at least Justice Douglas has proved that Supreme Court justices are human beings, and somebody else said yes, isn't it a pity? But isn't there something in this, that people want to think of this as a temple with rather disembodied great wisdom residing there?

DOUGLAS: It may be that there are some people who think that is the best way. That's really a symbolism of authority. I don't think so. We're all human and the decisions we make are profoundly important to the people, and the reasons we give. And I think that the person who goes there and stays ten, twenty, thirty years, should be very active in life. Otherwise, he'll end up a dried husk unrelated to anything that's going on in the world except his own personal experience that may be wholly irrelevant.

SEVAREID: You don't feel you're echoing Commodore Vanderbilt who for different reasons said, "The public be damned"?

DOUGLAS: No, I'm very respectful of the public. I'd like to educate them on what judges are, what judges should be, what civic affairs should be, and I'd like to see our people very stoutly independent of judges, of bureaucrats, of presidents, of congressmen and governors, and so on. I'd like to see our people very assertive and not submissive.

And the great danger is that with the surveillance and all the pressures for conformity, the data bank that we have, they run through: How many times was Eric Sevareid arrested? Out it comes, and so he's denied a job.

SEVAREID: But on the other hand, it seems to me, I've never seen such freedom of speech and action of theater, books, demonstrations [in] this country [as] we've seen in recent years. And that's resulting in a kind of a backlash, a fear of a kind of fragmentation and anarchy in the country.

DOUGLAS: But I think that's good. Not the reaction to it, but the fact that it's going on. I have great hope in the young people. I've been criticized—I wrote a couple of articles for *Playboy*. The reason I wrote for *Playboy* was because *Playboy* reaches eighteen million youngsters. And they're the minds that I'd like to reach. People of my generation are bankrupt—politically bankrupt. They're philosophically bankrupt. Look at what they've produced. A system that makes war the alternative. A system that's highly stratified, that just pays off great sums of money. This is to the rich people, this is socialism for the rich. I'd just like to reach the minds of the youngsters because it need not be that way. Not to have them take guns and start shooting people, but start voting and getting active. . . . They're doing it now.

SEVAREID: I want to talk to you, Mr. Justice, a bit about the court system as a whole. Not just the Supreme Court, but to a great extent it's bogged down, almost broken down, in one area after another in this country. These fantastic delays and congestion backlogs. It seems to a lot of us who've gone into this thing that it has quite a bit to do with the crime problem. How do you resolve this thing?

DOUGLAS: One of the reasons is that we as a people have a great propensity to make everything that somebody objects to on some moral ground a crime. And a lot of the stuff that's going on in our courts involved only people but no victims.

SEVAREID: Crime without victims, like vagrancy, drunkenness, or prostitution. You think too much has been loaded on the courts?

DOUGLAS: Yes, too much minutiae of the lower things. They should save their energies for the big things. On the big things, the problem has been greatly exaggerated. Roughly 90 percent of all the criminal cases in the federal courts are disposed of on pleas of guilty.

SEVAREID: Well, now, is that your answer to the complaint that various Supreme Court decisions to protect defendants have contributed to this congestion and difficulty of prosecutors?

DOUGLAS: Well, they haven't contributed. The FBI works under the Constitution. It's the best police force in the world. [The] *Miranda* [decision] is cursed and denounced by local police. FBI lives under *Miranda*. FBI is highly trained; they're efficient.

SEVAREID: [*Miranda*] is the right of counsel at the beginning?

DOUGLAS: No, not at the beginning of the investigation, but once they decide to hold a man, that's the start of the criminal prosecution. And our Constitution says a man has a right to a lawyer. Man is presumed to be innocent. Government must prove beyond a reasonable doubt. There must be an indictment. Right to jury trial. Those are all very important safeguards, because I tell you, once this powerful government—I don't mean this administration, but a government that is as powerful as ours, as it is now—gets after the individual, he's cooked. Unless he has Edward Bennett Williams, or Clarence Darrow, or somebody, to defend him.

SEVAREID: Chief Justice Burger said that criminal trials now take twice as long as they did ten years ago. Is this a good thing?

DOUGLAS: I don't know if that's true, generally or not.

SEVAREID: On an average, I mean.

DOUGLAS: In New York State, 95 percent of all criminal cases are disposed of on pleas of guilty. In California, 74.4 percent last year were disposed of on pleas of guilty. We're talking about a relatively small number of cases, although these are important cases. There's a great rush on in some areas to get rid of the jury to speed things up. But to send these poor devils down to trial by a judge against their will is a horrible thing. I think judges get to be calloused. They see so many of these and so they become sort of law-and-order automatons.

SEVAREID: Well you've been worried about the rights of minorities and what courts can do with it under these rules. Look at all these cases: Angela Davis case, Berrigan brothers, and others. They've been getting a pretty fair deal from juries in this country.

DOUGLAS: That's right. The jury reflects the conscience of America. Not every jury, but by and large, and that is a much better testing ground, I think, than the testing ground of a judge.

SEVAREID: Well, now, your Court has decided recently that state courts, anyway, don't have to have unanimity on a jury to find guilty.

DOUGLAS: And that was a very tragic decision.

SEVAREID: I don't know what exempted the federal courts—but they did.

DOUGLAS: That's a mystery because they both come from the Sixth Amendment.

SEVAREID: Well, if the jury splits and a majority of, say, two or three, four members of the jury say they don't think the man's guilty, then you'd assume there's a reasonable doubt. What happens to the principle of "beyond reasonable doubt"?

DOUGLAS: You're interviewing the wrong judge. I don't know the answer to that. I don't think it can be answered. . . . The principle is—well, not perhaps abrogated, but it's eroded.

SEVAREID: I think Chief Justice Burger said that a lot of things like environmental cases, consumer class actions, ought not to come to the courts. The courts are overburdened. . . . You'd take more of these things as I understand it.

DOUGLAS: If Congress should redesign the jurisdiction of federal courts so as to leave out of them the environmental questions, then we go down the drain really very fast. Because we then would be victims of the administrative agencies. And these administrative agencies, though they're high-minded and though they're not venal, are very oppressive. There must be some check on them. There must be, unless they're going to be abolished. I always thought that they should be abolished. I told FDR he never should create an agency unless he abolished it in ten years, because at the end of ten years, it becomes a monster.

SEVAREID: Well, a lot of people around the Court talk so very different from you on this subject. The Court's got more money this year; you got more clerks per justice and so on.

DOUGLAS: Yes, but we don't need clerks.

SEVAREID: And you've got a great big backlog. All this talk of too big a load—overwork. You're out here weeks before the Court even adjourns.

DOUGLAS: Well, we got a bigger backlog in the sense of more filings. When I went on the Court we had 1,800 cases a year—a term. And now we're having about 4,200.

SEVAREID: That you hear.

DOUGLAS: No, that are filed and we have to screen them. But of those 4,200, most of them come from prisons, and 98 or 99 percent of them are frivolous. We read them all because they produce classic situations like *Gideon* and *Miranda*, and so on. We're actually hearing and deciding fewer cases now than we were when I went on the Court.

SEVARIED: Why? Still got nine men.

DOUGLAS: Still have nine men, but the selective process has changed. The judges have changed, the idea of what is important has changed in the minds of the judges—a highly subjective consideration. Is this case

fit to take—should we take it? And we take fewer and fewer. When I
went on the Court, we sat six days a week. Under Warren we sat five
days a week, a conference on Friday. And now it looks as if our trend
will be to three days a week, with a conference on Saturday. The job
takes about four days a week.

SEVAREID: Well, it does for you. But some of the others complain
they're working eighteen hours a day every day to keep up.

DOUGLAS: Well, you need the week to think about these problems,
but you can be hiking while you're—you don't need to stop thinking.

SEVAREID: Can you keep the facts of a specified complicated case in
your head as you're walking through the woods here, for example?

DOUGLAS: Oh, sure. It's best way to solve a problem if you're confused. But when I talk to lawyers I tell them that you're never confused
if you read the Constitution the right way.

SEVAREID: Well, you said a moment ago you don't need clerks. And
now you get more clerks than ever. Why don't you need clerks?

DOUGLAS: Because these are highly individual decisions. Nobody in
my office can tell me or should tell me how I should vote.

SEVAREID: Don't you have somebody look up precedents and what
not?

DOUGLAS: Oh, I assign them to do research and they submit research
to me in addition to the briefs, and they're helpful in that way. But
we're surfeited with law clerks. We don't need the law clerks.

SEVAREID: You mean you'd be prepared to do all the looking up of
precedents yourself? You're not going to sell that to many judges.

DOUGLAS: No. But I'm entitled to my First Amendment rights.

SEVAREID: Well, you've turned out just about more formal written opinions than anyone on that Court ever, or you must be close to that record.

DOUGLAS: I have no idea.

SEVAREID: There has been some criticism by some legal scholars that you're really too hasty. Don't pay enough attention to precedents. . . .

DOUGLAS: That means they don't like my decisions.

SEVAREID: Well, they're saying that you think sociologically, politically—you decide what's fair in those terms in your mind, then you find precedents to suit that. That's been a running criticism of you.

DOUGLAS: Well, I've always thought that on a constitutional decision, that *stare decisis*, that is, established law, was really no sure guideline because what did the guys—the judges who sat there in 1875—know about, say, electronic surveillance? They didn't know anything about it. Why take their wisdom? That's why I once said, to the consternation of a group of lawyers, that I'd rather create a precedent than find one. Because the creation of a precedent in terms of the modern setting means the adjustment of the Constitution to the needs of the time.

SEVAREID: There's been scuttlebutt around Washington now for months . . . about a lot of abrasiveness inside the Court. A lot of unhappiness. Conflicts, personalities and what not. I don't expect you to talk about the personalities, but there is a different atmosphere now, isn't there?

DOUGLAS: There's no abrasiveness. There's no discord or ill will. It's a different group of men with different habits. You see, the distinctive thing about the Court and its history is that it's a circle of men with fierce ideological differences. Fierce. With every man willing to die for his point of view, but as a group, harmonious. Which is unusual to find.

SEVAREID: Would you say today it's harmonious?

DOUGLAS: Yes, it's harmonious.

SEVAREID: What do you think about these popular terms that have been used? President Nixon said he wants strict constructionists on the Court. Well, Justice Black, regarded himself as the strictest of constructionists, but he was not Nixon's kind of judge. What does that mean?

DOUGLAS: I told Hugo, when we read that in the paper, "He's talking about us. About you and me." And Hugo laughed and said, "I don't think so." Well, I said, "Congress shall pass no law abridging freedom of speech or press." And you and I take it to mean what it says. That's strict construction. Other members of the Court over the years have said that when the Constitution says Congress shall make no law abridging freedom of speech or press, it really means Congress may make *some* laws abridging freedom of speech and press. Now if you go off on that tangent, then it takes you a long time to make your decision. You have to do an awful lot of research. You work eighteen hours a day, write fifty-eight-page opinions.

SEVAREID: Would you say that's an absolute, as Black said?

DOUGLAS: Yes, in terms of if it's good or bad.

SEVAREID: Well, is that phrase "strict constructionist" confused with judicial restraint, meaning that the courts ought to leave more things to Congress, administration, and what not? What's the difference in the two phrases?

DOUGLAS: It's very difficult. I think it means that the gut reaction of the speaker indicates that he disagrees with the Court. The Constitution is not designed to leave things to Congress. In certain areas, yes. Should the president send a man to the Vatican as ambassador? That's none of the Court's business. But, as I said before, if the president or the governor or a general or anybody else takes somebody by the neck and says: Go to jail or go to Vietnam, or what not—that's the business of the courts, that's not for the president or the governor or the general alone to decide. You have a justiciable controversy. And if you intrude as a judiciary, like we did in the steel seizure case by Harry Truman, you upset a president. Harry Truman was very upset. . . . He was so upset that Hugo Black gave him a party. And we all went and poured a lot of bourbon down Harry Truman.

SEVAREID: Did he change his mind at all?

DOUGLAS: He didn't change his mind, but he felt a little better, at least for a few hours.

SEVAREID: Well, you said once somewhere that the Court must not be bound by the fears and illusions of the past. . . . But what about the fears and the illusions of the present? You can go too far with that, can't you?

DOUGLAS: Sure.

SEVAREID: Wasn't there some truth in the past?

DOUGLAS: Sure, and these are values that the oncoming members have to weigh, and it's very difficult to know what a new member will be like until he's there for five or ten years, because very few new members have been free and independent before. Now all the layers of prejudices of clients and what not have been peeled off, and there the man is. And what does he basically think in the terms of constitutional values? It takes time. And once he finds out what it is, then he either embraces the old precedent or he overrules it.

SEVAREID: But Black said the law changed because the judges changed.

DOUGLAS: That's right.

SEVAREID: There is now going on a pretty big general mood not only against impersonality of government, big institutions, but a move towards decentralization. Let people in the local communities take more into their own hands, and so on, whether school prayer or obscenity cases, where one community may feel different about it. Haven't you been against diversity at that level?

DOUGLAS: Well, obscenity is a separate and distinct problem, in my point of view, because I don't think that the First Amendment gives the states or the Congress any power to legislate as to what is poor literature.

SEVAREID: Not even by communities that may be very puritanical in outlook? Shouldn't they have the power to decide that for themselves?

DOUGLAS: Maybe so, but then we need a constitutional amendment because the First Amendment applies to the states as well as the federal government. And obscenity, at the time the First Amendment was adopted, was practically unknown in this country. It all came later on. As the nineteenth century developed, 1859, we had federal legislation on obscenity. So you can't say historically that speech and press excluded obscenity. The human race has been obscene from the beginning, and this is a matter of taste and, you know, culture. And what would pain you and me might be a lyric to somebody else. To get into this field, I think, is a great mistake unless we have a constitutional amendment. If people want to do it, to suppress it, then you can have a constitutional amendment and vote it up or vote it down, but I don't think, with Hugo Black, that it's barred by the Constitution. Is the "Song of Solomon" obscene? Some people think it's very suggestive.

SEVARIED: Well, what about the big '54 school desegregation decision? Do you have any cause to regret the way the Court went on that? I think Mr. Justice Black said that the "all deliberate speed" phrase probably could have been left out of it. What have been your thoughts since that? It's an awful mess now.

DOUGLAS: Well, "all deliberate speed" is an old, conventional equity term. If I should tear down your fence, the judge would direct me to restore the fence "with all deliberate speed," which meant that I could wait until the ground thawed out, you see. We didn't give too much thought about it. As it worked out, it wasn't a very happy choice because the resistance was great, and furthermore, the president in the White House at the time [Eisenhower] didn't think very much of the decision. . . . And it took him some time to move into action. If he'd sold off some of his great prestige by going to the people and saying, whether you agree with it or not, this is the law and we're going to have one nation out of many diverse people, and we're going to start with the schools, we could be much better off. But no president did that.

SEVAREID: Now, the administration is moving against it here in many ways with these new messages to Congress which attempt to have prohibitions against court moratoriums, court actions, and what not. Is this a serious threat to the independence of the judiciary, do you think?

DOUGLAS: The Court has a great tradition of independence. Whatever president names them, or whatever their party or background may be. And I think that this Court will be independent. In my years there, there's been no president who has talked to any member of the [Supreme] Court about any case or any problems. . . .

SEVAREID: Well, do you feel at all in the dark of the night that that decision which you approved, like all the other justices, eighteen years ago has really got us in a mess here now and that no one can find a way out of? That it doesn't work in many places. . . .

DOUGLAS: Well there's nothing that works perfectly. It's working pretty well in most places; it's sticky in other places. We hear mostly about the trouble spots. Busing is an old problem here. We're sitting at Goose Prairie, Washington. Now Goose Prairie has children, and a bus comes down the road here a spell and picks them up and drives them about forty-two miles to school so they can attend a consolidated school and get a better school. . . . Then they bus them back at night so these kids at Goose Prairie ride eighty some miles a day in a bus. Now the black schools have notoriously been inferior. The school boards in this country have never had blacks on them to any great extent. . . .

SEVAREID: A lot do now, though.

DOUGLAS: Well, you'd be surprised if you looked at the national statistics. It's moving in that direction, but what I'm trying to say is that the financing of the black schools has been inferior—with the result of inferior staffs, inferior library facilities, and so on. I think that probably the most important thing is association with a competitive group.

Where there is some of their own age setting a pace. That's probably the most important factor, and that's why I think, from an educational point of view—not a constitutional point of view—but from an educational point of view, why the mixture of the races is very good.

SEVAREID: Let's get back to the Bill of Rights. Do you have any ominous feelings about what's going on? You've just had a decision today on the rights of reporters. They can be compelled to testify about their sources in certain cases. People in my business are getting their wind up very high.

DOUGLAS: I was opposed to that decision. I think it was wrong. I think what we need, as poor as our press is, that it should be independent of government, completely independent, for all the reasons stated by Jefferson. When government can say what you can publish or what you can't publish, then the press is no longer free and independent; and then the people don't know; and then it depends upon the handout of some information; what the administration in power thinks is suitable for the people to know, and that's not healthy.

SEVAREID: Isn't broadcasting part of the free press?

DOUGLAS: I think so.

SEVAREID: But we've been put now, by the Court, in a second-class citizenship category, very specifically—in the *Red Lion* decision— and we're trapped! Why should the most pervasive medium of information, ideas, not have full protection of the Bill of Rights as the less pervasive have?

DOUGLAS: I think they should.

SEVAREID: On the strength of what you've said, maybe we'll go back and try this one again?

DOUGLAS: I only have one vote.

SEVAREID: But your feeling is the Bill of Rights has a real priority in the Constitution?

DOUGLAS: Well, a priority in the sense that it's filled with "thou shalt nots" and those are the absolutes.

SEVAREID: What is the basic picture in your mind of what this society ought to be?

DOUGLAS: Well, I think of this country ideally as a nation of very independent, vigorous, nonsubmissive people sticking to their own ideals, their own religion, their own political beliefs and campaigning, and so on. I look upon this nation as a place for free enterprise to flourish and that means the absence of monopoly, the nongrowth of these conglomerates that are bigger than European nations. . . . That's been going on, but that can't go on without eventually the people rising up and taking it over and becoming a socialist state. Maybe we're doomed for that. I think there's something better than that if we stick to small, private enterprise and break up the conglomerates.

SEVAREID: You think bigness is really a real curse, don't you?

DOUGLAS: Yes, because there's nobody smart enough to be able to run all these twenty, thirty, forty different industries that are put together. Nobody is smart enough. And these separate industries have great values. Brandeis used to lecture me on this, and I believed him. He said if we continue in the way in which we're going, this nation will become a nation of clerks—submissive clerks—rather than independent, free men. And, he was quite right.

SEVAREID: You want responsive government. You believe in the one-man, one-vote principle, in the majority rule principle; yet the Court is the great exception to this. Nobody elects people like yourself. You can hardly be removed. Should there be a different way of electing or choosing the Supreme Court?

DOUGLAS: Well, I've thought about that a lot. I don't know how members of our Court would run for office and campaign. I shudder to think of it. I don't know what kind of a Court you'd get. I'm sure you wouldn't get a Hugo Black or an Oliver Wendell Holmes. I don't know what you'd get. The Court is really the keeper of the conscience. And the conscience is the Constitution. And it's very important to have a keeper of the conscience, an independent group, above the storm, free from political influence.

SEVAREID: Thank you, Mr. Justice.

Conclusion — The Continuing Debate

ROBERT H. KELLER, JR.

10

Both the Supreme Court opinions and the nonlegal writings of William O. Douglas, and the way in which he lived his life off the bench, reveal a passionate and consistent social philosophy. For participants in the Douglas Symposium, that philosophy was the touchstone for their exploration of the complex ideas clustered around the theme "Individual Freedom and the Government." The variety of ideas upon which Douglas brought his philosophy to bear was mirrored by the array of issues expressed, debated, and discussed by the cross section of citizens who shared the weekend of April 15–17, 1977.

For some, the conference motif became the Emerson–Graglia dispute over the nature of the Constitution and the purpose of the Court. For others, the dominant issue became women's rights, affirmative action, and the ERA. Still others would have agreed with a person who later wrote of the Symposium, "I regret that Justice Douglas could not be present in body; he certainly was present in spirit." Much of the Douglas spirit—the sense that law ultimately is personal, that judges are human, that "we're all human and the decisions we make are profoundly important to the people," that a judge must not allow himself to "end up a dried husk unrelated to anything"—came out in thirty hours of small seminars and community workshops. Perhaps the following selected transcriptions from workshops and seminars can begin to suggest what people experienced.

SEATTLE ATTORNEY: Courts are two kinds of institutions. They are legal institutions, but perhaps more importantly they are social institutions. And if there's any one thing the United States Supreme Court does, it is set a tone for our society regarding certain kinds of social movement or lack of movement. In 1954, *Brown* decided that some black children would go to school, but it decided a hell of a lot more too. It set a tone in our society, it said the chief legal agency in our country will no longer allow people to be treated as second-class citizens. Everybody has a right to be treated equally. That tone permeated our society and has permeated it for over twenty years. We saw the growth of the civil rights movement, the youth movement, the peace movement, Native Americans, the women's movement. They are all related by one common thread: "We have not been part of the mainstream of American society. . . ."

* * *

THOMAS EMERSON: The law, including constitutional law, is based on the system of moral values. If it does not reflect that system, it has no relationship to society. But it never incorporates all those moral values. That's the key to a great justice or a great judge—that he knows where to draw the line, not too far ahead, and not too far behind. He can operate on moral principles and the objective legal system at the same time: He can make the proper balance.

* * *

SUPERIOR COURT JUDGE: There have been cases in my court where I screamed for a certain result. Literally, I wanted to have a certain result. But as I read the law, I could not get there. I would have loved to figure out a way, but I simply couldn't get there. . . . The law does impose itself, and the rules do impose themselves. There are those cases where, despite one's personal views, because of the rules of the game, and because of the predictability which society needs in playing the game, whether or not you like the rules, you follow them. But there are times when the law is not so clear, where it's ambiguous enough so that you can push the law forward a little bit, as you see forward. Then your personal values have an impact on the decision.

SEATTLE ATTORNEY: If the judges are wrong, they can be appealed. Except, of course, the only appeal from the Supreme Court is to God, or to a constitutional amendment.

THOMAS EMERSON: Or to a constitutional law professor!

* * *

MODERATOR: And let me quote from Douglas' opinion in *Belle Terre* v. *Boraas*[1] concerning what Douglas understood the town and the law to be protecting: "A quiet place where yards are wide, people few, and motor vehicles restricted. . . . zones where family values, youth values, and the blessings of quiet seclusion and clean air make the area a sanctuary for people." It used to be that we put birds in sanctuaries, but now Douglas is saying that we need people sanctuaries.

ENVIRONMENTALIST: In the conflict between individual rights and environmental regulation we are rapidly approaching a juncture where the courts must make a decision based on values. To what extent will people be permitted to move about freely, to have big automobiles, to bring big oil tankers into Puget Sound? We have to decide, I think, whether we will maximize individual freedom or maximize environmental protection.

* * *

TELEVISION EXECUTIVE: There's a problem here. Why shouldn't the Socialist Labor Party have an opportunity to put out their message during an election? That's the only reason they run. They don't really think that they can win. They've got a political point of view, and they use the election as a platform. On the other hand, to suggest that the Social Labor Party is of equal importance to you, to your decision between the two major candidates, one of whom will be governor, that claim, it seems to me, is spurious.

* * *

VINCE BLASI: Suppose you move past these lawyer arguments about not drawing the line, and you move past the question whether certain portrayals are sexist. Assume we can determine that certain materials—violent, sexist, or racist—are in our view unmistakably evil. Is it then correct to regulate them? To say that other people cannot be exposed to this literature or this appeal, because *we* know it's noxious, that in the long run society will be harmed if it is circulated? Can libertarians really say [socially dangerous] attitudes are individual and not subject to government regulation? Can government ever regulate with the avowed purpose of trying to exterminate or perpetuate attitudes?

* * *

PHILOSOPHER: What Douglas brought to government and law was a certain conception of the person: *of being a person with values.* When it came to how government should be structured, he did not care so long as it furthered values which had to do with the nature of the individual and his or her life. And I suspect that Douglas was a man of enormous vitality and power, and he was committed to promote the values he held most deeply. He found himself on the Court, and he was able to use that Court to achieve his values, to open up the social process, to make it possible for more individuals to participate, to make their voices felt, make their weight felt. . . .

* * *

INDIAN TRIBAL ATTORNEY: There is a collision here. We have our cherished idea that this is an open society of equal opportunity where each of us is awarded according to our merit. And we have the actual facts. Take a hard look at our history. It has not worked out equally. American history is not uniformly pretty. We see long episodes of which we, today, are ashamed. And there are continuing consequences. To ignore those consequences means preserving injustice. It means saying, "Well, we stopped doing that and now we will pretend that it never happened." That ignores justice. And it is not merely a question of the benevolence of the majority, but one of hardheaded realism: Can our society function if large segments remain left out? Sooner or later we have to pay the price. You don't have generations of one class singled out for oppression and exploitation and suffering without someday reaching an accounting.

* * *

DONALD HOROWITZ: If Moses had simply bargained with the pharaoh to stop discrimination against the Hebrews, they would still be building pyramids. He had to part the Red Sea. And that's what affirmative action is all about.

SEATTLE ATTORNEY: With affirmative action there's bound to be some incompetence. And to some extent that incompetence was caused by the very racism and sexism we are trying to alleviate. Professor Emerson's right—there have to be some sacrifices. There were involuntary sacrifices by blacks and Indians for hundreds of years. There's going to be some involuntary sacrifices in the future to equalize things.

COLLEGE PROFESSOR: At one time I gather we tried to achieve a just society and claimed constitutional backing for it in the equal protection clause. Then we prohibited discrimination on the basis of race. Are we now appealing to that very same equal protection clause to allow discrimination on the basis of race, to require it? Is *that* the shift? Are we still appealing to the same clause but saying that the facts have changed?

ANITA MILLER: I think that everyone would admit that there is [reverse] discrimination. And that we are working toward a situation where ultimately we will not have preferential treatment. The distance between today, with blatant discrimination, and the time when we do not need preferences, is the burden we face. I also insist on not just equal opportunity, but at some point in time, evident results. Until we see evident results, equal opportunity is just a catchword.

BELLINGHAM INSURANCE AGENT: I think that affirmative action in and of itself is claptrap, primarily because it's not law, secondly because it's from the executive branch, and thirdly because it reminds me of a bunch of social planners watching black and white mice running around in the maze looking for the right pedal to push for the peanut.

* * *

ENVIRONMENTALIST: Douglas saw people as creatures who need conditions which allowed them to be autonomous, self-directing persons. That was one of the touchstones of this man's values. But he was unable to separate the possibility of autonomous self-directing people from our need to live in an environment which had certain aesthetic characteristics. It's not accidental that he used the word "sanctuary." He felt that people *needed* sanctuaries. His own sanctuaries were the mountains, and these sanctuaries were readily available to him. I am sure that no one in our time would deplore more than Justice Douglas that, to preserve adequate sanctuaries to nourish the spirit, we have to enforce laws which zone and restrict human freedom. Now I think that the man was probably just straightforwardly inconsistent in this case.

* * *

COMMERCIAL FISHERMAN: We seem to be way up in the sky with a lot of this discussion when we should be getting down to the roots that must be discussed right here in this actual community. I'm a non-Indian fisherman, and I have about 3,400 buddies of mine out there who feel the same way I do, that we have reverse discrimination against us, that the Indians have more rights to fish than we do. If we don't solve this in the very near future, it's going to lead to catastrophe.

INDIAN TRIBAL ATTORNEY: If I sell you my property with the proviso that I can always come back to it and fish in a little stream on it, and that my children and their children's children forever can fish there, and you say, "That's a good deal, okay, I'll buy your property on those terms," and we write it into the deed, that my children's children can return here to fish, and it's a matter of public record, and everyone in the country knows it, is it reverse discrimination when someone buys that property with that encumbrance on it? If *you* buy and don't know it, it's your fault. That property is this whole country. And you're living in the wealthiest nation on the face of the earth, the highest living standards in the world, built on a land base that is the result of that kind of basic transaction. It was an exchange. The United States once thought the exchange was fair and proper, even though the Indians later discovered that it wasn't such a good deal for them. You say that the fishermen are now getting the brunt of it. Well, you apparently don't know about all the Indian people who have died on America's skid roads because they didn't get any justice at all. Nobody threatens to drive you away from your fishing. I talked to you yesterday, and I asked if you could go trolling, and you said, "Well, that takes me too far from home. I want to fish where I want to fish." The Indians have been zoned out of their homes for the past 100 years. People have to wake up and learn what they should have been taught in school, what the United States should have told them for 100 years. There is a sin here, a dereliction by the government when it did not tell us what our obligations were. Treaty and fishing rights are a *legal* obligation. Not moral. Not ethical. Not do-good or let's-help-our-poor-Indian-brother. But a pure and simple economic transaction, a contract.

* * *

SEATTLE ATTORNEY: The United States is living through a period of quiet revolution. Certain conditions evolved in the past—power and powerlessness, wealth and lack of it, freedom and lack of freedom—and until twenty years ago we just took inequality for granted and said everyone had to accept their fate and live with the old rules. Then in the sixties a lot of people said, "We don't accept your rules anymore." And to its credit, the dominant society, men such as Justice Douglas, responded. That revolution is still going on, more quietly, but not without pain and anger. America is trying to come to grips with its history. And at any given point in history, it's hard for any of us to think historically about ourselves. Why should we be held responsible for what happened 100 years ago, even though we are the beneficiaries of it, even though we profit from it? And we are perfectly willing to keep right on profiting from the past actions until the guy whose toes we are now crushing under our heel wakes up and yells. Eventually, we have to learn that history is continuous and connected.

* * *

The Symposium's multiplicity of interests also characterizes this book. Yet three generalizations seemed to develop throughout the various lectures, panels, and debates. These were the continuity of American political thought, the common assumptions about the nature of government, and the need to resolve the problem of legal authority.

Whatever side one took in the debates between Graglia and Emerson—judicial activism v. restraint, a broad versus narrow construction of the Constitution—it was reassuring to realize that with punctual regularity this debate recurs in American history, almost as if the disagreement were a natural law or inherent in any system based on a written constitution. It is the way in which our form of government compels us to argue, a casting of social disagreement into battles over the meaning and limits of constitutional language and judicial authority. Graglia and Emerson carried the tradition forward with eloquence, fervor, and insight.

Throughout the weekend, common assumptions regarding the nature of government were made and repeated. Almost all of these assumptions reflected classical constitutional arguments that began with the Continental Congress and Constitutional Convention, gained refinement in the *Federalist Papers*, and influenced American history through Jefferson, Marshall, Calhoun, Stephen Douglas, Lincoln, Holmes, Roosevelt, and Frankfurter. Federal–state relations, the necessity of balancing freedom and security, the need for checks and balances, the dangers of an established military, and the necessity and limits of the judiciary, are matters of debate for Emerson, Graglia, Blasi, and Morris as they were for Hamilton, Madison, and Jay, and as they continue to be for concerned American citizens.[2]

Whatever their other disagreements, most speakers at the Douglas Symposium were surprisingly close to the Founding Fathers in their conception of government as dangerous. The nature of politics, for the pessimistic and Calvinist authors of the *Federalist Papers*, was determined by human nature. And humans, especially when entrusted with the power to govern others, were not considered trustworthy. In the first three pages of a single essay, Alexander Hamilton used all of the following words and phrases to describe human relations and human history: "frequent and violent contents," "men are ambitious, vindictive, and rapacious," "hostility," "love of power," "jealousy of power," "enmities," "fears," "blood," "attack, vanquished and destroyed," "private pique," "theft," "dissipating," "fatal war," "viscissitudes," "ruin," "ambitious," "vanity," "intrigues," "bigotry," "petulence," "cabals," "ferments," "civil war."[3] An equally negative assessment of human nature was made by James Madison, though he wrote in more moderate terms:

. . . latent causes of faction are thus sown in the nature of man . . . the propensity of mankind to fall into mutual animosities . . . it is in vain to say that enlightened statesmen will be able to adjust these clashing interests. . . . If the impulse and the opportunity be suffered to coincide, neither moral nor religious motives can be relied on as an adequate control.[4]

This creates one of the unresolved dilemmas in American government, one that Madison isolated in his comment about men and angels: A strong central government is required to restrain human nature (Hamilton), but that very human nature makes a strong central government dangerous (Jefferson). Few thinkers have resolved this dilemma. Professor Emerson, a revered champion of liberal causes, is in this sense rooted in the *Federalist* tradition. In discussing government secrecy, he described the large and powerful modern state as a problem if not a threat. Yet, for Emerson, increased federal authority and power are necessary to ensure the civil rights of minorities. And even though Professor Graglia disputed Emerson's faith in the

Supreme Court as an antidote to the abuses of power, he shared Emerson's distrust of federal bureaucracy and of established authority. So did Professors Blasi and Morris, with Blasi arguing that the primary function of the First Amendment is to curb the constant temptation of government officials to destroy popular government. Almost all contributors to the Symposium viewed the state as a potential adversary, a view frequently expressed by Justice Douglas. In Vince Blasi's words, Americans in the 1970s have "a pathological view of government" and are prepared to assume the worst about public officials. That skepticism is not simply a reaction to the political crises of the 1970s; it consistently follows from a 200-year tradition of skepticism about government and human nature.

The contributors to the Douglas Symposium had different palliatives for this condition: a new value system in American culture (Emerson); reliance on state legislatures and public common sense (Graglia); deeper exposure of lawyers to the humanities (Murphy); constitutional mandates from the Supreme Court (Emerson); creation of an autonomous Fourth Estate (Blasi); a constitutional amendment and more frequent appointment of women as judges (Miller). Whatever their solutions, everyone shared a commitment to limited government, to checks and balances against concerted power. Everyone could endorse the conclusion that James Madison reached after reading Montesquieu and listening to Thomas Jefferson: "The accumulation of all powers, legislative, executive, and judiciary, in the same hands, whether of one, a few, or many, and whether hereditary, self-appointed, or elective, may justly be pronounced the very definition of tyranny."[5] In the American political system, that conclusion is part of the solution.

These misgivings about government pose another question: By what authority does anyone govern at all? By what sanction do codes, rules, regulations, and court decisions limit human behavior and determine our lives?[6] On the last day of the Symposium a panel addressed this question and produced four conflicting answers. Thomas Emerson argued that the ultimate sources of legal authority were reason and intuition expressing themselves through a people's cultural and moral values. Lino Graglia insisted that all government ultimately depends upon force—the point of a bayonet or the barrel of a gun. Attorney Donald Horowitz's answer was practical: Any law has authority if it helps to create a civil, democratic society in which guns and bayonets are unnecessary. Judge Marshall Forrest said that classical culture and the humanities, especially history and philosophy, provide an understanding of life that qualifies some men and women to decide the fate of other persons. Even if one disagreed with all of the panelists, their convictions moved the audience to continue seeking satisfactory answers. After a decade of assassinations, Vietnam, and Watergate, an examination of the foundations of our political system seemed essential to thoughtful Americans.

Whatever theories of authority and jurisprudence one adopts, pure ideas must be exposed to the tests of practice and experience. "Experience is the oracle of truth," Madison and Hamilton wrote. Yet experience itself must be subjected to study and reflection. The papers in this book are intended mainly as invitations to think and inquire. The reader will have noted that the authors' biases are legal and logical, with most of the papers being short on historical, psychological, and economic analysis.

Beyond these papers and the planned discussions, much else happened during the three days of the Douglas Symposium. Most of it is unrecorded, but we know from letters and comments that the conference inspired a considerable number of people to think earnestly about their own relationship to government and society, about the Constitution and the Supreme Court, and about the continuing debate over the nation's past and its future. We hope that this book has had a similar effect. Insofar as the Symposium and the book accomplish this, they achieve their goal of honoring Justice Douglas.

Notes

1. *Belle Terre* v. *Boraas*, 416 U.S. 1 (1974).
2. *The Federalist*, Nos. 8, 14, 16, 22, 29, 41, 51, 78–82.
3. Ibid., No. 6.
4. Ibid., No. 10.
5. Ibid., No. 47.
6. For a recent argument favoring the return to Federalist and Burkean concepts of government, see Alexander M. Bickel, *The Morality of Consent* (New Haven, Conn.: Yale University Press, 1975). For a reconstruction of democratic theory, see John Rawls, *A Theory of Justice* (Cambridge, Mass.: Harvard University Press, 1971).

Appendix A
William O. Douglas:
A Chronology
KENNETH OTT_____

Born: Maine, Minnesota, October 16	1898
Suffers polio	1904
Family moves to Cleveland, Washington (near Yakima, Washington); father dies	1904
Graduates valedictorian, Yakima High School	1916
Enters Whitman College, Walla Walla	1916
Joins Army ROTC	1918
Graduates from Whitman College	1920
Yakima high school teacher	1920–22
Enters Columbia Law School	1922
First marriage (to Mildred Riddle)	1923
Graduates from Columbia Law School, LL.B., second in class	1925
Practices law with Cravath, deGersdorf, Swain, and Wood, New York City	1925
Practices law in Yakima, Washington	1926
Returns to Columbia Law School as professor	1927
Resigns professorship	1928
Professor of law, Yale University	1928–34
Publishes *Cases and Materials on the Law of Corporate Organizations*	1931
Publishes *Cases on the Law of Partnership, Joint Stock Associations, Business Trusts and Other Non-corporate Business Organizations*	1932

Appointed by FDR to Securities and Exchange Commission (assumes chairmanship, 1936)	1934
Appointed by FDR to the United States Supreme Court, April 17	1939
Publishes *Of Men and Mountains*	1950
Publishes *Beyond the High Himalayas*	1952
Grants stay of execution to the Rosenburgs	1953
Establishes Goose Prairie, Washington, as home during early Supreme Court years	
Publishes *My Wilderness: The Pacific West*	1960
Publishes *A Wilderness Bill of Rights*	1965
Article, *Playboy* 16:143, "The Public Be Damned"	1966
Marries fourth wife (Cathleen Hefferman)	1966
Publishes *Toward a Global Federalism*	1968
Publishes *Points of Rebellion*	1970
Then U.S. Representative Gerald Ford introduces the Douglas impeachment resolution into the House	1970
Establishes the longest record of service in the Court's history, October 29	1973
Publishes *Go East, Young Man*	1974
Suffers stroke, January	1975
Resigns from the Supreme Court, November 17	1975

Appendix B
William O. Douglas:
A Bibliography
CHARLES R. BULGER_____

A swift way to glimpse the humanism of William O. Douglas is to study the titles and publishers of his writings, a forty-five year collection that includes forty-three books and over two hundred articles and published speeches. Recognizing the value of a thorough compilation of Douglas texts, Fairhaven College student Charles Bulger agreed to produce a bibliography for the Douglas Symposium. The following collection of data on essays, newspaper articles, speeches, books, and book reviews by and about Douglas is the result of Bulger's research. Not included are citations to the more than 1,200 opinions that Douglas wrote for the Supreme Court. Persons interested in that source should consult the Table of Cases in Vernon Countryman's *Judicial Record of William O. Douglas* (pp. 385–405) or, for a convenient selection, see Countryman's anthology, *The Douglas Opinions.*

Few if any justices in the history of the Court published so much outside the Court. Few have had so much published about them before they retired. The following bibliography provides an outline of Douglas' career, a stunning catalog of his diverse interests, and a concrete record of the public's reaction to his activities and opinions.

As one examines the bibliography, it becomes evident that Douglas' main interest before 1939 was the federal government's regulation of finance. Until his appointment to the Supreme Court, Douglas' published writings were scholarly and formal, consisting almost entirely of law school casebooks. Nevertheless, the press of the time described him as an angry Scotsman, a Wall Street cop, a fighter and "hard-hitter" who could "tame the bulls and bears," discipline the brokers of high finance, and "wash Wall Street's face."

During the forties and early fifties as Douglas began to write for mass circulation, lauding American democracy and describing his world travels, his writing became more personal, and his public image mellowed. The Democratic Party recognized him as a possible leader; others praised his long hikes and horseback rides and named him the Father of the Year in 1950. By the 1960s more awards and honors had come, especially from conservationists. Law review articles on his judicial thought grew common. At the same time, however, Douglas the angry Scotsman returned. His travels in foreign countries and his strong reaction against McCarthyism contributed to a growing disillusionment with the directions of postwar American culture, a disillusionment clearly reflected in the bibliography. His concerns for traditional civil liberties, for rivers and forests, and for world peace produced increasingly furious critiques of the United States. His views boiled out in titles such as *Points of Rebellion, Farewell to Texas: A Vanishing Wilderness, The Three Hundred Year War: A Chronicle of Ecological Disaster*, and *Holocaust or Hemispheric Cooperation*. Douglas' outspoken toleration for non-Western and noncapitalistic social systems, his deep skepticism about the U.S. military establishment, and his insistence upon libertarian goals, not to mention the event of his fourth marriage, inspired a partisan effort to impeach him in the early 1970s, an effort that only served to make Douglas more unconventional and abrasive during his final years on the Court. Typically, the last item in the list of his publications shows Douglas writing about the unorthodox field of CB radios and the First Amendment.

Besides providing this career overview, Bulger's bibliography also portrays the breadth of Douglas' interests and abilities. Of his forty-three books, a dozen concern law; there are six each about patriotism, the natural environment, travel, and international relations. He wrote two autobiographies and one biography, the latter an excellent children's book on John Muir. Of his published articles and essays, nearly one-third appeared in law reviews, two dozen in scholarly and legal journals, including four in the *National Lawyer's Guild Review* and nine in the *American Bar Association Journal*. Over a dozen of his essays appeared in environmental magazines. A partial list of other periodicals that published his writing includes: *Reader's Digest* (six articles), *National Geographic* (five articles), *Playboy* (five articles), *Vital Speeches* (ten speeches), *Ladies' Home Journal, Mademoiselle, Redbook, Holiday, Collier's, Life, Time, Newsweek, The Rotarian, The Progressive, The Nation, U.S. News & World Report, New Republic, Harper's, Saturday Review* (twelve articles), *Field and Stream, Bulletin of the Atomic Scientists, Today's Health, Science Digest*.

Certainly, Douglas has heeded his own advice in *Go East, Young Man* and in his interview with Eric Sevareid. He has eschewed narrow professional specialization that shrivels the human spirit. Many do not rank him among the

Supreme Court's great scholarly jurists, this being the price perhaps of his breadth and far-flung humanism. If his writing at times appears verbose, opaque, or superficial, it seems a small price to pay for the enormous quantity of opinion he addressed to the American public. The courts, lawyers, and law schools do not represent the crucial audience in a democracy; for William O. Douglas, one suspects, the rewards of humanism, activism, and full citizenship have been well worth the costs.

BOOKS BY WILLIAM O. DOUGLAS

Cases and Materials on the Law of Corporate Reorganizations (with Carrol M. Shanks). St. Paul, Minn.: West Publishing Co., 1931.

Cases and Materials on the Law of Financing of Business Units (with Carrol M. Shanks). Chicago: Callaghan and Co., 1931.

Cases and Materials on the Law of Management of Business Units (with Carrol M. Shanks). Chicago: Callaghan and Co., 1931.

Cases and Materials on Business Units, Losses, Liabilities and Assets (with Carrol M. Shanks). Chicago: Callaghan and Co., 1932.

Cases on the Law of Partnership, Joint Stock Associations, Business Trusts, and Other Non-corporate Business Organizations (with Charles E. Clark). St. Paul, Minn.: West Publishing Co., 1932.

Democracy and Finance: The Addresses and Public Statements of William Douglas as Member and Chairman of the S.E.C. (James Allen, ed.). New Haven, Conn.: Yale University Press, 1940.

Being an American (collection of speeches). New York: J. Day Co., 1948.

Democracy Charts Its Course. Gainesville: University of Florida, 1948.

Education for Citizenship and Dialectical Materialism. Los Angeles: Occidental College Press, 1949.

Stare Decisis. New York: Association of Bar of the City of New York, 1949.

Of Men and Mountains. New York: Harper, 1950.

Strange Lands and Friendly People. New York: Harper, 1951.

Beyond the High Himalayas. Garden City, N.Y.: Doubleday, 1952.

North from Malaya: Adventure on Five Fronts. Garden City, N.Y.: Doubleday, 1953.

An Almanac of Liberty. Garden City, N.Y.: Doubleday, 1954.

From Marshall to Mukherjea: Studies in American and Indian Constitutional Law. Calcutta: Eastern Law House Ltd., 1956 (Indian edition of *We the Judges* [1956]).

Russian Journey. Garden City, N.Y.: Doubleday, 1956.

We the Judges: Studies in American and Indian Constitutional Law from Marshall to Mukherjea. Garden City, N.Y.: Doubleday, 1956.

Exploring the Himalaya. New York: Random House, 1958.

The Right of the People. Garden City, N.Y.: Doubleday, 1958.
West of the Indus. Garden City, N.Y.: Doubleday, 1958.
The Mind and Faith of Powell Davies, by Powell Davies (Douglas, ed.). Garden City, N.Y.: Doubleday, 1959.
America Challenged. Princeton, N.J.: Princeton University Press, 1960.
My Wilderness: The Pacific West. Garden City, N.Y.: Doubleday, 1960.
A Living Bill of Rights. Garden City, N.Y.: Doubleday, 1961.
Muir of the Mountains. Boston: Houghton Mifflin, 1961.
My Wilderness: East to Katahdin. Garden City, N.Y.: Doubleday, 1961.
Democracy's Manifesto. Garden City, N.Y.: Doubleday, 1962.
Freedom of the Mind. Garden City, N.Y.: Doubleday, 1962.
The Anatomy of Liberty: The Rights of Man Without Force. New York: Simon and Schuster, 1963.
Mr. Lincoln and the Negroes: The Long Road to Equality. New York: Atheneum, 1963.
A Wilderness Bill of Rights. Boston: Little, Brown, 1965.
The Bible and the Schools. Boston: Little, Brown, 1966.
America Revisits Asia: A Critique of U.S. Policy. New York: City College (City College Papers No. 7), 1967.
Farewell to Texas: A Vanishing Wilderness. New York: McGraw-Hill, 1967.
Towards a Global Federalism. New York: New York University Press, 1968.
The Beautiful Land. New York: Scribner's, 1970 (pictorial book of the United States, with introduction by Douglas).
International Dissent. New York: Random House, 1970.
Points of Rebellion. New York: Random House, 1970.
Holocaust or Hemispheric Co-op: Crosscurrents in Latin America. New York: Random House, 1971.
International Dissent: Six Steps Toward World Peace. New York: Random House, 1971.
The Three Hundred Year War: A Chronicle of Ecological Disaster. New York: Random House, 1972.
Go East Young Man: The Early Years. New York: Random House, 1974.

ARTICLES BY WILLIAM O. DOUGLAS

"Functional Approach to the Law of Business Associations." *Illinois Law Review*, 23:673–82 (March 1929).
"Insulation from Liability Through Subsidiary Corporations" (with Carrol M. Shanks). *Yale Law Journal*, 39:193–218 (December 1929).

"Vicarious Liability and Administration of Risk." *Yale Law Journal*, 38:584–604, 720–45 (March–April 1929).

"Equity Receiverships in the United States District Court for Connecticut, 1920–29" (with J. H. Weir). *Connecticut Bar Journal*, 4:1–30 (January 1930).

"Business Failures Project—a Problem in Methodology" (with W. Clark and D. S. Thomas). *Journal of the National Association of Referees in Bankruptcy*, 5:142–6 (April 1931).

"Business Failures Project—an Analysis of Methods of Investigation" (with D. S. Thomas). *Yale Law Journal*, 40:1034–54 (May 1931).

"A Factual Study of Bankruptcy Administration and Some Suggestions" (with J. H. Marshall). *Columbia Law Review*, 32:25–59 (January 1932).

"Secondary Distribution of Securities, Problems Suggested by *Kinney* v. *Glenny*" (with G. E. Bates). *Yale Law Journal*, 41:949–1004 (May 1932).

"Some Functional Aspects of Bankruptcy." *Yale Law Journal*, 41:329–64 (January 1932).

"Federal Securities Act of 1933" (with G. E. Bates). *Yale Law Journal*, 43:171–217 (December 1933).

"Landlord's Claims in Reorganizations" (with J. Frank). *Yale Law Journal*, 42:1003–50 (May 1933).

"Some Effects of the Securities Act upon Investment Banking" (with G. E. Bates). *University of Chicago Law Review*, 1:283–306 (November 1933).

"Stock 'Brokers' as Agents and Dealers" (with G. E. Bates). *Yale Law Journal*, 43:46–62 (November 1933).

"A Symposium on Credit for the Urban Employee" (with Abe Fortas, W. H. Hamilton, et al.). *Yale Law Journal*, 42:473–642 (February 1933).

"Directors Who Do Not Direct." *Harvard Law Review*, 47:1305–34 (June 1934).

"Protecting the Investor." *Yale Review*, 23:521–33 (March 1934).

"Protective Committee in Railroad Reorganizations." *Harvard Law Review*, 47:565–89 (February 1934).

"The Lawyer and the Federal Securities Act" (address). *Duke Bar Association Journal*, 3:66–71 (Spring 1935).

"Legal Problem of Control over Protective Committees for Municipal and Quasi-Municipal Obligations." *Legal Notes on Local Government*, 2:81–9 (September 1936).

"Securities Acts and the Investment Market." *Vital Speeches of the Day*, 2:715–17 (August 15, 1936).

"Termites of High Finance." *Vital Speeches of the Day*, 3:86–93 (November 15, 1936).

"The Lawyer and Reorganizations" (address). *National Lawyer's Guild Quarterly*, 1:31–7 (December 1937).

"Your Securities: Their Future Protection." *Vital Speeches of the Day*, 3:436–42 (May 1, 1937).

"Improvement in Federal Procedure for Corporate Reorganizations." *American Bar Association Journal*, 24:875–9 (November 1938).

"Scatteration v. Integration of Public Utility Systems." *American Bar Association Journal*, 24:800–6 (October 1938).

"Address." *Texas Law Review*, pp. 81–90 (October 1940).

"The Lawyer and the Public Service" (address). *American Bar Association Journal*, 26:633–6 (August 1940).

"Pre-trial Procedure" (address). *American Bar Association Journal*, 26:693 (August 1940).

"The Bar's Responsibility" (address). *Tennessee Law Review*, 17:49–55 (December 1941).

"Dynamics of Democracy." *Rotarian*, 59:7 (August 1941).

"No Mental Coddling About the War." *Reader's Digest*, 41:1 (September 1942).

"Press Must Be America's Wartime University." *Life*, 13:11–12 (July 13, 1942).

"Challenge to Our Age." *Vital Speeches of the Day*, 10:11–14 (October 15, 1943).

"Silent Millions at the Council Table." *Free World*, 6:545–50 (December 1943).

"A Free Society—at Home and Abroad." *Lawyer's Guild Review*, 4:1–2 (November–December 1944).

"Freedom From and Freedom For." *Free World*, 8:49–52 (July 1944).

"Chief Justice Stone." *Columbia Law Review*, 46:693–5 (September 1946).

"The Lasting Influence of Mr. Justice Brandeis." *Temple Law Quarterly*, 19:361–70 (April 1946).

"Symposium on World Organization" (foreword). *Yale Law Journal*, 55:865–9 (August 1946).

"Harlan Fiske Stone—Teacher." *California Law Review*, 35:4–6 (March 1947).

"Most Important Single Job in the World" (with biographical sketch). *United Nations World*, 1:36–7 (April 1947).

"My Current Reading." *Saturday Review of Literature*, 30:8 (September 27, 1947).

"Democracy Charts Its Course." *University of Florida Law Review*, 1:133–48 (Summer 1948).

"Dissenting Opinion." *Lawyer's Guild Review*, 8:467–9 (November–December 1948).

" 'Law in Eruption': A Concept of Lawyer's Duty in a Time of Change." *American Bar Association Journal*, 34:674–6 (August 1948).

"Liberal Leadership." *New Republic*, 118:11 (June 14, 1948).

"Max Radin." *California Law Review*, 36:163–8 (June 1948).

"Our Bill of Rights." *Vital Speeches of the Day*, 14:238–42 (February 1, 1948).

"Our Bill of Rights" (excerpts). *New Republic*, 118:6 (January 12, 1948).

"Our Political Competence." *Vital Speeches of the Day*, 14:645–9 (August 15, 1948).

"Our Political Competence" (excerpts). *Time*, 51:14 (May 31, 1948).

"Procedural Safeguards in the Bill of Rights." *Journal of the American Judicature Society*, 31:166–70 (April 1948).

"Way to Win Without War." *Reader's Digest*, 53:87–94 (July 1948).

"Dialectical Materialism." *Vital Speeches of the Day*, 15:359–63 (April 1, 1949).

"Human Welfare State." *Survey*, 85:207–10+ (April 1949).

"The Human Welfare State." *University of Pennsylvania Law Review*, 97:597–607 (April 1949).

"Peace Within Our Grasp." *Nation*, 168:497–8 (April 30, 1949).

"*Stare Decisis*." *Columbia Law Review*, 49:735–58 (June 1949).

"*Stare Decisis*." *The Record of the Bar of the City of New York*, 4:152–79 (May 1949).

"People v. Trout: A Majority Opinion." *New York Times Magazine*, pp. 22+ (April 2, 1950).

"Two Boys on a Mountain" (excerpts from *Of Men and Mountains*). *Harper's*, 200:60–5 (April 1950); abridged version, *Reader's Digest*, 56:141–4 (June 1950).

"Baboquivari." *Arizona Highways*, 27:16–25 (April 1951).

"Underhill Moore." *Yale Law School*, 59:187–8 (January 1950).

"Honesty in Government" (address). *Oklahoma Law Review*, 4:279–85 (August 1951).

"How to Win Friends in Asia" (interview). *U.S. News & World Report*, 30:42–5 (June 22, 1951).

"Justice Douglas on Iron" (excerpts from *Strange Lands and Friendly People*). *Life*, 30:120+ (June 18, 1951).

"Recent Trends in Constitutional Law." *Oregon Law Review*, 30:279–88 (June 1951).

"Tennessee Across the World" (address). *Tennessee Law Review*, 21:797–802 (June 1951).

"Way to Win in the East" (with a biographical sketch). *Rotarian*, 78:6–9+

(June 1951).

"America's Power of Ideals" (reprint). *Social Research*, 19:269–76 (September 1952).

"Black Silence of Fear." *New York Times Magazine*, pp. 7+ (January 13, 1952).

"How to Win Peace with Point Four." *Newsweek*, 40:42 (July 7, 1952).

"My Favorite Vacation Land." *American Magazine*, 154:38–41+ (July 1952).

"New Law Review." *Utah Law Review*, 3:1–2 (Spring 1952).

"Power of Righteousness." *New Republic*, 126:9–13 (April 28, 1952).

"Revolution Is Our Business." *Nation*, 174:516–19 (May 31, 1952).

"We Are Losing Asia." *United Asia*, 4(3):142–4 (1952).

"A Wedge of Freedom in a One-Party State." *Reporter*, pp. 9–12 (February 5, 1952).

"World in Revolution." *New Republic*, 124:9–11 (March 12, 1951).

"World's Most Amazing Horses." *Science Digest*, 32:17–21 (October 1952).

"Address Before the American Law Institute, Washington, D.C., May 20, 1853." *Lawyer's Guild Review*, 13:145–8 (Winter 1953).

"Communists Here and Abroad." *U.S. News & World Report*, 35:110–12 (December 4, 1953).

"Essence of Due Process." *Vital Speeches of the Day*, 19:554–7 (July 1, 1953).

"Hard Unpartisan Thought." *New Republic*, 128:18 (May 25, 1953).

"Indo-China: A House Divided." *Reader's Digest*, 62:144–8 (March 1953).

"Man Who Saved the Philippines." *Reader's Digest*, 62:91–4 (January 1953).

"Some Antecedents of the Due Process." *American Bar Association Journal*, 39:871–5 (October 1953); *Notre Dame Lawyer*, 28:497–508 (Summer 1953).

"Too Many Shortcuts." *New Republic*, 129:9–11 (November 23, 1953).

"Douglas v. Felix." *Outdoor Life*, 113:24–5+ (January 1954).

"French Are Facing Disaster Again in Morocco." *Look*, 18:33–7 (October 19, 1954).

"High Adventure." *Saturday Review*, 37:18 (November 13, 1954).

"Jiberabu." *Colliers*, 134:28–31 (November 26, 1954).

"Light on the Lama." *Saturday Review*, 37:19 (March 6, 1954).

"Bill of Rights, Due Process, and Federalism in India." *Minnesota Law Review*, 40:1 (December 1955).

"Curmudgeon Goes to War." *Saturday Review*, 38:33+ (January 22, 1955).

"In Memoriam: George H. Dession" (Douglas et al.). *Buffalo Law Review*, 5:3 (Fall 1955).

"Independence and Survival." *Saturday Review*, 38:10–11 (April 23, 1955).

"Soviet Colonialism, Product of Terror." *Look*, 19:35–43 (December 13, 1955).

"Wilderness Trails of the Pacific Northwest." *Mademoiselle*, 40:140–1+ (April 1955).

"Durham Rule: A Meeting Ground for Lawyers and Psychiatrists." *Iowa Law Review*, 41:485 (Summer 1956).

"Impressions of a Visit to the Soviet Union." *United Asia*, 8:390–5 (December 1956).

"Interposition and the *Peters* Case, 1778–1809." *Federal Rules Decisions*, 19:185 (September 1956); *Stanford Law Review*, 9:3 (December 1956).

"Man's Inhumanity to Land." *American Forests*, 62:9 (May 1956).

"Mr. Justice Black—a Symposium" (foreword). *Yale Law Journal*, 65:449 (February 1956).

"Quiet Revolutionist." *Saturday Review*, 39:18 (June 2, 1956).

"Religion in the Godless State." *Look*, 20:11–16 (January 10, 1956).

"Understanding of Asia." *Rotarian*, 89:8–10+ (December 1956).

"War or Peace." *Look*, 20:66–73 (January 24, 1956).

"America's Ace in Asia." *Progressive*, 21:8–11 (March 1957).

"Asian Revolutions" (address, January 26, 1957). *Vital Speeches of the Day*, 23:272–4 (February 15, 1957).

"Down the River Rapids." *Look*, 21:106–10 (May 14, 1957).

"Jerome N. Frank." *University of Chicago Law Review*, 24:625 (Summer 1957); *Journal of Legal Education*, 10:1 (1957).

"Hazards to Liberty." *Decalogue Journal*, 7:1 (June 1957).

"Unlimited Horizons for Free Expression: The Right to Be Let Alone." *Progressive*, 21:7–10 (December 1957); 22:12–15 (January 1958).

"West from the Khyber Pass." *National Geographic Magazine*, 114:1–44 (July 1958).

"Books Break Barriers." *Wilson Library Bulletin*, 33:473–6 (March 1959).

"From Justice Douglas: A Dissent; Excerpts from Opinion." *U.S. News & World Report*, 47:143 (November 23, 1959).

"*In Forma Pauperis* Practice in the United States." *New Hampshire Bar Journal*, 2:5 (October 1959).

"Means and the End." *Washington University Law Quarterly*, 1959: 103 (April 1959).

"On Misconception of the Judicial Function and the Responsibility of the

Bar." *Columbia Law Review*, 59:227 (February 1959).

"Role of the Lawyer." *Oklahoma Law Review*, 12:1 (February 1959).

"Seekers of the Farthest Reaches." *Saturday Review*, 42:17 (February 28, 1959).

"Station-Wagon Odyssey: Baghdad to Istanbul." *National Geographic Magazine*, 115:48–87 (January 1959).

"Symposium on the Securities and Exchange Commission" (foreword). *George Washington Law Review*, 28:1 (October 1959).

"Arizona's New Judicial Article." *Arizona Law Review*, 2:159 (Winter 1960).

"Dissent in Favor of Man." *Saturday Review*, 43:59–60 (May 7, 1960).

"Mr. Justice Cardozo." *Michigan Law Review*, 58:549–56 (February 1960).

"Public Trial and the Free Press." *American Bar Association Journal*, 46:840 (August 1960); *Rocky Mountain Law Review*, 33:1 (December 1960).

"Russia and the Superman Myth." *Saturday Review*, 43:17–19+ (October 15, 1960).

"Supreme Court and Its Case Load." *Cornell Law Quarterly*, 45:401–14 (Spring 1960).

"Vagrancy and Arrest on Suspicion." *Yale Law Journal*, 70:1 (November 1960).

"Friendly Huts of the White Mountains." *National Geographic Magazine*, 120:202–39 (August 1961).

"My Island" (excerpts from *My Wilderness: East to the Katahdin*). *Saturday Evening Post*, 234:20–1+ (August 19, 1961).

"Right to Counsel: A Foreword." *Minnesota Law Review*, 45:693 (April 1961).

"Towards a Rule of Law in World Affairs." *Saturday Review*, 44:19–21+ (March 11, 1961).

"U.S. and the Revolutionary Spirit." *Saturday Review*, 44:17–19+ (June 10, 1961).

"Dedication: Charles Evans Whittaker: The Supreme Court Years." *Texas Law Review*, 40:742 (June 1962).

"Journey to Outer Mongolia." *National Geographic Magazine*, 121:289–345 (March 1962).

"Karl N. Llewellyn" (Douglas, Clark, et al.). *University of Chicago Law Review*, 29:611 (Summer 1962).

"Law and the American Character." *Journal of the State Bar of California*, 37:753 (September–October 1962).

"Law Day—U.S.A. 1962" (Clark, Harlan, and Douglas). *Connecticut Bar Journal*, 36:4 (March 1962).

"Lawyers of the Peace Corps." *American Bar Association Journal*, 48:909–13 (October 1962).

"People of Cades Cove." *National Geographic Magazine*, 122:60–95 (July 1962).

"Sewage Treatment Plants, Not Dams" (address). *National Parks Magazine*, 36:14–15 (March 1962).

"Visit with Tito" (interview, ed. by Douglas). *Look*, 26:23–5 (February 13, 1962).

"Walk in the Woods." *Redbook*, 119:44–7 (May 1962).

"Bill of Rights and the Free Society: An Individual View." *Buffalo Law Review*, 13:1 (Fall 1963).

"Bill of Rights Is Not Enough." *New York University Law Review*, 38:207 (April 1963).

"Freedom Declining? Jurist Says Yes" (excerpts from interview). *U.S. News & World Report*, 54:14 (January 14, 1963).

"The Erosion of Liberty" (address). *New Politics*, 2:16–18 (Fall 1963).

"Judge Clark." *Yale Law Journal*, 73:1 (November 1963).

"Right of Association." *Columbia Law Review*, 63:1361–83 (December 1963).

"Wesley A. Sturges: In Memoriam." *Yale Law Journal*, 72:639 (March 1963).

"Why We Must Save the Allagash." *Field and Stream*, 68:24–9+ (July 1963).

"America's Vanishing Wilderness." *Ladies' Home Journal*, 81:37–41+ (July 1964); abridged version, "To Preserve America's Glories," *Reader's Digest*, 86:146–54 (January 1965).

"Archeologist on an Oriental Journey." *Saturday Review*, 47:59 (November 14, 1964).

"Banks Island: Eskimo Life on the Polar Sea." *National Geographic Magazine*, 125:702–35 (May 1964).

"In Honor of Adolph A. Berle; Dedication." *Columbia Law Review*, 64:1371 (December 1964).

"Animal Man Needs to Hike." *New York Times Magazine*, pp. 34–5 (March 21, 1965).

"Excerpts from the Opinion of the Court, June 7, 1965." *Congressional Digest*, 44:222–3 (August 1965).

"Land Despoiled." *Holiday*, 38:171–4 (October 1965).

"Law and Survival" (address). *Vital Speeches of the Day*, 31:400–3 (April 15, 1965).

"Law Reviews and Full Disclosure." *Washington Law Review*, 40:227 (June 1965).

"North River, Town of Norwell, Plymouth County, Mass." *Bulletin of the*

Atomic Scientists, 21:11 (May 1965).

"Phil S. Gibson." *Law in Transition Quarterly*, 2:129 (Summer 1965).

"Rule of Law in World Affairs." *Kansas Law Review*, 13:473 (May 1965); *Washington Law Review*, 40:673 (October 1965).

"Our Wilderness Rights Are Missing" (excerpt from *A Wilderness Bill of Rights*) (ed. by R. D. Butcher). *Audubon Magazine*, 68:85 (March 1966).

"Amen, Mr. Justice." *American Forests*, 73:30–1+ (November 1967); 74:2 (February 1968).

"The Attack on the Right to Privacy." *Playboy*, 14:189+ (December 1967).

"Computerized Man." *Vital Speeches of the Day*, 33:700–4 (September 1, 1967).

"Discurso." *Revista del Colegio Abogados de Puerto Rico*, 27:485 (August 1967).

"Is the War Legal?" (Two justices pose questions: summary of testimony). *U.S. News & World Report*, 63:16 (November 20, 1967).

"C&O Canal as a National Historic Park." *Parks and Recreation*, 3:24–6+ (April 1968).

"Computerization of Government Files: What Impact on the Individual?" *U.C.L.A. Law Review*, 15:1371 (September 1968).

"Dedication to Chief Justice Earl Warren." *Nebraska Law Review*, 48:3 (November 1968).

"Future Lawyer's Role in Solving Local and International Problems." *University of San Fernando Valley Law Review*, 1:101 (January 1968).

"An Inquest on Our Lakes and Rivers." *Playboy*, 15:96–8, 177–81 (June 1968).

"Juvenile Courts and Due Process of Law." *Juvenile Court Judges Journal*, 19:9 (Spring 1968).

"Living Under Our Bill of Rights." *Soundings*, 51:390–401 (Winter 1968).

"Reflections on International Human Rights." *Columbia Forum*, 11:8–12 (Winter 1968).

"Their Glory Is in Danger." *Holiday*, 43:65 (May 1968).

"Civil Liberties: The Crucial Issue." *Playboy*, 16:93+ (January 1969).

"Federal Courts and the Democratic System." *Alabama Law Review*, 21:179–90 (Spring 1969).

"The Public Be Damned." *Playboy*, 16:143 (July 1969).

"Conservation of Man." *Journal of Public Law*, 19:3–12 (1970).

"Managing the Docket of the Supreme Court of the United States." *Record of the Association of the Bar of the City of New York*, 25:279 (May 1970).

"Points of Rebellion" (excerpt from *Points of Rebellion*). *Playboy*, 17:163–4+ (January 1970).

"Press and First Amendment Rights." *Idaho Law Review*, 7:1 (Spring 1970).

"Redress and Revolution." *Evergreen Review*, 77:41–43+ (April 1970).

"Some Dicta on Discrimination." *Loyola University of Los Angeles Law Review*, 3:207 (April 1970).

"C&O Canal Becomes a Park." *National Parks & Conservation Magazine*, 45:4–8 (May 1971).

"Environmental Problems of the Oceans; the Need for International Controls." *Environmental Law*, 1:149–66 (Spring 1971).

"In Honor of Chief Justice Stanley H. Fuld" (Douglas et al.). *Columbia Law Review*, 71:531 (April 1971).

Symposium on International Protection of the Environment, "Pollution: An International Problem Needing International Solution." *Texas International Law Journal*, 7:1 (Summer 1971).

"Future of Law in a Multicultural World." *Political Science Quarterly*, 87(1):90 (1972).

"Grand Design of the Constitution." *Gonzaga Law Review*, 7:239 (Spring 1972) (the inaugural address in the William O. Douglas Lecture Series at Gonzaga University).

"Justice Brennan as a Jurist." *Rutgers Camden Law Journal*, 4:5 (Fall 1972).

"Mr. Justice Douglas, Dissenting." *Living Wilderness*, 36:19–29 (Summer 1972).

"Samuel M. Chapin." *California Western Law Review*, 8:185 (Winter 1972).

"Symposium: Law and Technology. Preface." *Southern California Law Review*, 45:i (Spring 1972).

"Freight Train to Optimism" (interview, ed. D. Beckwith). *Time*, 102:93 (November 12, 1973).

"Harlan Fiske Stone Centennial Lecture: The Meaning of Due Process." *Columbia Journal of Law and Social Problems*, 10:1–14 (Fall 1973).

"Liberty—John Stuart Mill." *Journal of Social Issues*, 29(3):227 (1973).

"Nature's Constitutional Rights." *North American Review*, 258:11–14 (Spring 1973).

"Remarks of Associate Justice William O. Douglas." *Rutgers Law Review*, 28:616–24 (Winter 1975).

"Remarks on Law Day 1973." *Syracuse Law Review*, 24:1209–15 (1973).

"Symposium: The Denver Public Defender: Forword." *Denver Law Journal*, 50:1 (1973).

"Toward Greater Vitality." *Today's Health*, 51:54–7 (May 1973).

"Dedication to Ernest Gruening" (Douglas et al.). *U.C.L.A.-Alaska Law*

Reviews, 4:1–11 (Fall 1974).

"In Honor of Fred Rodell: Foreword." *Yale Law Journal*, 84:1–8 (November 1974).

"Tribute: Simon E. Sobeloff" (by Warren Burger, Douglas et al.). *Maryland Law Review*, 34:483–540 (1974).

"World of Earl Warren—as Chief Justice." *American Bar Association Journal*, 60:1228–36 (October 1974).

"First Amendment and the Media: Chaos on the Citizens Band—Regulatory Solutions for Spectrum Pollution" (Douglas' article is the last of the series). *Hastings Law Journal*, 26:631–821 (January 1975).

BOOKS AND STUDIES ABOUT WILLIAM O. DOUGLAS

Brownfeld, Allan C. *Dossier on Douglas*. Washington, D.C.: New Majority Book Club, 1970.

Countryman, Vernon (ed.). *Douglas of the Supreme Court; a Selection of His Opinions*. Garden City, N.Y.: Doubleday, 1959.

_____. *The Judicial Record of Justice: William O. Douglas*. Cambridge, Mass.: Harvard University Press, 1974.

_____. *The Douglas Opinions*. New York: Random House, 1977.

Evans, Luther Harris. *Writings By and About William O. Douglas*. New York: Columbia Law Library International and Legal Collections, 1965.

Hopkirk, John William. "William O. Douglas—Individualist: A Study in the Development and Application of a Judge's Attitudes." Unpublished Ph.D. dissertation, Princeton University, 1958.

James, Dorothy Buckton. "Judicial Philosophy and Accession to the Court: The Cases of Justices Jackson and Douglas." Unpublished Ph.D. dissertation, Columbia University, 1966.

Hoyt, Edwin P. *William O. Douglas: A Biography*. Middlebury, Vt.: Eriksson, 1978.

McBride, H. E. *Impeach Justice Douglas*. New York; Exposition Press, 1971.

Meek, Roy Lee. "Justices Douglas and Black: Political Liberalism Judicial Activism." Unpublished Ph.D. dissertation, University of Oregon, 1964.

Oddo, Gilbert Lawrence. *Mr. Justice Douglas and the Roosevelt Court*. Washington, D.C., 1952.

_____. *The Judicial Opinions of Mr. Justice Douglas Concerning the Question of Civil Liberty*. Washington, D.C., 1950.

Pollock, Paul King. "Judicial Libertarianism and Judicial Responsibilities:

The Case of Justice William O. Douglas." Unpublished Ph.D. disser-
    tation, Cornell University, 1968.
Resnik, Solomon. "Black and Douglas: Variations in Dissent." Unpublished
    Ph.D. dissertation, New School for Social Research, 1970.
Rodell, Fred. *Woe unto You Lawyers!* New York: Reynal & Hitchcock,
    1939.
Williams, Julian E. *The Case Against William O. Douglas*. Tulsa, Okla.:
    Christian Crusade Publications, 1970.
Wolfman, Bernard, et al. *Dissent Without Opinion: The Behavior of Justice
    William O. Douglas in the Federal Tax Cases*. Philadelphia: Uni-
    versity of Pennsylvania Press, 1975.

BOOKS HAVING SIGNIFICANT REFERENCES TO WILLIAM O. DOUGLAS

Asch, Sidney H. *Supreme Court and Its Greatest Justices*. New York: Arco,
    1971. Pp. 204–17.
Brant, Irving. *Impeachment: Trials and Errors*. New York: Knopf, 1972. Pp.
    84–121.
Frank, John Paul. *The Warren Court*. New York: Macmillan, 1964. Pp.
    57–76.
Hazeltine, Alice Isabel. *We Grew Up in America: Stories of American Youth
    Told by Themselves*. New York: Abingdon Press, 1954. Pp. 207–14.
Lash, Joseph P. *From the Diaries of Felix Frankfurter*. New York: W. W.
    Norton & Co., 1975. Pp. 309–38.
McCune, Wesley. *The Nine Young Men*. New York: Harper, 1947. Pp.
    116–27.
Rodell, Fred. *Nine Men*. New York: Random House, 1955. Pp. 273–77.

ARTICLES AND ESSAYS ABOUT WILLIAM O. DOUGLAS

Wisehart, M. K. "Have You the Right to Be in Business?" (interview).
    American Magazine, 110:26–7 (August 1930).
Creel, G. "Young Man Went East." *Collier's*, 97:9+ (May 9, 1936).
"Portrait." *Business Week*, p. 46 (January 25, 1936).
"Portrait." *Fortune*, 13:198 (March 1936).
"Portrait." *Time*, 27:51 (June 29, 1936).
"Walla Walla to Washington." *Time*, 27:50 (January 27, 1936).
"Bill and Billy." *Time*, 30:61–2+ (October 11, 1937).
"Cynic on Grumpsters; Remaking the Country's Investment Business."
    Time, 29:71 (April 5, 1937).

"Douglas Heads S.E.C." *Business Week*, p. 60 (September 25, 1937).

"Financing Reforms Under Fire; Investment Bankers Cite S.E.C.'s Own Rules Against Douglas." *Business Week*, p. 34 (April 3, 1937).

Lerner, M. "Wall Street's New Mentor." *Nation*, 145:429–32 (October 23, 1937).

"New Chairman of the S.E.C." *Nation's Business*, 25:94 (November 1937).

"New S.E.C. Chairman a Pretty Conservative Fellow." *Newsweek*, 10:37 (October 4, 1937).

"People." *Review of Reviewers*, 95:24 (May 1937).

"S.E.C.'s New Chairman." *Literary Digest*, 124:33 (October 9, 1937).

"Wall Street Cop." *Scholastic*, 31:28 (October 30, 1937).

Britt, G. "Wall Street vs. Washington." *Literary Digest*, 125:12–13 (January 29, 1938).

Flynn, J. T. "Washing Wall Street's Face" (interview). *Collier's*, 101:12–13+ (January 29, 1938).

"Portrait." *Business Week*, p. 16 (July 2, 1938).

"Portrait." *Fortune*, 18:162 (December 1938).

"Portrait." *Newsweek*, 11:35 (May 30, 1938).

"Portrait." *Newsweek*, 12:37 (August 1, 1938).

"Portrait." *Time*, 31:59 (June 13, 1938).

Rodell, F. "Douglas Over the Stock Exchange." *Fortune*, 17:64–5+ (February 1938).

Childs, M. W. "Mr. Justice Douglas." *Reader's Digest*, 34:58–60 (June 1939).

"Douglas, Jurist; Appointment to Supreme Court Puts Hard Hitter on the Bench." *Newsweek*, 13:13 (March 27, 1939).

"Exchanges Wonder About S.E.C.; Chairman Douglas' Sharp Rejection of Their Suggestion." *Business Week*, p. 17 (March 25, 1939).

"No Monkey Business." *Time*, 33:12–13 (March 27, 1939).

"Nominated to Supreme Court." *Christian Century*, 56:405 (March 29, 1939).

"Portrait." *Fortune*, 19:122 (January 1939).

"Portrait." *Christian Science Monitor Magazine*, p. 7 (April 8, 1939).

"S.E.C. Head Named to High Court; Rebuffs Brokers." *Scholastic*, 34:11 (April 1, 1939).

Smith, B. "Tamer of Bulls and Bears." *American Magazine*, 127:20+ (May 1939).

"Portrait." *Business Week*, p. 44 (November 30, 1940).

"Portrait." *New York Times Magazine*, p. 9 (February 18, 1940).

Janeway, E. "Bill Douglas, Fighter." *Nation*, 152:48–50 (January 11, 1941).

"Portrait." *Time*, 37:15 (March 10, 1941).

Alexander, J. "Washington's Angry Scotsman." *Saturday Evening Post*, 215:9–10+ (October 17, 1942).

"At Home with Two Justices of the United States Supreme Court." *House & Garden*, 82:13 (August 1942).

Neurberger, R. L. "Mr. Justice Douglas." *Harper's Magazine*, 185:312–21 (August 1942).

_____. "Much-Discussed Bill Douglas." *New York Times Magazine*, pp. 10–11 (April 19, 1942).

"*United States* v. *Pink*; Text of Decision in the First Russian Insurance Company Case." *American Journal of International Law*, 36:309–24 (April 1942).

"Meet Supreme Court Justice Douglas' Family of Washington, D.C." *Ladies' Home Journal*, 60:99–102+ (March 1943).

"Portrait." *Time*, 41:66 (March 29, 1943).

"Portrait." *Time*, 43:81 (January 17, 1944).

Rodell, F. "Bill Douglas: American." *American Mercury*, 61:656–65 (December 1945).

Fraser, H. R. "Bill Douglas: American; Reply." *American Mercury*, 62:251 (February 1946).

"Superseniority." *U.S. News & World Report*, 20:39 (June 7, 1946).

Marx, H. L., Jr. "Youngest of the Nine Mr. Justices." *Senior Scholastic*, 51:20 (October 13, 1947).

Schlesinger, A. M., Jr. "Supreme Court: 1947." *Fortune*, 35:73–9+ (January 1947).

Bendiner, R. "Putting Douglas on Ice." *Nation*, 166:650–1 (June 12, 1948).

"Bonfire." *Time*, 51:22 (January 26, 1948).

Fuller, H. "Douglas: Issue of Principle." *New Republic*, 118:10–12 (June 14, 1948).

Janeway, E. "Ideas of the Future." *Saturday Review of Literature*, 31:15–16 (August 21, 1948).

"Jurist's Political Lure." *U.S. News & World Report*, 24:37 (January 30, 1948).

"Portrait." *Life*, 25:37 (December 6, 1948).

Weschler, J. A. "Douglas: The Best Hope." *Nation*. 167:34–6 (July 10, 1948).

"Biographical Note." *U.S. News & World Report*, 27:20 (August 5, 1949).

Epstein, L. D. "Economic Predilections of Justice Douglas." *Wisconsin Law Review*, 1949:531–62 (May 1949).

"Have We Lost the Peace? Japanese Convicted in War Crime Trials." *Christian Century*, 66:838–9 (July 13, 1949).

"Life Congratulates." *Life*, 27:55 (December 5, 1949).

"Portrait." *New York Times Magazine*, p. 12 (September 18, 1949).

"Portrait." *Time*, 54:30 (November 28, 1949).

"With Justice Douglas in Iran." *Life*, 27:59–61 (August 15, 1949).

Lerner, M. "Supreme Court." *Holiday*, 7:82 (February 1950).

Morse, R. "Justice in the Wallowas." *Christian Science Monitor Magazine*, p. 10 (April 8, 1950).

"Named Father of the Year." *Publisher's Weekly*, 157:2297 (May 27, 1950).

"Portrait." *Newsweek*, 35:28 (April 3, 1950).

Sanderson, I. T. "Memories of a Supreme Court Justice." *Saturday Review of Literature*, 33:53 (April 15, 1950).

Coon, C. S. "Justice on Horseback." *Nation*, 173: 476–8 (December 1, 1951).

"Digs at Douglas." *Newsweek*, 38:27 (September 10, 1951).

Epstein, L. D. "Justice Douglas and Civil Liberties." *Wisconsin Law Review*, 1951:125–57 (January 1951).

"People of the Week." *U.S. News & World Report*, 31:50+ (September 14, 1951).

"Portrait." *Saturday Review of Literature*, 34:17 (November 10, 1951).

"William, Meet Julius." *Time*, 58:33 (September 17, 1951).

"Justice Douglas Is Available." *Nation*, 174:73 (January 26, 1952).

"Justice Travels." *Newsweek*, 40:116+ (September 22, 1952).

"Laughter Award." *Publisher's Weekly*, 162:240 (July 19, 1952).

"Our Readers Prefer Bill Douglas." *Nation*, 174:444–5 (May 10, 1952).

"People of the Week." *U.S. News & World Report*, 32:49 (May 16, 1952).

Rodell, F. "I'd Prefer Bill Douglas." *Nation*, 174:400–2 (April 26, 1952).

"Crime and Punishment of Julius and Ethel Rosenberg." *New Republic*, 128:6 (June 29, 1953).

"A Crusade for the Bar." *American Bar Association Journal*, 39:871–5 (October 1953).

Irish, M. D. "Mr. Justice Douglas and Judicial Restraint." *University of Florida Law Review*, 6:537–53 (Winter 1953).

"Justice Douglas and the Rosenberg Case." *Commonweal*, 58:312–13 (July 3, 1953).

"A New Voice for America." *Progressive*, 17:6–9 (November 1953).

"Off the Cuff; Talk at National Book Awards Gathering." *New Yorker*, 28:21–2 (February 7, 1953).

"Portrait." *Illustrated London News*, 222:1095 (June 27, 1953).

"Portrait." *Saturday Review*, 36:13 (June 20, 1953).

"Portrait." *Saturday Review*, 36:15 (June 27, 1953).

"Portrait." *U.S. News & World Report*, 34:32 (June 26, 1953).

"Portrait." *U.S. News & World Report*, 35:38 (September 18, 1953).

"C&O Walkathon." *American Forests*, 60:18–19+ (May 1954).

"End of the Trial." *Time*, 63:21 (April 5, 1954).

"Justice Douglas, Journalists Debate C&O Canal Plans on 189-Mile Hike."
    American Forests, 60:42 (April 1954).

"Solitary Dissent: Chesapeake and Ohio Canal Parkway." *Time*, 63:15
    (February 1, 1954).

"Woods Walkers." *Time*, 63:20 (March 29, 1954).

"Dissenter on the Bench and on World Policy Too." *U.S. News & World Report*, 38:78+ (February 11, 1955).

"People." *Time*, 66:37 (July 18, 1955).

"People of the Week." *U.S. News & World Report*, 38:16 (March 11, 1955).

"Justice Douglas: Headline Hunter." *American Mercury*, 83:121–6 (August 1956).

Kunitz, J. "Justice Douglas on Russian Imperialism." *Monthly Review*, 8:273–82 (December 1956).

Mandel, S. "Biographical Sketch." *Saturday Review*, 39:12 (June 9, 1956).

"Photo That Caused Trouble." *U.S. News & World Report*, 41:20 (December 7, 1956).

"Portrait." *Saturday Review*, 39:16 (February 4, 1956).

"Portrait." *U.S. News & World Report*, 40:66 (June 15, 1956).

"Soviet Safari." *Time*, 67:110+ (June 11, 1956).

"Travelers in the Russian Backlands." *U.S. News & World Report*, 39:16 (August 5, 1956).

"Travelling Judge." *Newsweek*, 47:122 (June 11, 1956).

"Nine Justices." *Time*, 70:12 (July 1, 1957).

"Warren Court." *Life*, 43:35 (July 1, 1957).

Cohen, W. "Justice Douglas: A Law Clerk's View." *University of Chicago Law Review*, 26 (Autumn 1958).

Lewis, A. "Portraits of Nine Men Under Attack." *New York Times Magazine*, p. 14 (May 18, 1958).

"Portrait." *Saturday Review*, 41:14 (January 18, 1958).

Rodell, F. "Gallery of Justices." *Saturday Review*, 41:9–11+ (November 15, 1958).

———. "Justice Douglas: An Anniversary Fragment for a Friend." *University of Chicago Law Review*, 26:2 (Autumn 1958).

Bickel, A. M., Jr. "Justices on Display." *New Republic*, 141:20–1 (September 14, 1959).

"New Look at the Warren Court." *U.S. News & World Report*, 47:75 (July 13, 1959).

Harris, S. J. "Justice Pleads for Excellence." *Saturday Review*, 43:21 (July 2, 1960).

Smith, E. W. "Jake's Rangers vs. the Supreme Court." *Field & Stream*, 65:44–6+ (May 1960).

"Horace Marden Albright Medal Awarded to Justice Douglas." *National Parks Magazine*, 35:10 (April 1961).

Smith, E. W. "Douglas Down the Allagash." *Field & Stream*, 66:41–3+ (May 1961).

"C.I.A. Secrecy Under Fire; Justice Douglas Is Critical." *U.S. News & World Report*, 53:12 (December 24, 1962).

"Douglas v. Black: Old Friends Fall Out." *U.S. News & World Report*, 54:20 (June 17, 1963).

"Greatest Honor, Says Justice Douglas of Audubon Medal." *Audubon Magazine*, 65:113 (March 1963).

Resnik, S. "Black and Douglas: Variations in Dissent." *Western Political Quarterly*, 16:305–22 (June 1963).

"Sequel to Springtime: Marriage to Joan Martin." *Time*, 82:17 (August 16, 1963).

"Third Wife for Justice Douglas." *U.S. News & World Report*, 55:16 (August 19, 1963).

Black, H. L. "William Orville Douglas." *Yale Law Journal*, 73:915+ (May 1964).

Countryman, V. "The Constitution and Job Discrimination." *Washington Law Review*, 39 (Spring 1964).

Fortas, A. "Mr. Justice Douglas." *Yale Law Journal*, 73 (May 1964).

Jennings, R. W. "Mr. Justice Douglas: His Influence on Corporate and Securities Regulation." *Yale Law Journal*, 73 (May 1964).

Linde, H. "Justice Douglas on Freedom in the Welfare State." *Washington Law Review*, 39 (Spring 1964).

Louisell, D. W. "The Man and the Mountain: Douglas on Religious Freedom." *Yale Law Journal*, 73:975–98 (May 1964).

Manning, L. F. "The Douglas Concept of God in Government." *Washington Law Review*, 39 (Spring 1964).

"The Other Eight—Libertarian vs. Conservative." *Newsweek*, 63:27 (May 11, 1964).

Warren, E. "Introduction—a Tribute to Justice Douglas." *Washington Law Review*, 39 (Spring 1964).

Williams, J. S. "Critique of 'the Constitution and Job Discrimination.' " *Washington Law Review*, 39 (Spring 1964).

"Dangerous Climb: Storm Traps Justice Douglas." *U.S. News & World Report*, 58:16 (March 1, 1965).

"Emanations from a Penumbra." *Time*, 85:47–8 (June 18, 1965).

"For Justice Douglas, a Third Divorce Suit." *U.S. News & World Report*, 59:11 (December 27, 1965).

Hopkirk, J. W. "William O. Douglas—His Work in Policing Bankruptcy Proceedings." *Vanderbilt Law Review*, 18:663 (March 1965).

Kauper, P. G. "Penumbras, Peripheries, Emanations, Things Fundamental and Things Forgotten: The *Griswold* Case." *Michigan Law Review*, 64:235+ (December 1965).

Linde, H. A. "Constitutional Rights in the Public Sector: Justice Douglas on Liberty in the Welfare State." *Washington Law Review*, 40:10 (April 1965).

Ritter, C. "Walkin' and Hollerin'." *American Forests*, 71:6–7+ (June 1965).

Thomas, H. S. "Justice William O. Douglas and the Concept of a 'Fair Trial.' " *Vanderbilt Law Review*, 18:701 (March 1965).

Ace, G. "Boy Meets Girl." *Saturday Review*, 49:6 (August 13, 1966).

Beaney, W. M. "The *Griswold* Case and the Expanding Right to Privacy." *Wisconsin Law Review*, 1966:979+ (Fall 1966).

"Honeymooners." *Newsweek*, 68:21 (August 1, 1966).

North, S. "Justice Douglas' Twenty-three Year Old Bride Talks About Her Marriage." *Ladies' Home Journal*, 83:92+ (November 1966).

Ostrow, R. J. "New Controversy Involving Justice Douglas" (reprint from *Los Angeles Times*, October 16, 1966; and excerpts from address by J. J. Williams, October 17, 1966). *U.S. News & World Report*, 61:66–8 (October 31, 1966).

"People of the Week—Justice Douglas Weds Fourth Time." *U.S. News & World Report*, 61:12 (August 1, 1966).

Romero, P. "A Look at Supreme Court Justice William O. Douglas." *Negro History Bulletin*, 29:129–30+ (March 1966).

"September Song." *Time*, 88:17 (July 29, 1966).

Gross, H. "The Concept of Privacy." *New York University Law Review*, 42:34+ (March 1967).

"Profiles of the Nine Justices." *Senior Scholastic*, 91:36 (October 5, 1967).

"Shift in the Supreme Court; What One Justice Can Mean." *U.S. News & World Report*, 62:67–8 (April 24, 1967).

"As Fortas Court Will Look: A Report on All Nine Justices." *U.S. News & World Report*, 65:33 (July 8, 1968).

"Help for the Heart of an Active Justice." *U.S. News & World Report*, 64:14+ (June 24, 1968).

Countryman, V. "Justice Douglas: Expositer of the Bankruptcy Law." *U.C.L.A. Law Review*, 16 (June 1969).

Deedy, J. "Political Pornography." *Commonweal*, 91:266 (November 28, 1969).

Deschin, J. "Justice Douglas as a Contest Judge." *Popular Photography*, 65:28+ (September 1969).

Frank, J. P. "William O. Douglas." In Friedman, L., and Israel, F. L., eds., *The Justices of the United States Supreme Court, 1789–1969: Their Lives and Major Opinions*. 4 vols. New York: Chelsea House in association with Bowker (1969). Vol. 4, pp. 2247–490.

"Justice Douglas Quits Foundation." *U.S. News & World Report*, 66:8 (June 2, 1969).

"Justice Douglas' Letter." *Newsweek*, 73:36–7 (June 9, 1969).

Karst, K. L. "Invidious Discrimination: Justice Douglas and the Return of the 'Natural-Law-Due-Process Formula.' " *U.C.L.A. Law Review*, 16:716+ (June 1969).

"Now, Douglas' Dealings." *Time*, 93:23 (June 6, 1969).

"Outside Income." *New Republic*, 160:5–6 (June 7, 1969).

"Parvin Who?" *Newsweek*, 73:72 (June 2, 1969).

Rodell, F. "As Justice Douglas Completes His First Thirty Years on the Court: Herewith a Random Anniversary Sample, Complete with Casual Commentary, of Diverse Scraps, Shreds, and Shards Gleaned from a Forty-Year Friendship." *U.C.L.A. Law Review*, 16:704+ (June 1969).

Van Alstyne, W. W. "The Constitutional Rights of Public Employees: A Commentary on the Inappropriate Use of an Old Analogy." *U.C.L.A. Law Review*, 16 (June 1969).

Warren, E., and Cohen, W. "Mr. Justice Douglas: Three Decades of Service." *U.C.L.A. Law Review*, 16:699 (June 1969).

Crawford, K. "Impeach Douglas?" *Newsweek*, 75:37 (May 4, 1970).

"Crude Plot: Crude Plotters: Impeachment Move." *Nation*, 210:483–4 (April 27, 1970).

"Douglas Case." *Time*, 95:78 (May 11, 1970).

"Douglas Dossier." *Newsweek*, 75:29–30+ (April 27, 1970).

Forkosch, M. D. "The 'Rebellion' of William O. Douglas." *Georgia Law Review*, 4:830 (Summer 1970).

Haag, E. van den, "Here Comes Da Judge." *Georgia Law Review*, 4 (Summer 1970).

Hook, S. "Points of Confusion." *Encounter*, 35:45–6+ (September 1970).

"Impeach Douglas?" *Time*, 95:21–2 (April 27, 1970).

"Impeaching Justice Douglas" (with excerpts from address by G. R. Ford). *U.S. News & World Report*, 68:25–6+ (April 27, 1970).

"House Committee Studies Charges Against Douglas." *Congressional*

Quarterly Weekly Report, 28:2786–9 (November 13, 1970).

"Justice Douglas and the Supreme Court." *America*, 122:464 (May 2, 1970).

"Justice Douglas—Evergreen Case." *Writer's Digest*, 50:44+ (June 1970).

"Justice for Douglas?" *Economist*, 237:34–5 (December 26, 1970).

"Let's Get Douglas." *New Republic*, 162:9 (May 2, 1970).

"Mr. Douglas' Revolution." *National Review*, 22:481 (May 5, 1970).

"Open Letter to: Norman Cousins, and Others, from the Editors of *National Review* Concerning *Points of Rebellion*." *National Review*, 22:293–4 (March 24, 1970).

"Representative Ford's Charges Against Justice Douglas" (text of section of address to House of Representatives, April 27, 1970). *U.S. News & World Report*, 68:67–71 (April 27, 1970).

Resnik, S. "Black, Douglas, and Absolutes: Some Suggestions for a New Perspective on the Supreme Court." *Journal of Urban Law*, 47(4):765–95 (1970).

"Reston Replies." *National Review*, 22:446+ (May 5, 1970).

"Revolution: What Douglas Foresees." *U.S. News & World Report*, 68:17 (February 16, 1970).

Seligman, D. "Revolution, Rant, and Justice Douglas." *Life*, 68:4 (May 1, 1970).

U.S., Congress, House. "Report by the Special Subcommittee on House Resolution 920, on Its Investigation into the Possible Impeachment of Associate Justice William O. Douglas" (91st Cong., 2d sess.). *House Committee Print*, Y4.J89/1:D74 (June 20, 1970).

U.S., Congress, House. "Final Report by the Special Subcommittee on House Resolution 920" (91st Cong., 2d sess.). *House Committee Print*, Y4.J89/1:D74/2 (September 17, 1970).

Viorst, M. "Bill Douglas Has Never Stopped Fighting the Bullies of Yakima." *New York Times Magazine*, pp. 8–9+ (June 14, 1970).

"Where Douglas Impeachment Case Stands Now." *U.S. News & World Report*, 69:91 (December 14, 1970).

"Wit and Wisdom of Justice Douglas." *National Review*, 22:191 (February 24, 1970).

"Justice Douglas; No Evidence to Support Impeachment." *New Republic*, 164:13–14 (January 2, 1971).

Way, H. F., Jr. "Study of Judicial Attitudes: The Case of Mr. Justice Douglas." *Western Political Quarterly*, 24:12–23 (March 1971).

Sevareid, E. "Mr. Justice Douglas Speaks His Mind: Eric Sevareid." *Bill of Rights Journal*, 5:17–37 (December 1972). (The original CBS interview, *Mr. Justice Douglas*, may be rented from Carousel Films, Inc., 1501 Broadway, NYC, 10036.)

Booker, J. L. "Justice William O. Douglas at Bat." *The Shingle* (April 1973).

Emerson, T. "Douglas: The Longest and Youngest." *Bill of Rights Journal*, 6:3–7 (December 1973).

"Justice Douglas." *Nation*, 217:485 (November 12, 1973).

"Newsmakers: Surpassed." *Newsweek*, 82:69 (November 12, 1973).

"Odd Pause That Wasn't." *Time*, 102:7 (August 13, 1973).

Wolfman, B., et al. "Behavior of Justice Douglas in Federal Tax Cases." *University of Pennsylvania Law Review*, 122:235–365 (December 1973).

Yarbrough, T. E. "Justices Black and Douglas—Judicial Function and Scope of Constitutional Liberties." *Duke Law Journal*, 1973(2):441 (1973).

Young, R. L. "Justice Douglas Reaches a Milestone." *American Bar Association Journal*, 59:282 (March 1973).

Ares, C. "Constitutional Criminal Law." *Columbia Law Review*, 74(3) (April 1974).

Burger, W. E., Chief Justice. "Tribute to Mr. Justice Douglas" (on Douglas' thirty-fifth year on the Court, April 17, 1974). 416 *U.S. Reports* v–vi.

Countryman, V. "Douglas, Justice: Contribution to Law—Business Regulation." *Columbia Law Review*, 74(3):366 (1974).

———. "Justice Douglas and Law of Business Regulation." *Banking Law Journal*, 91(4):312–19 (1974).

"The Dissenting Opinions of William O. Douglas (1948–72)." *Lithopinion*, 8:31–3 (Winter 1974).

Dorsen, N. "Mr. Justice Douglas' Contribution to the Law—'Equal Protection of the Laws.' " *Columbia Law Review*, 74(3) (April 1974).

Dunne, G. T. "Justice Douglas and the Law of Banking." *Banking Law Journal*, 91(10):307–11 (April 1974).

Emerson, T. "Douglas, Justice: Contributions to Law—the First Amendment." *Columbia Law Review*, 74(3):353 (April 1974).

Francke, L. "Most Surprising Happy Marriage in Washington." *McCalls*, 101:16+ (April 1974).

Graham, M. "State v. Douglas—Judicial Revival of an Unconstitutional Statute." *Louisiana Law Review*, 34(4):851 (1974).

Hechinger, F. M. "Justice Douglas' Dissent in the DeFunis Case." *Saturday Review World*, 1:51–2+ (July 27, 1974).

Powe, L. A. "Evolution to Absolutism—Douglas, Justice and First Amendment." *Columbia Law Review*, 74(3):371 (1974).

Warren, E., and Burger, W. "In Honor of Mr. Justice William O. Douglas." *Columbia Law Review*, 74:341+ (April 1974).

Weaver, W. "Now That Marco DeFunis Has His Law Degree." *Education Digest*, 40:50–2 (November 1974).

Baude, P. "An Appreciative Note on Mr. Justice Douglas' View of the Court's Role in Environmental Cases." *Indiana Law Journal*, 51 (Fall 1975).

Beaney, W. M. "Justice William O. Douglas: The Constitution in a Free Society." *Indiana Law Journal*, 51:18–21 (Fall 1975).

Berry, J. "Debt to William O. Douglas." *Library Journal*, 100:2277 (December 15, 1975).

"Beyond the Call of Duty." *Nation*, 221:452 (November 8, 1975).

"Can Douglas Cope?" *Time*, 105:58 (April 7, 1975).

"Choose Wisely, Mr. Ford." *Economist*, 257:61–2 (November 22, 1975).

Clark, M. "Stroke Clinics." *Newsweek*, 86:90 (December 8, 1975).

"Douglas Digs In." *Economist*, 256:61 (July 12, 1975).

"Douglas Finally Leaves the Bench." *Time*, 106:69–70 (November 24, 1975).

"Douglas Returns." *Newsweek*, 86:37 (October 13, 1975).

Dunne, G. T., "Fed as Symbol." *Banking Law Journal*, 92(10):1051–2 (1975).

Elliot, J. M. "Douglas, W. O." *New Republic*, 173(25):32 (1975).

Fortas, A. "William O. Douglas—Appreciation." *Indiana Law Journal*, 51:1 (1975).

Howard, L., and Camper, D. "Douglas the Durable." *Newsweek*, 86:46 (July 7, 1975).

Karst, K. L. "Justice Douglas and the Equal Protection Clause." *Indiana Law Journal*, 51 (Fall 1975).

Keller, R. H., Jr. "William O. Douglas, the Supreme Court, and American Indians." *American Indian Law Review*, 3(2):333–60 (1975).

Lewin, N. "William O. Douglas." *New Republic*, 173:7–9 (November 29, 1975).

Mathews, T., et al. "Final Judgement." *Newsweek*, 86:45–6 (November 24, 1975).

"Mooting Justice Douglas." *Time*, 106:44–5 (July 7, 1975).

Peer, E. "Mind of a Maverick." *Newsweek*, 86:46–8 (November 24, 1975).

"Puzzle over Role of Justice Douglas." *U.S. News & World Report*, 78:69 (May 26, 1975).

Rabinove, S. "Justice Douglas and the *DeFunis* Case: A Critique." *Humanist*, 35(2):25–6 (March 1975).

"Remarks of Associate Justice William O. Douglas." *Rutgers Law Review*, 28:616–24 (Winter 1975).

"Retirement of Mr. Justice Douglas" (comments of Chief Justice Warren Burger, a letter from the Court to Douglas, and a letter from Douglas to the Court, November 17, 1975). 423 *U.S. Reports* vii–x.

Sprecher, R. A. "Mr. Justice Douglas." *Indiana Law Journal*, 51 (Fall 1975).

"Time to Step Down." *Christianity Today*, 20:31 (October 24, 1975).

"Tribute." *New Yorker*, 51:18–19 (December 29, 1975).

"Verdict on Douglas." *Time*, 106:82–3 (October 13, 1975).

"Will Douglas Quit?" *Time*, 105:78 (February 17, 1975).

"With Douglas Gone, How Court May Shift." *U.S. News & World Report*, 79:41 (November 24, 1975).

Ares, C. E. "Mr. Justice Douglas." *Harvard Civil Rights Law Review*, 11 (Spring 1976).

Burleson, B., and Bowmer, J. D. "William O. Douglas—in Retrospect; Introduction." *Baylor Law Review*, 28:211 (Spring 1976).

Clark, R. "William O. Douglas: Daring to Live Free." *Progressive*, 40:7–9 (January 1976).

Clark, T. C. "Bill Douglas—a Portrait." *Baylor Law Review*, 28 (Spring 1976).

Countryman, V. "Contributions of the Douglas Dissents." *Georgia Law Review*, 10:331–52 (Winter 1976).

———. "Even-handed Justice." *Harvard Civil Rights Law Review*, 11 (Spring 1976).

"Douglas the Pioneer Departs: Stevens the Pragmatist Arrives." *Trial; The National Legal Magazine*, 12:3 (January 1976).

Duke, S. "Mr. Justice Douglas." *Harvard Civil Rights Law Review*, 11(2):241–2 (1976).

———. "Tribute to Mr. Justice Douglas." *Akron Law Review*, 9:399–401 (Winter 1976).

Fleishman, F. "Mr. Justice Douglas on Sex Censorship." *Los Angeles Bar Journal*, 51:560–2+ (May 1976).

Glennon, R. J. " 'Do Not Go Gentle': More Than an Epitaph." *Wayne Law Review*, 22:1305–34 (September 1976).

Goldberg, A. J. "Tribute to Justice Douglas." *Hastings Constitutional Law Quarterly*, 3:1–18 (Winter 1976).

Huber, R. B. "William O. Douglas and the Environment." *Environmental Affairs*, 5:209–12 (Spring 1976).

"Justice Douglas Retired from the Supreme Court, Ending the Longest Tenure as an Active Justice." *American Bar Association Journal*, 62:87–9 (January 1976).

Kilpatrick, J. J. "Love Affair with the Supreme Court." *Nation's Business*, 64:9–10 (January 1976).

Martin, E. W. "Justice Douglas and Education for Severely-Profoundly Handicapped." *Journal of Special Education*, 10(2):123–6 (1976).

Maverick, M. "Douglas and the First Amendment—Visiting Old Battlegrounds." *Baylor Law Review*, 28 (Spring 1976).

Mendelson, W. "Mr. Justice Douglas and Government by the Judiciary." *Journal of Politics*, 38:918–37 (November 1976).

Mosk, S. "William O. Douglas." *Ecology Law Quarterly*, 5(2):229–32 (1976).

"Mr. Justice Douglas: One Man's Opinions." *Hastings Constitutional Law Quarterly*, 3:3–18 (Winter 1976).

"Remember the Golden-Mantled Ground Squirrels." *Forbes*, 117:138 (May 15, 1976).

Richards, D. R. "Justice Douglas and the Availability of the Federal Forum to Civil Rights Litigants." *Baylor Law Review*, 28 (Spring 1976).

"C&O Canal Dedicated to Justice Douglas" (includes text of Douglas' speech). *National Parks and Conservation Magazine*, 51:20 (August 1977).

Countryman, V. "Justice Douglas: Expositor of the Bankruptcy Law" (revision of 1969 article). *American Bankruptcy Law Journal*, 51:127–94,247–75 (Spring–Summer 1977).

Goldman, S. "In Defense of Justice: Some Thoughts on Reading Professor Mendelson's 'Mr. Justice Douglas and Government by the Judiciary.' " *Journal of Politics*, 39:148–58 (February 1977).

"Last Word." *Time*, 109:80+ (April 11, 1977).

Mendelson, W. "A Response to Professor Goldman." *Journal of Politics*, 39:159–65 (February 1977).

Adler, S. S. "Toward a Constitutional Theory of Individuality: The Privacy Opinions of Justice Douglas." *Yale Law Journal*, 87:1579–1600 (July 1978).

"Center Begins New Program: Inquiry into State of Freedom Will Honor William O. Douglas." *Center Magazine*, 11:2–4 (September 1978).

SELECTED NEWSPAPER ARTICLES ABOUT WILLIAM O. DOUGLAS

"Appointment as S.E.C. Chairman Likely." *New York Times*, p. 35 (January 14, 1937).

"Election as S.E.C. Chairman Foreseen; Unpopular with Wall Street." *New York Times*, p. 25 (August 10, 1937).

"Elected S.E.C. Chairman; New York Stock Exchange Heads Approve; Career." *New York Times*, p. 41 (September 22, 1937).

"Editorial." *New York Times*, p. 26 (September 23, 1937).

"Douglas Makes Statement on S.E.C. Policies and Progress and His Own Views on Market Regulation." *New York Times*, p. 41 (September 23, 1937).

"W. O. Douglas Hinted as Successor (to Retired Justice Brandeis)." *New York Times*, p. 1 (February 15, 1939).

"Senator Schwellenbach, Dean W. B. Rutledge, and Douglas Lead Candidates." *New York Times*, p. 3 (February 18, 1939).

"Business Believed to Favor Appointment of W. O. Douglas or Dean W. B. Rutledge." *New York Times*, p. 10 (March 13, 1939).

"Douglas Appointed; Comment." *New York Times*, p. 1 (March 21, 1939).

"Krock Comments." *New York Times*, p. 22 (March 21, 1939).

"Editorial on Douglas' Youth." *New York Times*, p. 22 (March 23, 1939).

"Appointment Approved by Senate Subcommittee." *New York Times*, p. 3 (March 25, 1939).

"Comment by D. Dinwoodey." *New York Times*, sec. 4, p. 7 (March 26, 1939).

"Feature Article." *New York Times*, sec. 8, p. 4 (March 26, 1939).

"Appointment Approved by Senate Committee." *New York Times*, p. 17 (March 28, 1939).

"Senate Debate; Douglas Confirmed." *New York Times*, p. 17 (April 5, 1939).

"Douglas Sworn In." *New York Times*, p. 17 (April 18, 1939).

"Douglas Orders Stay of Rosenbergs' Execution to Permit Litigation of Death Sentences; Chief Justice Vinson Calls Supreme Court to Review Order." *New York Times*, p. 1 (June 18, 1953).

"Text of the Order." *New York Times*, p. 16 (June 18, 1953).

"Supreme Court Vacates Stay; Douglas Dissents." *New York Times*, p. 1 (June 20, 1953).

"Text of Dissent." *New York Times*, p. 7 (June 20, 1953).

"House Republicans Set Serious Bid to Impeach Supreme Court Justice William Douglas." *Wall Street Journal*, p. 22 (April 10, 1970).

"Douglas Attends . . . Symposium on His Latest Book, *Points of Rebellion*; Which Some House Republican Members Cite as Grounds for Removal from Supreme Court." *New York Times*, p. 33 (April 11, 1970).

"Justice Douglas Would Be Object of Possible Impeachment Under a Planned Bill." *Wall Street Journal*, p. 1 (April 14, 1970).

"Representative Ford Says Decision by Partisan Group in House to Press for Investigation of Douglas' Fitness to Serve on Supreme Court Was Sparked by His Article Taken from *Points of Rebellion*." *New York Times*, p. 27 (April 14, 1970).

"Editorial on Validity of House Republican's Claim That Talk of Impeaching Douglas in No Way Stems from Senate's Rejection of Two Presidential Nominees to High Court." *Wall Street Journal*, p. 18 (April 15, 1970).

"J. Reston's Comments on Possible Impeachment Against Douglas; Sees Little Chance of Impeachment." *New York Times*, p. 42 (April 15, 1970).

"Representative Ford Questions Record." *Christian Science Monitor*, p. 2 (April 16, 1970).

"Editorial: The Douglas Issue." *Christian Science Monitor*, editorial page (April 16, 1970).

"Ouster Doubted." *Christian Science Monitor*, p. 1 (April 18, 1970).

"House Judiciary Committee Named Panel to Investigate Charges Against Justice Douglas." *Wall Street Journal*, p. 6 (April 22, 1970).

"House to Probe Charges." *Christian Sciene Monitor*, p. 2 (April 22, 1970).

"Setback to Anti-Douglas Move?" *Christian Science Monitor*, p. 2 (April 25, 1970).

"Editorial: On the Impeachment." *Christian Science Monitor*, editorial page (May 5, 1970).

"Douglas Files Report with Supreme Court Clerk Disclosing (His Assets, Income, and Associations with Organizations)." *New York Times*, p. 15 (August 5, 1970).

"Douglas Reports Earnings." *Christian Science Monitor*, p. 7 (August 10, 1970).

"Justice Douglas Shouldn't Be Impeached, Special Five-Man Committee Concluded." *Wall Street Journal*, p. 1 (December 1, 1970).

" 'No Grounds' Against; (Impeachment)." *Christian Science Monitor*, p. 2 (December 2, 1970).

"Announces His Intention to Remain on Court." *New York Times*, p. 43 (December 17, 1970).

"Douglas Intends to Remain." *Christian Science Monitor*, p. 2 (December 17, 1970).

"Douglas in Serious Condition, Suffers Stroke on December 31. President Ford's Unsuccessful Effort as House Minority Leader to Impeach Douglas Recalled." *New York Times*, p. 31 (January 2, 1975).

"Douglas Will Probably Not Rejoin Court Before Mid-March. Court Appears to Be Delaying Some Cases Until Return." *New York Times*, p. 34 (January 31, 1975).

"Hospitalization of Supreme Court Justice Marshall Raises Cloud of Uncertainty Around Operations of Court During Remaining Months of Term." *New York Times*, p. 25 (February 16, 1975).

"Douglas Returns to Bench for First Time Since Suffering Stroke." *New York Times*, p. 42 (March 21, 1975).

"Douglas Says Idea of Resigning Has 'Never Entered My Mind.' " *New York Times*, p. 24 (March 26, 1975).

"Ailing William Douglas Fails to Participate in Supreme Court Action; He Is Voting in Decisions, But Not Writing Opinions." *Wall Street Journal*, p. 1 (May 23, 1975).

"Douglas Says He Will Not Retire from Supreme Court." *New York Times*, p. 47 (July 16, 1975).

"Douglas Says He Intends to Stay on Supreme Court 'As Long as Work Remains Interesting and Challenging.' " *New York Times*, p. 14 (September 13, 1975).

"Justice Douglas Determined to Continue on Bench: His Health and Its Impact on Court Are Critical Questions Confronting Court." *New York Times*, p. 28 (September 30, 1975).

"The Douglas Case." *Christian Science Monitor*, p. 35 (October 20, 1975).

"Douglas Hospitalized in Washington, D.C., for 'Slight Fever'; Growing Concern over Douglas' Ability to Continue." *New York Times*, p. 41 (October 30, 1975).

"Douglas on November 12 Retires from Bench Because of Failing Health, Ending Record Thirty-six and One-half Years on Court; Statements of Praise from President Ford, Burger, and Fellow Justices: Speculation on Whom Ford Will Appoint." *New York Times*, p. 1 (November 13, 1975).

"William O. Douglas Resigned from Supreme Court, Due to Ill Health; Gives President Ford First Chance to Name Justice." *Wall Street Journal*, p. 2 (November 13, 1975).

"Texts of Letters from Douglas to President Ford; Ford's Letter of Reply; Statement by Chief Justice Burger." *New York Times*, p. 60 (November 13, 1975).

"Anthony Lewis Article on Douglas' Career." *New York Times*, p. 60 (November 13, 1975).

"Editorial on Douglas' Retiring from Bench; Says That Douglas Rendered Final High Service to Country He Loves and Served Well." *New York Times*, p. 40 (November 13, 1975).

"Mrs. Douglas Comments on Douglas' Retirement." *Christian Science Monitor*, p. 2 (November 14, 1975).

"Editorial: Douglas' Role: Unconventionality." *Christian Science Monitor*, p. 34 (November 14, 1975).

"Well Done, Mr. Douglas." *Christian Science Monitor*, editorial page (November 14, 1975).

"Douglas' Career as Justice Noted." *New York Times*, p. 1 (November 16, 1975).

"Anthony Lewis' article on Mr, Douglas: 36 Years Out on the Frontier." *New York Times*, sec. 4, p. 2 (November 16, 1975).

"Text of Letter to Douglas Regarding Retirement from Eight Other Justices; Read at Court by Chief Justice Burger; Douglas' Letter of Reply." *New York Times*, p. 18 (November 18, 1975).

"Chesapeake and Ohio Canal Historic Park dedicated to William O. Douglas." *New York Times*, sec. 2, p. 1 (May 18, 1977), p. 26 (May 18, 1977).

BOOK REVIEWS BY WILLIAM O. DOUGLAS

New York Law of Damages, 1925 (by Briscoe Baldwin Clark). *Columbia Law Review*, 26:780–2 (June 1926).

Student's Manual of Bankruptcy Law & Practice, 1925 (by Lee E. Joslyn). *Illinois Law Review*, 22:347–8 (November 1927).

Cases on Law of Bankruptcy, 1927 (by Holbrook and Aigler). *Yale Law Journal*, 37:685–7 (March 1928).

Cases on Damages, 1928 (by Judson Crane). *Yale Law Journal*, 38:608–9 (March 1929).

Cases on the Measure of Damages, 1928 (by Joseph Henry Beale). *Yale Law Journal*, 38:698–9 (March 1929).

Cases on the Law of Bankruptcy, 1928 (by William E. Britton). *Illinois Law Review*, 24:121–2 (May 1929).

Treatise on the Law and Practice of Receivers, 1929 (by Ralph E. Clark). *Yale Law Journal*, 39:592–3 (February 1930).

Cases and Materials on Corporate Finance, 1930 (by Adolph A. Berle, Jr.). *Virginia Law Review*, 17:625–6 (April 1931).

Law of Insolvency in British India, 1929 (by Sir Dinshah Fardunji-Mullah). *Yale Law Journal*, 40:840 (March 1931).

Lawful Pursuit of Gain, 1931 (by Max Radin). *Harvard Law Review*, 44:1164–5 (May 1931).

Bonds and Bondholders, Rights and Remedies, with Forms, 1934 (by Sylvester E. Quindry). *Columbia Law Review*, 34:1391 (November 1934).

Shareholder's Money, 1933 (by Horace B. Samuel). *Columbia Law Review*, 34:787–93 (April 1934).

Twentieth-Century Capitalist Revolution, 1954 (by Adolph A. Berle, Jr.). *University of Pennsylvania Law Review*, 103:1108 (June 1955).

Approach to Self-government, 1956 (by Ivor W. Jennings). *Tulsa Law Review*, 32:788 (June 1958).

Blue Sky Law, 1958 (by Louis Loss and Edward M. Cowett). *Harvard Law Review*, 73:1235 (April 1960).

SELECTED REVIEWS ON WILLIAM O. DOUGLAS' BOOKS

Cases and Materials on the Law of Corporate Reorganizations (with Carrol M. Shanks) (1931):

> Blackstock, L. G. *Texas Law Review*, 10:396–7 (April 1932).
> Crimmins, J. M. *Notre Dame Lawyer*, 7:132–3 (November 1931).
> *Detroit Law Review*, 2:144–5 (March 1932).
> Dewing, A. S. *Harvard Law Review*, 45:1138–9 (April 1932).
> Dodd, E. M., Jr. *Cornell Law Quarterly*, 17:317–19 (February 1932).
> Evans, A. E. *Kentucky Law Journal*, 20:188–9 (January 1932).
> Finletter, T. K. *University of Pennsylvania Law Review*, 80:624–5 (February 1932).
> Harvey, R. S. *Georgia Law Review*, 20:571–4 (May 1932).
> Johnson, S. *Virginia Law Review*, 18:472–3 (February 1932).
> Peppin, J. C. *California Law Review*, 20:347–54 (March 1932).
> Shapiro, W. H. *St. John's Law Review*, 6:197–9 (December 1931).
> Swaine, R. T. *Columbia Law Review*, 32:402–3 (February 1932).

Cases and Materials on the Law of Financing of Business Units (with Carrol M. Shanks) (1931):

> Payne, P. M. *Virginia Law Review*, 18:593–5 (March 1932).
> Root, E., Jr. *Yale Law Journal*, 41:481 (January 1932).

Cases and Materials on the Law of Management of Business Units (with Carrol M. Shanks) (1931):

> Isaacs, N. *Yale Law Journal*, 41:150–2 (November 1931).
> O'Keefe, A. J., Jr. *Southern California Law Review*, 5:176–7 (December 1931).

Democracy and Finance: The Addresses and Public Statements of William Douglas as Member and Chairman of the S.E.C. (1940):

> Abel, A. S. *Washington University Law Quarterly*, 26:289–90 (February 1941).
> Ballantine, A. A. *Michigan Law Review*, 39:951–61 (April 1941).
> Dean, A. H. *Yale Law Journal*, 50:725–6 (February 1941).
> Eaton, C. S. *University of Chicago Law Review*, 8:195–201 (February 1941).
> Frank, J. *Harvard Law Review*, 54:905–15 (March 1941).
> Katz, W. G. *American Bar Association Journal*, 27:118 (February 1941).

Larson, A. *Tennessee Law Review*, 16:890–3 (April 1941).

MacChesney, B. *Illinois Law Review*, 36:247–8 (June 1941).

Being an American (1948):

    Burns, J. J. *American Bar Association Journal*, 34:815–17 (September 1948).

    Byse, C. *University of Pennsylvania Law Review*, 97:452–4 (February 1949).

    Donnelly, R. C. *Virginia Law Review*, 34:864–6 (October 1948).

    Landis, E. S. *Cornell Law Quarterly*, 34:285–6 (Winter 1948).

    Maurer, R. A. *Georgia Law Journal*, 37:284–7 (January 1949).

    Rodell, F. *University of Pittsburgh Law Review*, 10:605–10 (May 1949).

    Schleicher, C. P. *Oregon Law Review*, 28:88–9 (December 1948).

    Schlesinger, A., Jr. *Iowa Law Review*, 34:729–30 (May 1949).

    White, W. H. *Fordham Law Review*, 17:317–18 (November 1948).

Of Men and Mountains (1950):

    Hass, V. P. *Chicago Sunday Tribune*, p. 4 (April 23, 1950).

    Henderson, R. W. *Library Journal*, 75:776 (May 1, 1950).

    Hutchens, J. K. *New York Herald Tribune Book Review*, p. 1 (April 9, 1950).

    Sanderson, I. T. *Saturday Review of Literature*, 33:53 (April 15, 1950).

    Sawyer, R. *Christian Science Monitor*, p. 5 (April 15, 1950).

    Stewart, G. R. *New York Times*, p. 3 (April 9, 1950).

Strange Lands and Friendly People (1951):

    Casgrain, J. D. *Catholic World*, 174:318 (January 1952).

    Coon, C. S. *Nation*, 173:476 (December 1, 1951).

    Harrison, J. G. *Christian Science Monitor*, p. 11 (November 1, 1951).

    Reynolds, Q. *New York Herald Tribune Book Review*, p. 1 (November 4, 1951).

Beyond the High Himalayas (1952):

    Hass, V. P. *Chicago Sunday Tribune*, p. 3 (September 7, 1952).

    Krader, L. *Harvard Law Review*, 66:382–4 (December 1952).

    MacEoin, G. *Commonweal*, 57:124 (November 7, 1952).

    Sawatzky, G. *Kansas Law Review*, 1:381–4 (May 1953).

    Trumbull, R. *New York Times*, p. 3 (September 21, 1952).

North from Malaya: Adventure on Five Fronts (1953):

    Durdin, T. *New York Times*, p. 3 (May 31, 1953).

    McSorley, J. *Catholic World*, 178:237 (December 1953).

    Michener, J. A. *New York Herald Tribune Book Review*, p. 1 (May 31, 1953).

U.S. Quarterly Book Review, 9:273 (September 1953).

Walker, G. *Christian Science Monitor*, p. 11 (May 28, 1953).

An Almanac of Liberty (1954):

    Breakey, J. R., Jr. *University of Detroit Law Journal*, 18:347 (March 1955).

    Dennon, L. E. *American Bar Association Journal*, 41:254–5 (March 1955).

    Duncan, J. P. *Oklahoma Law Review*, 8:258–60 (May 1955).

    North Dakota Law Review, 31:209–10 (April 1955).

    Rodell, F. *Yale Law Journal*, 64:1099 (June 1955).

    Rodgers, W. D. *Iowa Law Review*, 40:674 (Summer 1955).

    Stumpf, S. E. *New York University Law Review*, 30:1459 (November 1955).

Russian Journey (1956):

    Harrison, J. G. *Christian Science Monitor*, p. 7 (June 7, 1956).

    Higgins, M. *New York Herald Tribune Book Review*, p. 4 (June 24, 1956).

    Salisbury, H. E. *New York Times*, p. 3 (June 10, 1956).

    Stevens, L. C. *Saturday Review*, 39:12 (June 9, 1956).

    Time, 67:110 (June 11, 1956).

We the Judges: Studies in American and Indian Constitutional Law (1956):

    Clark, C. E. *Texas Law Review*, 35:470 (February 1957).

    Fahy, C. *Notre Dame Lawyer*, 32:353 (March 1957).

    Freund, P. A. *Iowa Law Review*, 42:141 (Fall 1956).

    Garcia-Mora, M. R. *University of Detroit Law Journal*, 34:203 (November 1956).

    Gertz, E. *Decalogue Journal*, 7:16 (September–October 1956).

    Gledhill, A. *Northwestern University Law Review*, 51:506 (September–October 1956).

    McCloskey, R. G. *Harvard Law Review*, 70:189 (November 1956).

    Merril, M. H. *Oklahoma Law Review*, 9:357 (August 1956).

    Ramaswamy, M. *Stanford Law Review*, 8:756 (July 1956).

    Sivasubramanian, L. R. *University of Chicago Law Review*, 23:563 (Spring 1956).

    Stumberg, G. W. *Law Library Journal*, 50:60 (February 1957).

Exploring the Himalaya (1958).

    Berkvist, R. *New York Times*, p. 40 (February 15, 1959).

    McFate, M. *Library Journal*, 83:3006 (October 15, 1958).

    Taylor, M. *Christian Science Monitor*, p. 15 (November 26, 1958).

West of the Indus (1958):

    Arnold, S. *San Francisco Chronicle*, sec. 3, p. 3 (December 11, 1958).

Godsell, G. *Christian Science Monitor*, p. 15 (November 26, 1958).

Ozbekkan, H. *New York Times*, p. 6 (November 9, 1958).

Schmidt, D. A. *Saturday Review*, 41:18 (November 22, 1958).

The Right of the People (1958):

Andersen, W. R. *Kentucky Law Journal*, 46:648 (Summer 1958).

Denonn, L. E. *American Bar Association Journal*, 44:675 (July 1958).

Howe, M. D. *Harvard Law Review*, 71:1377 (May 1958).

Manning, L. F. *Fordham Law Review*, 27:141 (Spring 1958).

Matson, M. H. *University of Pittsburgh Law Review*, 19:834 (Summer 1958).

Murphy, J. W. *Villanova Law Review*, 3:591 (June 1958).

Rice, W. G. *Lawyers Guild Review*, 18:169 (Winter 1959).

Sobolik, D. M. *North Dakota Law Review*, 34:274 (July 1958).

Traynor, R. J. *California Law Review*, 46:301 (May 1958).

America Challenged (1960):

Cahn, E. *New York Herald Tribune Book Review*, p. 5 (June 12, 1960).

Davis, S. R. *Christian Science Monitor*, p. 7 (July 7, 1960).

Harris, S. J. *Saturday Review*, 43:21 (July 2, 1960).

Kramer, E. F. *Christian Century*, 77:950 (August 17, 1960).

My Wilderness: The Pacific West (1960):

Borland, H. *New York Times Book Review*, p. 46 (November 20, 1960).

Foell, E. W. *Christian Science Monitor*, p. 16 (November 17, 1960).

Holbrook, S. *Chicago Sunday Tribune*, p. 6 (November 27, 1960).

Kirkus, 28:663 (August 1, 1960).

Zahniser, H. *New York Herald Tribune Book Review*, p. 3 (November 6, 1960).

A Living Bill of Rights (1961):

Harris, S. J. *Saturday Review*, 44:52 (May 13, 1961).

Kiley, R. J. *Chicago Sunday Tribune*, p. 6 (March 5, 1961).

Lefkowitz, L. J. *Fordham Law Review*, 30:209 (October 1961).

North Dakota Law Review, 37:306 (April 1961).

Notre Dame Lawyer, 36:455 (May 1961).

My Wilderness: East to Katahdin (1961):

Borland, H. *New York Times Book Review*, p. 7 (November 5, 1961).

Cowle, J. *Chicago Sunday Tribune*, p. 3 (October 22, 1961).

Henderson, R. W. *Library Journal*, 86:3488 (October 15, 1961).

Hogan, W. *San Francisco Chronicle*, p. 33 (October 24, 1961).

Muir of the Mountains (1961):

Christian Science Monitor, sec. B, p. 8 (May 11, 1961).

Fitch, V. K. *Library Journal*, 86:2362 (June 16, 1961).

Libby, M. S. *New York Herald Tribune Books*, p. 13 (August 27, 1961).

Democracy's Manifesto (1962):

Kirkus, 30:151 (February 1, 1962).

Henderson, R. W. *Library Journal*, 87:1471 (April 1, 1962).

Spencer, F. L. *Springfield Republican*, sec. D, p. 4 (April 22, 1962).

Freedom of the Mind (1962):

Henderson, R. W. *Library Journal*, 89:644 (February 1, 1964).

Rogat, Y. *New York Review of Books*, 3:5 (October 22, 1964).

Mr. Lincoln and the Negroes: The Long Road to Equality (1963):

Furnas, J. C. *New York Times Book Review*, p. 42 (September 29, 1963).

Littler, R. *Stanford Law Review*, 16:782 (May 1964).

Lowe, M. J. *Brooklyn Law Review*, 30:395 (April 1964).

Woodward, C. Vann. *Book Week*, 1:4 (September 22, 1963).

The Anatomy of Liberty: The Rights of Man Without Force (1963):

Baldwin, R. *Saturday Review*, 47:79 (January 4, 1964).

Henderson, R. W. *Library Journal*, 88:4782 (December 15, 1963).

Rogat, Y. *New York Review of Books*, 3:5 (October 22, 1964).

A Wilderness Bill of Rights (1965):

Beck, R. *Natural Resources Journal*, 7:456 (July 1967).

Harrison, G. *Book Week*, p. 10 (September 19, 1965).

Johnson, C. S. *Library Journal*, 90:4788 (November 1, 1965).

Sorenson, M. *Christian Science Monitor*, p. 9 (September 21, 1965).

Tarlock, A. D. *Stanford Law Review*, 19:895 (April 1967).

Weatherford, G. D. *Oregon Law Review*, 45:341 (June 1966).

The Bible and the Schools (1966):

Bernhard, H. A. *Law in Transition Quarterly*, 3:206 (Summer 1966).

Christian Century, 83:118 (January 26, 1966).

Richardson, D. *Christian Science Monitor*, p. 9 (March 26, 1966).

Farewell to Texas: A Vanishing Wilderness (1967):

Bogie, T. M. *Library Journal*, 92:1841 (May 1, 1967).

Dugger, R. *Book Week*, p. 3 (July 16, 1967).

Richardson, D. *Christian Science Monitor*, p. 7 (July 27, 1967).

Towards a Global Federalism (1968):

Deutsch, E. P. *University of Illinois Law Forum*, 1969:281 (1969).

Hay, P. *Journal of Law and Economic Development*, 4:386 (Fall 1969).

Points of Rebellion (1970):

Apple, J. G. *Kentucky Law Journal*, 59:573 (1970–71).

Davidow, R. P. *St. John's Law Review*, 45:179 (October 1970).

Eckstein, P. F. *Notre Dame Lawyer*. 46:643 (Spring 1971).

Grossman, G. S. *Library Journal*, 95:1388 (April 1, 1970).

Hayakawa, S. I. *Boston University Law Review*, 50:493 (Summer 1970).

Hermann, D. H. *Washington Law Review*, 46:195 (October 1970).

Howard Law Journal, 16:181 (Fall 1970).

Koplowitz, E. A. *Lincoln Law Review*, 5:80 (December 1970).

Leahy, J. E. *Brooklyn Law Review*, 37:258 (Fall 1970).

Manning, L. F. *Fordham Law Review*, 39:161 (October 1970).

Sedler, R. A. *Kentucky Law Journal*, 59:578 (1970–71).

Stephenson, D. G., Jr. *University of Pennsylvania Law Review*, 119:536 (January 1971).

Yoder, E. M. *Book World*, p. 6 (March 29, 1970).

Zinn, H. *Boston University Law Review*, 50:490 (Summer 1970).

Holocaust of Hemispheric Co-op: Crosscurrents in Latin America (1971):

Page, J. A. *New York Times Book Review*, p. 48 (November 28, 1971).

Silvert, K. H. *New York University Journal of International Law and Politics*, 4:519 (Winter 1971).

Snow, L. F. *Library Journal*, 96:3766 (November 15, 1971).

Williams, B. D. *Best Sellers*, 31:340 (November 1, 1971).

International Dissent: Six Steps Toward World Peace (1971):

Bingham, A. M. *Saturday Review*, 54:30 (May 8, 1971).

Choice, 8:1087 (October 1971).

Holtman, E. *Library Journal*, 96:1988 (June 1, 1971).

Lopatkiewicz, S. M. *Harvard International Law Journal*, 12:609 (Summer 1971).

The Three Hundred Year War—a Chronicle of Ecological Disaster (1972):

New York Times Book Review, p. 38 (October 8, 1972).

Nygaard, A. *Library Journal*, 97:2633 (August 1972).

Reed, K. R. *Arizona Law Review*, 14:877 (1972).

Go East Young Man: The Early Years (1974):

Bliven, N. *New Yorker*, 50:74 (July 8, 1974).

Bost, W. L., Jr. *Emory Law Journal*, 23:781–6 (Summer 1974).

Botein, S. *Yale Law Journal*, 84:151–66 (November 1974).

Fortas, A. *New York University Law Review*, 49:374–6 (May–June 1974).

Higginbotham, P. E. *American Bar Association Journal*, 60:896 (August 1974).

Joseph, P. *Nation*, 219:26 (July 6, 1974).

Latham, E. *Michigan Law Review*, 72:1656–67 (August 1974).
Morrissey, D. *Commonweal*, 100:527–8 (September 27, 1974).
Vichich, J. J. *Duquesne Law Review*, 13:406–10 (Winter 1974).

Index

ABOUT THE EDITOR

Robert H. Keller, Jr. is Associate Professor of History at Fairhaven College, Western Washington University, Bellingham, Washington. He has contributed to the *American Indian Journal, Ethnohistory,* the *American Indian Law Review*, the *Smithsonian Handbook of North American Indians*, and many other journals.

Contributions in Legal Studies
Series Editor: *Paul L. Murphy*

Stability, Security, and Continuity: Mr. Justice Burton and Decision-Making in the Supreme Court 1945–1958
Mary Frances Berry

Philosophical Law: Authority, Equality, Adjudication, Privacy
Richard Bronaugh, editor

Law, Soldiers, and Combat
Peter Karsten

Appellate Courts and Lawyers: Information Gathering in the Adversary System
Thomas B. Marvell

Charting the Future: The Supreme Court Responds to a Changing Society, 1890–1920
John E. Semonche

The Promise of Power; The Emergence of the Legal Profession in Massachusetts, 1760–1840
Gerard W. Gawalt

Inferior Courts, Superior Justice: A History of the Justices of the Peace on the Northwest Frontier, 1853–1889
John R. Wunder

Antitrust and the Oil Monopoly: The Standard Oil Cases, 1890–1911
Bruce Bringhurst

They Have No Rights: Dred Scott's Struggle for Freedom
Walter Ehrlich

Popular Influence Upon Public Policy: Petitioning in Eighteenth-Century Virginia
Raymond C. Bailey